Enrollment Strategies for a Maturing Population

GEN

X

ers

RETURN TO
COLLEGE

AACRAO®
1 9 1 0

AMERICAN ASSOCIATION OF COLLEGIATE
REGISTRARS AND ADMISSIONS OFFICERS

American Association of Collegiate
Registrars and Admissions Officers
One Dupont Circle, NW, Suite 520
Washington, DC 20036-1135

For a complete listing of AACRAO publications, visit www.aacrao.org/publications.

The American Association of Collegiate Registrars and Admissions Officers, founded
in 1910, is a nonprofit, voluntary, professional association of more than 9,300 higher
education administrators who represent more than 2,400 institutions and agencies
in the United States and in twenty-eight countries around the world. The mission
of the Association is to provide leadership in policy initiation, interpretation, and
implementation in the global educational community. This is accomplished through the
identification and promotion of standards and best practices in enrollment management, information technology, instructional management, and student services.

Library of Congress Cataloging-in-Publication Data

Black, Jim, 1959-
    Gen Xers return to college : enrollment strategies for a maturing population / Jim Black and associates.
    p. cm.
    Includes bibliographical references and index.
    ISBN 1-57858-054-4
    1. Continuing education—United States. 2. Generation X—Education (Higher)—United States. 3.
    College student orientation—United States. I. Title: Generation-Xers return to college. II. American
    Association of Collegiate Registrars and Admissions Officers. III. Title.

LC5251.B54 2003
    374'.973—dc22

                                2003018459

In loving memory of

Kathryn Douglas Smith
August 27, 1957 – February 5, 2001

Kathy, as she was best known to her friends and family, was a valued member of the Enrollment Services team at The University of North Carolina at Greensboro. She demonstrated an unparalleled capacity to manage details while never losing sight of the people associated with the details. The courage and grace with which she lived will always be remembered.

Jim Black and Associates

DEDICATION

GEN X

Enrollment Strategies for a Maturing Population

Contents

Copyeditor — Karen Haywood
Content Editor — Jim Black

GEN X

Enrollment Strategies for a Maturing Population

Preface

As colleges and universities embrace a new generation, the Millennials, few institutions can afford to ignore the Generation Xers. Indeed, some 6.2 million college students in the United States are adults, most of whom are Xers (National Center for Education Statistics, 2002). Though Generation X, also known as the 13th Generation, is relatively small compared to the Boomers before them or the Millennials currently flooding the higher education pipeline, they include 41 million people in the United States alone (U.S. Census Bureau, 2000).

Beyond their sheer numbers and impact on the higher education landscape, Gen Xers have been maligned as "self-absorbed slackers" who are often depicted as unmotivated, unambitious individuals with short attention spans (Brown, 1997; Kraus, 2000; Smith, 2000). Such stereotypes have been proven largely inaccurate. In fact, more recent literature has described Gen Xers as self-reliant, entrepreneurial, positive thinkers, who are extremely mentally agile (Kraus, 2000; Audibert & Jones, 2002). The truth is that this generation, like all others before it, cannot be pigeonholed. Like other generations, Gen Xers are individuals first and part of a group second.

Within the context of returning to college, it is imperative for enrollment managers to be cognizant that Gen Xers are individuals who are enrolling for different reasons. Marketing to them as a narrowly defined segment is only effective to a point. Understanding their individual motivators and barriers to enrolling tends to be more productive.

The chapters in this book, however, largely deal with stereotypes. Consider the observations and strategies presented here within that framework; but never lose sight of the individual stories that affect each Gen Xer. Their goals are generally career oriented and often financially motivated, yet they are most concerned about maintaining a balanced life – family, work, leisure, community, and school (Ritchie, 1995; Silbiger & Brooks, 2002). As such, their stories are uniquely their own.

Part One of the book examines the characteristics that are common among Gen Xers with special attention to differences by gender, race, and sexual orientation. Given these characteristics, nontraditional students have specific needs and expectations related to their college experiences. These needs and expectations are described in Part One as well.

In Part Two, the focus shifts to marketing and recruitment. Beginning first with stories of Gen Xers returning to college, Part Two also describes specific marketing and recruitment strategies targeted at this population. Case studies from various institutions reveal unique approaches to recruiting Generation X.

Retention-related issues and strategies permeate Part Three. Everything from initial transition to persistence and graduation strategies is conveyed. Gen Xers going to college are particularly prone to stopping out and, in many cases, never returning; therefore, retention strategies for this population should be an institutional priority.

Finally, Part Four addresses operational issues and trends. Staffing, training, infrastructure, and technology are among the ingredients necessary for operationalizing the strategies discussed in previous chapters. In particular, the implications for enrollment managers of three mega trends in higher education that impact Gen Xers are explained.

About the Authors

Scott Amundsen is the associate director for advising of student academic services at The University of North Carolina Greensboro (UNCG). Prior to arriving at UNCG in 2000, Amundsen served as the head wrestling coach at Anderson College in South Carolina. Amundsen holds his master's from the University of South Carolina and is a Ph.D. candidate at The University of North Carolina at Greensboro. He is active in NACADA, currently serving as the North Carolina state representative, and is a frequent contributor at workshops and regional and national conferences. His interests include working with first-year and at risk students. Amundsen recently coauthored *First Things First: Your Transition to UNCG*.

Jim Black is the associate provost for enrollment services at The University of North Carolina at Greensboro. His areas of responsibility include undergraduate admissions, financial aid, registrar's office, student academic services (primarily responsible for advising and retention initiatives), student success center, evening university, and the student information system (SCT Banner). Black is the founder of the National Conference on Student Retention in Small Colleges and cofounder of the National Small College Admissions Conference and the National Small College Enrollment Conference. He is currently serving as the director of AACRAO's Strategic Enrollment Management Conference. Black has published numerous articles and book chapters. Among his other published works are a monograph titled *Navigating Change in the New Millennium: Strategies for Enrollment Leaders* and a book he recently edited, *The Strategic Enrollment Management Revolution* – considered to be a groundbreaking publication for the enrollment management profession. He has served as a consultant for more than sixty colleges, universities, professional organizations, and corporations and is currently one of only twenty-three IBM Best Practice Partners in the world.

Brad Burch is the registrar of Guilford Technical Community College and recently served as an assistant director of undergraduate admissions and 2Plus coordinator at The University of North Carolina at Greensboro. Burch also supervised transfer articulation in UNCG's registrar's office and worked as an academic advisor in student academic services. Burch has experience as a residence hall director, youth minister, and swim coach. Burch has presented at regional and national educational conferences, and published over 100 devotionals and fifteen articles on faith-related issues. Burch has a B.B.A. from Eastern Kentucky University, an M.Div. from The Southern Baptist Theological Seminary, and a Ph.D. from The University of North Carolina at Greensboro.

Stacy Fair serves as commencement coordinator in the registrar's office at The University of North Carolina at Greensboro. Previously, she worked in youth ministry, student services, and academic advising. As an academic advisor, Stacy was an active member of NACADA and in spring 2002 presented at the regional conference in Charlotte, North Carolina. She holds a B.A. in youth ministry from The Moody Bible Institute in Chicago and M.Ed. in higher education administration from UNCG, and has completed the Program for Management Development offered through UNCG's Bryan School of Business and Economics.

Trina Gabriel is a senior assistant director for undergraduate admissions at The University of North Carolina at Greensboro. Gabriel's current responsibilities include the coordination of minority recruitment activities. Gabriel received her bachelor's degree from Wake Forest University and her master's from The University of North Carolina at Greensboro.

Bryant Hutson is college and career information specialist and technology coordinator for the College Foundation of North Carolina Resource Center. A doctoral candidate in higher education and adult development at The University of North Carolina at Greensboro, he has been involved as an adjunct instructor in UNCG's Student Academic Success project for at risk students since the program's creation. Hutson was previously a history instructor at Guilford Technical Community College and Greensboro College, and director of a not-for-profit organization that focused on improving rural public education – positions that allowed him to closely observe the challenges faced by academically at risk college students.

Cindra Kamphoff is the retention coordinator in student academic services at The University of North Carolina at Greensboro. She works primarily with at risk students, including undergraduate students who are on academic probation or returning from suspension or dismissal. She is active in the National Academic Advising Association and has made several presentations on at risk students at regional and national conferences. Kamphoff is currently working toward her doctorate in exercise and sport science from UNCG with a post-graduate certificate in women's and gender studies. Kamphoff holds an adjunct faculty position at Greensboro College and also serves as a reviewer for Prentice Hall's Student Success and Career Development division.

Pete Lindsey is the director of the evening university at The University of North Carolina at Greensboro. He is responsible for marketing, recruiting, retention, and program development initiatives for seven undergraduate and nineteen master's and doctoral programs. Lindsey held the position of director of undergraduate admissions for three years at The University of North Carolina at Greensboro. He also served for thirteen years as dean of undergraduate admissions at St. John Fisher College, in Rochester, New York. He has ten years of experience working with adult and transfer students in his capacities as associate director of admissions at LeMoyne College in Syracuse, New York, and as assistant director of admissions at St. Bonaventure University in Olean, New York. He has served as a consultant for STAMATS Communications, Inc., in Cedar Rapids, Iowa, and has presented at the NACAC and NYSACAC conferences. Lindsey has extensive training in Total Quality Management and was featured in *TQM in Higher Education* as well as *Recruitment and Retention in Higher Education*. Lindsey holds a B.B.A. from St. Bonaventure University.

Micah Martin is assistant director of advising for student academic services at The University of North Carolina at Greensboro and an instructor in the first-year experience program. Prior to returning to UNCG, he taught creative writing in public and private high schools. Martin holds his master's in writing and editing from UNCG and has recently begun work on his Ph.D. in curriculum and instruction with a concentration in higher education. An active member of the National Academic Advising Association and a reviewer for the Houghton

Mifflin Student Success Program, he is also coauthor of the book *First Things First: Your Transition to UNCG.*

Kara Mohre is the associate manager of student marketing and communications for enrollment services at The University of North Carolina at Greensboro. Mohre served as an assistant director of undergraduate admissions at UNCG, coordinator of student orientation for student financial services at the University of Virginia, and student enrollment and recruitment specialist at Danville Community College prior to her current position. She holds a Master of Education in Counseling, with an emphasis in higher education, from the University of Virginia. Among her contributions to the profession, Mohre authored a chapter in *First Things First: Your Transition to UNCG*, a guide for freshmen transitioning into college, is a member of CACRAO, and recent presenter for VACRAO on student marketing and recruiting strategies. Mohre has served as an adjunct faculty member for Gardner–Webb University's Human Services undergraduate program. Her research and teaching interests focus on educational psychology and counseling.

Bob Roberts is the manager of organizational learning for enrollment services at The University of North Carolina at Greensboro. He has held a variety of positions including a college admissions officer, staff recruiter, and compensation analyst. Roberts holds a master's degree in human resource management and labor relations and a bachelor of science in business administration with a major in human resource management from West Virginia University. He is scheduled to receive a bachelor of arts in philosophy in May 2004 from The University of North Carolina at Greensboro.

PART 1

Characteristics of the Generation X Population

GEN X

Enrollment Strategies for a Maturing Population

PART I
Characteristics of the Generation X Population

CHAPTER ONE
Gen Xers: Who Are They and Why Are They Returning to College?

Jim Black

Though Coupland, Howe, Strauss, and others began writing about the Generation X population in the early 1990s, Peter Sacks first wrote about Gen X students in his book, *Generation X Goes to College: An Eye-Opening Account of Teaching in Postmodern America* in 1996. In his book, Sacks described this generation from the perspective of a college faculty member and former newspaper reporter. Sacks viewed these students as "a generation in trouble" (Sacks, 1996, p. xiii). Largely from his personal experience, he described Gen Xers as students who were disengaged, did not read assignments, had been "conditioned by an overly nurturing, hand-holding educational system not to take responsibility for their own actions," and believed that everything was negotiable – even grades (Sacks, 1996, p.10). Yet, Sacks did not blame the students entirely for their plight. He saw Gen X students as being influenced by cultural and economic forces as well as a rigid higher education system unwilling or unable to adapt to the reality inherent in such a diverse generation of learners.

Indeed, the academy was challenged by the initial entry of Generation X students onto college campuses. As many of these same students return to college years later to complete an unfulfilled or new educational goal, the challenges of educating them are no less daunting. In fact, some of their evolving learning needs and service expectations require even more radical institutional responses in order to ensure their success and satisfaction with the experience than in their first pass through the system. Of course, life circumstances and maturation have changed many Gen Xers since their days as traditional-age freshmen.

So, who are they now? And perhaps more importantly, why are they returning to college at this stage in their lives? These questions will be answered in the remainder of this chapter and the others that follow. Along with an illustrative profile of today's Gen X student, specific institutional responses will be illuminated throughout the book.

Demographic Characteristics

Sources differ regarding the exact years in which Gen Xers were born: Coupland (1991) 1960–1970; Bradford and Raines (1992) 1965–1975; and Howe and Strauss (1993) 1961–1981. "Whatever the birth years, it is their common life experiences that give the cohort an identity" (Lankard, 1995, p. 3). Through their life experiences and this general timeframe, the profile of Generation X is defined.

According to the United States Census Bureau (2000), the average age of Americans is 35.3 years. Of the 281,421,906 people accounted for in the April 2000 Census, 30.2% fell in the age range 25–44 and represent the bulk of the Generation X population. Correspondingly, 31.1% of all undergraduate students enrolled in U.S. higher education for fall 2000 were 25–44 years of age and 37.3% were 25 or older (U.S. Census Bureau, 2000). In contrast, adults 25 or older represented only 26% of U.S. undergraduate enrollments in 1968 (Council for Adult and Experimental Learning and the American Council on Education, 1993).

The general population of Gen Xers is distributed evenly across the U.S. based on the total population of a given state. South Dakota has proportionally the smallest representation of Gen Xers with only 27.3% of its residents being between the ages of 25 and 44. On the upper end of the continuum, Colorado has 32.6% of its population in this age range. One might conclude from this data that a relatively even distribution of the population translates into equal opportunity for colleges and universities to enroll Generation X students; however, intervening variables, such as economic status of the individual, the condition of the local economy, distance from home or work to the closest college or university, and the current educational level of a state's residents, largely determine enrollment opportunities with Gen Xers.

Gender is another intervening variable. Of the total U.S. population in 2000, 51.1% were women (U.S. Census Bureau, 2000). Thirty percent of all individuals in the U.S. population were in the age range 25–44 (15.3% women and 14.8% men). It is reasonable to infer from this data that a slight majority of Generation Xers are women. This is an important distinction for enrollment managers because 56.4% of all students enrolled in U.S. higher education in fall 2000 were women and 32.4% of all women enrolled in that year were between the ages of 25 and 44. This is a substantial market, particularly for part-time undergraduate enrollments in two- and four-year institutions as well as part-time and full-time enrollments in graduate programs. It also represents a shift in the market over the last twenty years when, in 1980, just 51.5% of the higher education student market were women. For many years now, women have been attending college at higher rates than men (59.8% of males compared to 63.6% of females in 2001) and completing undergraduate degrees at higher rates (National Center for Education Statistics, 2001; Postsecondary Education OPPORTUNITY, 2002).

However, most of the recent enrollment growth in the U.S. has been from the younger Millennials and the older Boomers. During the decade of the '90s, undergraduate enrollment rates for women between the ages of 25 and 34 have remained relatively flat and increased only modestly for men in the same age range (Postsecondary Education OPPORTUNITY, 2001). In comparison, U.S. college and university enrollments of 18–24 year olds grew by 12.5% and undergraduates 35 or older grew by 12.6% in the '90s (National Center for Education Statistics, 2001). Given the increasing sentiment of many college administrators that adult degree programs represent an institutional "cash cow" and subsequent increases in investments of time and resources to recruit adult students as well as the exponential growth of on-line degree programs and for-profit educational providers targeting these learners, it is particularly interesting that enrollment patterns have not increased correspondingly for Gen Xers, particularly Gen X women (Council for Adult and Experimental Learning and the American Council on Education, 1993). From 1999 to 2010, the National Center for Education Statistics (2001) projects a rise of 21% in enrollments of persons under 25 and an increase of 14% in the number of students 25 and over. During this period the number of women under 25 is expected to increase by 22.5% and the number of women 25 and over is predicted to increase by 21.4% (National Center for Education Statistics, 2001). In both age groups, the number of women enrolled in U.S. higher education is expected to continue increasing at a faster rate than their male counterparts.

Race and ethnicity also are reflected in enrollment patterns. The U.S. Census Bureau (2000) reported "Asian and Pacific Islanders have by far the highest undergraduate enrollment rates between the ages 18 and 29, but then have the lowest thereafter" (Postsecondary Education OPPORTUNITY, 2001, p. 5). Conversely, Hispanics have the lowest enrollment rates through age 30. White non-Hispanics represent the second largest rate of traditional-age students enrolled, the third largest between ages 25 and 30, but have similar enrollment rates to Hispanics and Asian and Pacific Islanders beyond the age of 30. Only blacks, who represent the third largest enrollment rate between 18 and 21, are significantly more likely than other groups to be enrolled beyond age 30 (Postsecondary Education OPPORTUNITY, 2001).

In sheer numbers, white non-Hispanics continue to far outpace other racial and ethnic groups in college enrollments (*The Chronicle of Higher Education*, 2002). According to *The Chronicle of Higher Education*, white non-Hispanics accounted for 10,262,100 (71.9%) college enrollments in fall 1999 compared to 1,640,700 blacks (11.5%), 1,316,000 Hispanics (9.2%), and 909,700 Asians (6.4%). American Indians represented 145,300 of college enrollments that year and international students totaled some 516,400 of the total U.S. college enrollment. So although blacks represent the largest growth market of Generation X students in terms of enrollment rates, white non-Hispanics remain an overwhelming majority of the market. Nonetheless, the diversity of this generation suggests natural market segments for defining and communicating to distinct audiences (Ritchie, 1995).

Educational Characteristics

From 1990 to 2000, the percentage of the U.S. population age 25 and older with a bachelor's degree or higher rose from 20.3% to 25.6% (National Center for Education Statistics, 2003). Among the causes for this upward shift in educational attainment of adults is the strong correlation between educational attainment and unemployment and median income earnings. According to Postsecondary Education OPPORTUNITY (2003), the median income earnings of individuals in 2001 who had earned a high school diploma was $29,187 compared to those who had earned a bachelor's degree at $46,969, a master's at $56,589, or a doctorate at $75,182. As one might conclude, an inverse relationship between educational attainment and unemployment exists. In 2002, persons who completed high school were unemployed at a rate of 5.3% compared to bachelor's degree recipients at 3.1%, master's degree recipients at 2.8%, and doctoral degree holders at 1.6% (Postsecondary Education OPPORTUNITY, 2003). While there are obviously no guarantees regarding employment or earnings that come with college degrees, the evidence is compelling.

Within this context, a particular concern is the disparity that exists between racial and ethnic groups regarding educational attainment. On average, 20.3% of U.S. citizens 25 or older have earned a bachelor's degree or higher (National Center for Education Statistics, 2003). Of those, Asian and Pacific Islanders have the highest percentage earning bachelor's degrees or higher (36.6%). Whites earn four-year degrees and higher at a rate of 21.5% compared to blacks at 11.4%, Americans Indians or Alaskan Natives at 9.3%, and Hispanics at 9.2%.

Contrary to the dominance of females in the total population earning bachelor's degrees, as cited in chapter three, there is essentially no difference in the number of bachelor's degree recipients who are 25 or older based on gender (National Center for Education Statistics, 2003). Parity begins to diminish, however, for females in this age group when comparing professional and doctoral degrees earned. Adult males outpace females nearly 2:1 for professional degrees and 3:1 for doctorates. Conversely, females 25 or older have a slight advantage in earning master's degrees (approximately 258,000 more are earned annually by women than men).

Obviously, such inequities have implications for individuals as well as the nation. But some differences in educational characteristics of Gen Xers affect states directly. By state, residents 25 and over who have earned a bachelor's degree or higher range from a high of 37.6% in Maryland to a low of 15.9% in West Virginia (Postsecondary Education OPPORTUNITY, 2003). Along with Maryland, the states of Colorado, Virginia, Massachusetts, Connecticut, New Jersey, Vermont, Minnesota, New Hampshire, and Rhode Island have adult populations with more than 30% having earned a bachelor's degree or higher. On another positive note, between 1989 and 2002, every state except Wyoming has experienced an increase in the percentage of the adult population earning such degrees (Postsecondary Education OPPORTUNITY, 2003). Alabama, Maryland, and Delaware have increased by more than 10% during this period.

Gen Xers return to college with a variety of educational goals, not just to complete a degree program. Some are seeking certification, job skills, self-enrichment, and even intellectual affirmation. Sometimes independent of their educational goals, they generally select fields of study that interest them. Among adults ages 30 to 49, the five most popular fields of study, listed in order of preference, are business, education, engineering, liberal arts, and the natural sciences (National Center for Education Statistics, 2003). The health sciences, social sciences, and psychology are also popular fields of study among Gen Xers.

Other educational characteristics of the Gen X population identified by the National Center for Education Statistics (1996) suggest that they often:

- have delayed enrollment into postsecondary education
- attend college part-time
- are financially independent of parents
- work full-time while enrolled
- lack a standard high school diploma

(Council for Adult and Experimental Learning, 2000).

Values, Beliefs, and Behaviors

In a twenty-five trend analysis published by the Cooperative Institutional Research Program (Dey, Astin, & Korn, 1991), data regarding the values, beliefs, and behaviors of college freshmen along with other descriptive information reveals insights into Gen Xers when they were in their late teens. By comparing this data with studies of their behavior now, the effects of the environment and maturation can be inferred. For example, approximately half of freshmen Gen Xers were willing to attend college more than fifty miles away from home (Dey, Astin, & Korn, 1991). However, today's adult students are geographically bound unless enrolled in distance learning programs. For these students, geographic convenience is often a major factor in the college selection process.

As freshmen, Gen Xers indicated that they decided to go to college largely because of the perceived value of a college degree when seeking a desirable job, making more money, or learning things that interest them (Dey, Astin, & Korn, 1991). Unquestionably, many adults are returning to college today for career-related reasons. A down economy has historically compelled adults to enhance their job prospects or security through education. In the twenty-first century, jobs increasingly require higher skills and individuals increasingly change careers multiple times throughout their lifetimes (Council for Adult and Experimental Learning and the American Council on Education, 1993; Zill & Robinson, 1995). The former has been driven by increased technology and automation, particularly in manufacturing. The loss of high-paying manufacturing jobs to automation and foreign competitors with lower labor costs has sent many less-educated workers to unemployment lines or to lower paying jobs (Zill & Robinson, 1995). As referenced in chapter four, many Gen Xers witnessed their parents fall victim to corporate takeovers and downsizing (Smith, 2000; Audibert & Jones, 2002). This left many distrusting corporate America and recent scandals with Enron, WorldCom, Martha Stewart Living Omnimedia, Inc., and others, have only heightened their distrust resulting in a growing unwillingness to invest in a single company or career as their parents did.

Generation X employees are often motivated more by an opportunity than a specific job (Smith, 2000). These opportunities are generally related to something that interests them and corresponds with their desire once as first-time freshmen and now as returning adults to enroll in college to learn about something that interests them. However, the economic prosperity the country experienced in the mid and late '90s gave some Gen Xers a false sense of potential opportunities and unrealistic career expectations (Audibert & Jones, 2002).

Sometimes dubbed the multitasking generation, they grew up watching television and doing homework at the same time (Kraus, 2000). A multitasking lifestyle is essential to their success as returning college students. They must balance school, work, family, church, community, and many more of life's daily demands. These oft-competing priorities frustrate the Gen Xer who is constantly striving to live a balanced life.

Due in part to the high rate of divorce experienced by their parents and the resulting instability in their family lives, Gen X adults tend to have traditional values related to marriage, sex, and commitment (Kraus, 2000; Yin, 2002). As teenagers, however, the majority of college bound Gen Xers believed that premarital sex was acceptable if people liked each other; couples should live together before marriage; and abortion should be legalized (Dey, Astin, & Korn, 1991). In the same study, slightly less than half felt that divorce laws should be liberalized. And, depending upon the cohort surveyed, Gen X freshmen who thought parents should be discouraged from having large families ranged from 36% to 69% of the respondents. Matured Gen Xers are cautious and judicious about entering into a stage of life that includes marriage and a family (Kraus, 2000). They are waiting longer to make such commitments than their parents. Their views on marriage and family often impact when and how they return to college. For some, the completion of a college degree calculatedly precedes marriage and family; others balance family life with college life; and some wait until "the nest is empty" again or their own divorce motivates them to pursue a new life direction through education. Whatever the case, marriage and family status is a factor that enrollment managers, admissions counselors, financial aid professionals, academic advisors, faculty, and others should consider when interacting with Gen Xers.

Similar to the delayed commitment with marriage and family, some research suggests that many Gen Xers make a slow transition into adulthood (Zill & Robinson, 1995). In the early stages of their adult lives, they are more likely than their predecessors to live with their parents (Zill & Robinson, 1995). Whether they reside with their parents or not, many are dependent on parents for financial support much like they were as traditional freshmen (Dey, Astin, & Korn, 1991; Ritchie, 1995).

Even though some Gen Xers are financially dependent upon their parents, as the nation's first generation of "latchkey kids," they grew up as independent thinkers (Smith, 2000;

Audibert & Jones, 2002). They are creative problem solvers (Smith, 2000). Changes in family composition, technology, the economy, and the like have thrust this generation into a state of constant mutation (Audibert & Jones, 2002). To survive, Gen Xers have had to be nimble – responding instantaneously to their environment. Their chameleonlike adaptability is considered by many employers to be an invaluable asset (Smith, 2000) and, indeed, can be an asset in a college classroom.

Perhaps, because everything around them is so fluid, Generation Xers have an unquenchable need to stay in touch with friends and family (Ritchie, 1995). Many are satisfying that need by moving closer to friends and family (Silbiger & Brooks, 2002). New technology such as cell phones, the Web, e-mail, instant messaging, text messaging, and video conferencing has allowed this generation to remain connected with a regularity from any distance. Following September 11th, some Gen Xers also are expressing a desire to reconnect with their local communities (Silbiger & Brooks, 2002).

Time is one of their most precious possessions (Bishop, 2002); so, staying connected in ways that are convenient and efficient is essential. Likewise, interactions with their college of choice must be convenient and efficient. From student services to instructional delivery, Gen Xers are busy people with zero tolerance for delays and institutional bureaucracy. The implications of student time to colleges and universities are written about extensively in chapter four.

Addressing the time constraints of Generation X students is just one visible sign that an institution recognizes that these students are savvy consumers (Ritchie, 1995). They have little patience for organizations that are not customer oriented. So, the elite in the academy can continue to pretend that students are not customers, but to do so is perilous.

Having been bombarded by advertising their entire lives, Gen Xers are leery of insincere marketing pitches and gimmicks (Ritchie, 1995). Their antiadvertising bent should be considered before investing significant institutional dollars in advertising campaigns. As savvy consumers, Gen Xers tend to spend their discretionary dollars on items that feed their need to stay in touch (primarily electronic devices), maintain a balanced life (e.g., leisure activities and family entertainment), and live practically (e.g., economical automobiles, functional clothes, health insurance, and education) (Ritchie, 1995). Interestingly, Gen Xers spend 78% more than the average American on personal services (Bishop, 2002). This dependency on personal services is likely driven by their need to safeguard their limited time.

Conclusion

Admittedly, college faculty and staff encounter Gen X students who resemble Sack's (1996) description of disengaged loafers with an entitlement mentality; however, returning Gen Xers are more likely to exhibit positive characteristics like those described in this chapter. Generally, they perform better academically than their younger counterparts, they are more motivated, and they enrich the classroom by sharing their life experiences.

Comparing twenty-five years of trend data of American freshmen to the lives of today's Gen Xers suggests that many have fulfilled their dreams. They have attended graduate or professional schools, owned successful businesses, earned substantial incomes, made a name for themselves in their chosen professions, and raised families (Dey, Astin, & Korn, 1991). But for some, there is still a void.

As freshmen, Gen Xers overwhelmingly indicated that they had aspirations of completing a bachelor's degree. For whatever reason, that aspiration was temporarily derailed. Now, more determined and motivated than ever, they are returning to college to complete unfinished business. True, many are driven by career and economic factors. Yet, a surprising number of Gen Xers return to college to prove something to themselves or others in their lives. Rightly or wrongly, they believe that their full potential will be unleashed or their lives enriched through further education. Their future and, to some degree, that of the country's depends on higher education's collective response to their return.

REFERENCES

Audibert, G., and Jones, M. (2002, March). The impact of a changing economy on Gen X job seekers. *USA Today Magazine*. 130(2682): 20–21.

Bishop, D. (2002, July/August). The Gen X budget. *American Demographics*. 24(7): S5.

Council for Adult and Experimental Learners & American Council on Education (1993, March). *Adult degree programs: Quality issues, problem areas, and action steps*. Chicago, IL & Washington, DC: Council for Adult and Experimental Learners & American Council on Education.

Council for Adult and Experimental Learning (2000). *Serving Adult Learners in Higher Education: Principles of Effectiveness*. Chicago, IL: Council for Adult and Experimental Learning.

Coupland, D., *Generation X*. New York, NY: St. Martin's Press, 1991.

Dey, E., Astin, A., & Korn, W. (1991). *The American Freshman: Twenty-five Year Trends*. Los Angeles, CA: Cooperative Institutional Research Program.

Kraus, S. (2000, June 5). Gen Xers' reinvented 'traditionalism.' *Brandweek*. 41(23): 28–30.

National Center for Education Statistics (2001). *Total fall enrollment in degree-granting institutions, by attendance status, sex, and age: 1970 to 2011*. [On-line]. Available: http://nces.ed.gov//pubs2002/digest2001/tables/dt174.asp.

National Center for Education Statistics (2003, June). *Digest of education statistics*. [On-line]. Available: http://nces.ed.gov/pubs2003/2003060a.pdf.

Postsecondary Education OPPORTUNITY (2001, November). *College enrollment by age, 1950 to 2000*. [On-line]. Available: http://www.postsecondary.org/last12/1131101Age.pdf.

Postsecondary Education OPPORTUNITY (2002, February). *Earned degrees conferred by gender, 1870–2000*. [On-line]. Available: http://www.postsecondary.org/archives/previous/116202GENDER.pdf.

Postsecondary Education OPPORTUNITY (2003, March). *Earnings by educational attainment*, 1958 to 2001. (129): 11–16.

Postsecondary Education OPPORTUNITY (2003, March). *Educational attainment, 1940 to 2002*. (129): 1–10.

Postsecondary Education OPPORTUNITY (2003). *Education and training pay*. [On-line]. Available: http://www.postsecondary.org/archives/Posters/Education%20and%20Training%20Pay02%20 poster.pdf

Ritchie, K. (1995). Marketing to Generation X: Marketing to the post-baby boom generation. *American Demographics*. 17(4): 34–40.

Sacks, P. (1996). *Generation X Goes to College: An Eye-opening Account of Teaching in Postmodern America*. Chicago and LaSalle, IL: Open Court.

Silbiger, S. & Brooks, C. (2002, March 11). Generation disconnext. *Brandweek*. 43(10): 22–24.

Smith, B. (2000, November). Managing Generation X. *USA Today Magazine*. 129(2666): 32–34.

The Chronicle of Higher Education (2002, August 30). *College enrollment by racial and ethnic group, selected years*. XLIX (1): 23.

U.S. Census Bureau (2000). *Census 2000 summary file 1, matrices PCT12 and P13*. [On-line]. Available: http://factfinder.census.gov/bf/_lang=en_vt_name=DEC_2000_SF1_U_GCTP5_US9_geo_ id=01000US.html.

U.S. Census Bureau (2000, March). *Population by age, sex, race and Hispanic origin*. [On-line]. Available: http://landview.census.gov/population/socdemo/gender/ppl-121/tab01.txt.

Yin, S. (2002, April). Career matters. *American Demographics*. 24(4): 18–20.

Zill, N. & Robinson, J. (1995). The Generation X difference. *American Demographics*. 17(4): 24–30.

CHAPTER TWO

Gen Xers of Color

Trina Gabriel

Changing Educational Landscape

Approaching the fiftieth-year anniversary of the Brown v. Topeka Board of Education decision provides educational institutions the opportunity to reflect upon and gauge their commitments to access and the "equality of education" for all students, more specifically students of color. Intermingled within these reflections undoubtedly will be the current debate/litigation regarding affirmative action. Education is political and extends far beyond the bounds of the classroom. As such, education can be contentious terrain. And in looking at the landscape, we find that it is ever changing. A more diverse body of students is entering higher education. Educational institutions, as agents of change, now have a greater charge to meet the needs of multiple communities.

Individuals twenty-five years of age or older account for more than 15% of full-time students and more than 60% of part-time first-year undergraduates (Osgood–Treston, 2001). These individuals are also racially and ethnically diverse. The multitude of varying ethnic students currently found in higher education was not present several decades ago. Students of color have been one of the fastest growing populations in higher education. Gen Xers comprise part of this growing population. Gen Xers have been referred to as "the most ethnically diverse generation in American history" (Saunders & Bauer, 1998, p. 8).

The purpose of this chapter is to examine the climate faced by Gen Xers of color as they return to higher education at the undergraduate level. Specifically, this chapter will focus on those students who return for academic credit, usually seeking to complete a degree at a traditionally white institution. This is a very limited look at native or naturalized African American and Latino/Hispanic citizens. It will not cover the additional challenges faced by Native American, Asian American, or international students.

Are they seen?

As an institution of higher education seeks to craft an institutional community, it must be cognizant of the challenges faced by members of its multiple communities. Community building requires colleges and universities to look at the campus culture and determine whether or not it embraces a culturally diverse adult population. The campus is constructed of multiple communities – students, faculty, staff, alumni, administrators. They each play a crucial role in creating an inclusive climate (Keeton & James, 1992).

Power and privilege are embedded within the manner in which this population is labeled or defined – often referred to as adult students of color. Much of the research concerning Generation X utilizes the terms adult or nontraditional students. Labeling the group as adult or nontraditional fails to note generational differences that may affect learning experiences. To reference the group as students of color often negates the complexities and distinctions found within and among various racial and ethnic groups.

Institutions typically focus on the term student, often silencing their students' voices as adults and dismissing their racial or ethnic identity. Students are viewed as dependent upon the institution and its personnel. The term adult involves the idea of independence and self-reliance (Schollsberg, Lynch, & Chickering, 1989); hence, in addressing their needs, institutions cannot simply replicate what is done for the traditional-age student of color. The policies and practices constructed for younger students of color may not work for Gen Xers of color.

There are a myriad of factors impacting this population. Adult students of color are not a homogeneous group. Keeton & James note "People of different ethnic groups may share a common culture, but a college or university serving substantial numbers of ethnically diverse students is likely also to be serving culturally diverse students" (1992, p. 9). Combined with the difference in race or ethnicity are the differences of gender, sexual orientation, socioeconomic status, familial obligations, geographical location, etc. These attributes are considered ways of knowing and they can't be parceled out when discussing this group.

Why should an emphasis be placed on Gen Xers of color?

To understand the ways in which populations of color will impact the country in the future, it is necessary to look at their educational opportunities. African Americans, American Indians, and Hispanic Americans have a higher population growth rate in comparison to whites (Raines, 1998). Latino/Hispanic students, most often, do not progress in the same educational manner toward college as do majority students. Sixteen percent of Latinos entered college after graduation from high school, while 44% of Asian Americans, 30% of whites, and 27% of African Americans entered college after graduation from high school (Hispanics, 1994).

Adult students of color may be products of an educational environment that left them unprepared to attain advanced education. African American and Hispanic students are more likely to attend secondary schools concentrated in areas of poverty. Even those who do well in inner city schools may have received an inferior education and may not have been adequately prepared for college-level work (O'Brien & Zudak, 1998).

As the population rates for communities of color exceed that of whites, the face of our work-place has changed (O'Brien & Zudak, 1998). For example, the Hispanic population has an average age of 29 and is evenly distributed between men and women. They are the fastest growing minority population in the United States (Laden, 2001). The academic well-being of this population affects the overall economic health of this country (Brown, Santiago, & Lopez, 2003). "When the educational, social, and economic attainment of large segments of any nation's population is low, the cultural and economic life of that nation is adversely affected and if the condition persists, placed in peril" (Maguire, 1988, p. 21). Hailed as the great equalizer, higher education remains one of the most viable means for continued social mobility and achievement for populations of color in the United States (Raines, 1998).

It is important to look at Gen Xers of color because they have multiple identities – related to both age and race. There may be multiple definitions of "the meaning and role of race as well as how these differences interact with specific contexts to affect academic outcomes" (Chavous, 2002, p. 145). There is no one way for members of various racial or ethnic groups to view the manner in which race or ethnicity affects their lives. "African Americans differ in the ways they see race as functioning in their lives, and these differences in belief systems should be related to how individuals experience and react to situations and experiences within their educational contexts" (Chavous, 2002, p. 145). These contexts are framed within individual experience, group experience, and the racial climate that exists on campus. Faculty, staff, and students must actively question the culture of the institution. Is it traditional-age and white? If so, what does this mean for the adult student of color?

A few issues to address …

The success of any student begins with his or her entrance into the institution. Taking note of student concerns at the admissions stage may likely increase retention and enhance the likelihood for matriculation (Johnson, Schwartz, & Bower, 2000). Particularly for adult students, the location of a college or university is frequently more important than academic reputation. Serving students of color necessitates knowing not only the campus community but also the larger community in which the institution is located. If a student selects an institution that can effectively meet his needs and desired goals, he is more likely to matriculate. If presented with an accurate picture of an institution, the student can make a more informed choice. For nontraditional students of color, traditional admission information is often inadequate. These students regularly are in search of information related to financial aid, personal/social support, and family concerns (Edwards & Person, 1997).

Similar to the concerns of many adult students, financial aid may be a priority for Gen Xers of color. Securing financial aid can be a complex process, as it tends to focus on traditional under-graduate students. For example, work-study programs, one federal source for education funding, are designed for full-time students aged 18–22 (Schollsberg, Lynch, & Chickering,

1989). For many Gen Xers of color, their attendance is on a part-time basis. As a part-time student, financial aid options are limited. Adult students typically seek the university's assistance in finding part-time employment and aid. This is important because many of these students are coming from disadvantaged backgrounds. Not all minorities are poor, but a large percentage comes from lower socioeconomic backgrounds (O'Brien & Zudak, 1998).

In assisting these students, an effort must be made to support them through various programs and services. Counseling services geared toward academic reentry, study techniques, and course selection can be very beneficial (Laden, 2001). Members of this community are often defined as minorities who are underprivileged and at risk. Not all are underachievers, but many are academically unprepared and have not received the support needed in the past (O'Brien & Zudak, 1998). College personnel must understand how circumstances outside of the classroom play out in the classroom for this growing population (Johnson-Bailey, 2002).

Even if they are actively recruited and persist, students of color could possibly still feel isolated on the campus because their cultural values may be different from the majority. They frequently feel overlooked or invisible. Often, their experiences are framed within those of majority students. To simply reference the student's behaviors, values, and experiences to that of white students diminishes those students of color and relegates them to the position of "other" (Gloria & Rodriguez, 2000). It is difficult to separate social adjustment from academic adjustment. Learning is best achieved in a respectful climate. As Chavous notes, students of color at traditionally white institutions often live within two realms – ethnicity and self-development – as well as the culture and values of the traditionally white environment (2002).

A face similar to one's own can be a source of lasting support. Utilizing current students as peer advisors or counselors can aid in the formation of a social network through which Gen Xers of color can gain answers to questions and seek advice from those who may be in a similar situation. How a student interacts with a campus has a lot to do with who already exists on that campus. Students need to feel a sense of value, respect, and appreciation. There must be a link that aids this population in carving an identity and that provides a sense of inclusion. Gen Xers of color may be seeking mentors or advisors not strictly limited to academics. Concerns related to collegiate progress do not center solely upon academics. Oftentimes, students leave school for economic reasons, personal reasons, family reasons, etc. (Gloria & Rodriguez, 2000).

As part of the campus community, faculty and staff must recognize potential barriers facing Gen Xers. Institutions of higher learning are now challenged to negotiate the balance between the "former majority" and its "new diverse constituents" (Keeton & James, 1992). Teaching faculty must recognize and implement strategies that are inclusive of all of their students. Bishop-Clark & Lynch (1992) suggest that they encourage personal contact, discuss differences, find similarities, and promote these among the individuals within the class. Difference doesn't necessitate a value judgment. It can be interesting. As it stands, students change to fit the college mold (Keeton & James, 1992). The curriculum should include literature on issues related to adult students of color in the classroom. Culturally responsive approaches must be designed for these students – synergy created between faculty and students (Johnson-Bailey, 2002).

Those faculty and staff who reflect the various cultures of students of color may be called upon to assist in the campus responsiveness. These persons may have a more acute awareness and comprehension of the "commitment" needed to meet students' social, cultural, and academic needs. Not many persons in positions of power at traditionally white institutions resemble these students. For example, Hispanic faculty accounted for 2.6% of all higher education faculty but Hispanic students (in 1996) comprised 10.3% of the undergraduate student population (Laden, 2001).

An adult student often has multiple roles or responsibilities. Time is limited. Keeton and James (1992) suggest that a one-way relationship between students and colleges or universities is no longer valid. Not only must students come into the campus community, but colleges and universities must go out into the world of the student. Faculty and staff must begin a dialogue with these students. Students become invested in the community when they interact with the community. Attending as part-time students, the majority of this population does not live on campus. To affect culture or be affected by a culture, one must see him or herself as a part of that culture, involved in that culture.

> It is not enough that the institution has programs and staff to support him; it must continually reaffirm its welcome. A commitment must be transmitted and a belief evoked in the student that he, in particular, will be a success. The college also must enable its diverse students to see the value of their contributions to the quality of the institution itself and thereby to accumulate real and lasting equity in its future (Keeton & James, 1992, p. 11).

Minority Serving Institutions: Implications for Serving Generation X

Minority-serving institutions (MSIs), defined as "the groups of institutions that enroll a high proportion of African American, Hispanic, and American Indian students" (O'Brien & Zudak, 1998, p. 5), have played crucial roles in educating populations of color. The National Center for Education Statistics (NCES) noted in 1994 that more than two-thirds of all students of color were enrolled in nearly 1,000 institutions (less than one-third of the total number of universities). The majority of these institutions were defined as minority-serving institutions (O'Brien & Zudak, 1998). It is important that increased understanding and recognition of the roles of MSIs takes place within the dialogue regarding Gen Xers of color. It is necessary to note that MSIs are not operating in "educational isolation" but in conjunction (whether cooperatively or competitively) with traditionally white institutions and each other.

Historically Black Colleges and Universities (HBCUs) are one category of MSIs. HBCUs are the oldest group of minority-serving institutions. They were developed in the nineteenth century as a means of educating African American students who were not allowed to enroll in traditionally white institutions in the southern and border states (O'Brien & Zudak, 1998).

Hispanic Serving Institutions (HSIs) are a second category of MSIs. HSIs are "2- and 4-year colleges and universities with 25% or more total undergraduate Hispanic full-time equivalent (FTE) enrollments" (Laden, 2001, p. 73). HSIs were developed due to geographic location –

most HSIs are located in the ten states with the largest number of Hispanic residents. More than 50% of all Hispanic students are enrolled in institutions of higher learning in Texas and California. HSIs differ from HBCUs in that their design was not specifically created to meet the needs of this population (Laden, 2001). HSIs serve nearly 40% of all Latino students — enrolling more than 1.4 million Hispanic students (as of 1997) (Laden, 2001). These 220 institutions comprise approximately 6% of all postsecondary institutions.

Roebuck and Murty (1993) note that black students feel a closer connection on black campuses since the collegiate experience encompasses more than just academics. This thought could be extended to Hispanic students at HSIs. Socially, students have the opportunity to be in the majority as opposed to the minority. Students are enveloped in an environment that contains a rich and positive history and tradition. Oftentimes, their experiences in the college environment are quite similar to those from their home environments (Sims, 1994). Although Gen Xers of color are often members of an ethnic or racial majority on the campus of an MSI, they soon discover their distinction as an "aged" minority. As Generation Xers of color seek to overcome the challenges faced in returning to higher education, MSIs must seek to craft a welcoming environment — an environment which recognizes these students have unique skills, interests, and motivations (Saunders & Bauer, 1998).

MSIs are said to provide more role models for students of color. The curriculum often centers on their culture and the skills needed for them to succeed in a predominantly white environment. The environment is one in which students feel safe to express and define themselves (Raines, 1998). MSIs must ensure that the safe environment extends to self-development for Gen Xers.

Access to higher education is often an issue for Gen Xers of color. For this reason, among many others, MSIs will play a critical role in the education of Gen Xers color. As Brown eloquently notes,

> … [T]he black college does not absolve higher education of its responsibility to explore the sociocultural, socioeconomic, political, and familial backgrounds that contribute to African American students' attrition, and the ramifications of the larger society that perpetuates these characteristics. However, the black college remains the academic home of the legacy of scholastic achievement in spite of inequitable resources (1999, p. 21).

These attributes are present in Hispanic Serving Institutions as well. MSIs are not the sole keepers of African American student success; however, they've been great facilitators. But as facilitators, they must recognize the generational differences that affect student success as well.

MSIs have a unique opportunity to study generational differences within their populations. Although students of color are not a homogeneous group, the environment of an MSI may allow for group identity where race is not the focal point. An opportunity is presented to discover the needs of different subgroups, specifically Gen Xers. As students feel that their racial or ethnic culture is celebrated, other issues come to the forefront. Many of these may be generation specific. The confluence of race and age is potentially muted (though not eliminated) at an MSI. MSIs are now challenged to look beyond the experience of race and account for generational differences. Gen Xers are unique. They are not the same as the generation that preceded them.

Community Colleges

Community colleges also play a crucial role in the educational development of adult students. Accounting for roughly 28% of the total number of all U.S. colleges and universities, two-year institutions enroll nearly 37% of all students. Community colleges have a large number of commuter students who attend on a part-time basis. They are often older, students of color who come from a working class background. Many adult students of color are attending local community colleges because they offer a convenient location, open admissions policy, affordable cost, and quality education, and allow for a balance with non-school commitments (Pascarella & Terenzini, 1998).

There is a climate of acceptance at community colleges for those who may be from a lower socioeconomic background, first generation, or academically ill-prepared (Laden, 2001). Financial concerns and the opportunity to remain close to home are two reasons Latino students often choose to attend a community college (Brown, Santiago & Lopez, 2003).

Community colleges operate under an open-door policy. Meeting students where they are, without requiring specific academic accomplishments, these institutions provide an arena where students learn to be successful, which may be critically important for underrepresented students (West, 1993). True to the mission under which they were created, community colleges provide access to higher education for all – even those who were previously excluded (Mellow, 2000). They serve as a connector between educational and economic opportunity for the masses.

Gail Mellow notes that community colleges are constantly changing. As these institutions respond to the needs of the community, they redevelop themselves. The nearly eleven hundred community colleges are responsible for enrolling nearly eleven million students, accounting for nearly 45% of all undergraduates – 42% of all African American students, 50% of all Native students, 55% of all Latino students, and 40% of all Asian and Pacific Islander students (2000).

As Saunders & Bauer reflected, "The climate encountered by the students will depend on the groups to which they belong, and how they interact with the institution" (1998, p. 13). Different subgroups will have different experiences on the community college campus. The average age of enrollees at the community college is twenty-nine (Saunders & Bauer, 1998). Combined with the racial or ethnic diversity of these students, one finds fertile ground for discovering the means by which to meet the needs of Generation X. As Gen Xers of color continue to choose community colleges as a primary means to attain higher education, community colleges will be challenged to ensure the success for this part-time, non-residential, time-constrained population.

Keep in Mind …

The adult population returning to higher education is steadily increasing, but many services are geared toward the traditional-age college student. Because the returning student may not be the primary focus, oftentimes his or her needs are not met. Gen Xers of color face many issues and have many needs that institutions must address. It is imperative that college personnel take a global look at the various ways in which they interact with these students. An institutional understanding of the climate of the campus can significantly better the educational experience. Gen Xers of color need support and encouragement from the college or university in order for them to succeed, and this support will be reflected through resources and attention.

Gen Xers of color must be viewed as individuals with different needs and concerns, not a homogeneous community. From faculty and administrators to staff, persons of color must be involved in the process of crafting a welcoming climate. Students must also be a part of the discussion. They must be given the opportunity to voice their concerns. It is important that we continue to hear from this group to learn what their perceived needs are. The impetus to hear and respond to the voice of this population is a necessity, not a choice. Sissel, Hansman, & Kansworm note that " … change requires more than assessing current support services; it requires political awareness of the privilege and power on campus and the willingness to challenge current conditions while proposing and implementing better resources for adult learners" (1993, p. 22), particularly adult learners of various racial and ethnic backgrounds.

This group of students should not simply be viewed as problematic. They are assets to the institution. If measures are taken to build a diverse institutional community, students have a rewarding experience and institutions can see the successful matriculation of its students. These students must be taken from the margins and made a central concern. There must be recognition of the role of power, privilege, and position within current institutions. Campus leaders must listen to the voice of Gen Xers and incorporate their perspective.

Recognizing difference does not necessitate a value judgment. Yet, it is an institutional responsibility to question if this population is receiving different responses than their younger counterparts. This population could become "hyperinvisible" because of their age as well as their race or ethnicity.

REFERENCES

Bishop-Clark, C., & Lynch, J. (1992). The mixed-age college classroom. *College Teaching*. 40(3): 114–117.

Brown, M. (1999). Public black colleges and desegregation in the United States: A continuing dilemma. *Higher Education Policy*. 12: 15–25.

Brown, S., Santiago, D., & Lopez, E. (2003). Latinos in higher education: Today and tomorrow. *Change*. 35(2): 40–46.

Chavous, T. (2002). African American college students in predominantly white institutions of higher education: Considerations of race and gender. *African American Research Perspectives*. 8(1): 142–50.

Edwards, R., & Person, D. (1997). Retaining the adult student: The role of admission counselors. *Journal of College Admission*. 154: 18–21.

Gloria, A., & Rodriguez, E. (2000). Counseling Latino university students: Psychosociocultural issues for consideration. *Journal of Counseling and Development*. 78: 145–154.

Hispanics trail in higher education. (1994, April). *USA Today Magazine*. 122: 13.

Johnson, L., Schwartz, R., and Bower, B. (2000). Managing stress among adult women students in community colleges. *Community College Journal of Research and Practice*. 24: 289–300.

Johnson-Bailey, J. (2002). Race matters: the unspoken variable in the teaching-learning transaction. *New Directions for Adult and Continuing Education*. 93: 39–49.

Keeton, M. & James, R. (1992). An uncertain trumpet. *Liberal Education*. 78(4): 8–12.

Laden, B. (2001). Hispanic-serving institutions: myths and realities. *Peabody Journal of Education*. 76(1): 73–92.

Maguire, J. (1988). Reversing the recent decline in minority participation in higher education. In *Minorities in Public Higher Education: At a Turning Point*. Washington, DC: AASCU Press.

Mellow, G. (2000, September). *The History and Development of Community Colleges in the United States*. Paper presented at New Options for Higher Education in Latin America: Lessons from the Community College Experience Conference, Cambridge, MA.

O'Brien, E. & Zudak, C. (1998). Minority-serving institutions: An overview. *New Directions for Higher Education*. 102: 5–15.

Osgood-Treston, B. (2001). Program completion barriers faced by adult learners in higher education. *Academic Exchange Quarterly*. 5(2): 120.

Pascarella, E. & Terenzini, P. (1998). Studying college students in the 21st century: Meeting new challenges. *The Review of Higher Education*. 21(2): 151–165.

Raines, R. (1998). Collaboration and cooperation among minority-serving institutions. *New Directions for Higher Education*. 102: 69–80.

Roebuck, J., & Murty, K. (1993). *Historically Black Colleges and Universities: Their Place in American Higher Education*. Westport: Praeger Publishers.

Saunders, L., & Bauer, K. (1998). Undergraduate students today: Who are they? *New Directions for Institutional Research*. 98: 7–16.

Schollsberg, N., Lynch, A., & Chickering, A. (1989). *Improving Higher Education Environments for Adults: Responsive Programs and Services from Entry to Departure*. San Francisco: Jossey–Bass.

Sims, S. (1994). *Diversifying Historically Black Colleges and Universities: A New Higher Education Paradigm*. Westport: Greenwood Press.

Sissel, P., Hansman, C., & Kasworm, C. (2001). The politics of neglect: Adult learners in higher education. *New Directions for Adult and Continuing Education*. 91: 17–27.

West, L. (1993). A view from the margins: Community colleges and access to higher education for adults in inner-city america. *Studies in the Education of Adults*. 25(2): 146–172.

CHAPTER THREE

The Influence of Gender and Sexuality Among Gen Xers

Cindra S. Kamphoff

Introduction

It is difficult to consider Gen Xers returning to college without consider-ing the influence of gender and sexuality. In fact, many would contend that gender and sexuality influences everything that we do in our lives. Gender influences our roles in society including the roles men and women play within families and work environments. These roles drasti-cally influence the Gen Xer's ability to return to college. Understanding how these roles influence being both men and women in Western society, particularly in a college environment, is essential. It is difficult, and almost impossible, to truly consider the impact of being a woman in college, without also understanding what it is like to be a man in college as well. In addition, there are universal categories of acceptable sexualities affecting all men and women in society, and if men and women do not fit into these socially constructed categories of femininity and masculinity, they feel marginalized. Heterosexuality has become naturalized in society, whereas homosexuality is seen as unnatural and wrong to many Ameri-cans. This chapter will discuss trends regarding gender and sexuality in higher education, issues for men and women when returning to college, GLBTQ (gays, lesbians, bisexuals, transsexuals, and questioning) individ-uals, how to make campuses more accommodating to all people, and current issues in higher education regarding gender and sexuality.

Separating Gender and Sexuality

Most scholars would argue that it is impossible to consider gender and sexuality without also considering how other social inequalities such as race, ethnicity, class, and ability impact men and women (Anderson, 1997; Zinn, Hondagneau-Sotelo, & Messner, 2000). Both sexuality and gender operate independently of each other, as well as interdependently with each other. In addition, both sexuality and gender interact with race, ethnicity, class, and ability. When considering gender and sexuality in college, these inequalities are also affected by race, ethnicity, class, and ability.

Trends in Gender and Sexuality Affecting Higher Education

THE GENDER SHIFT

The United States government has influenced the number of women Gen Xers that are returning to college. Specifically, both Title VII and Title IX have impacted the ability for women to attend college. Title VII of the Civil Rights Act of 1961 forbade discrimination on any term or condition of employment based on race, color, religion, sex, or national origin. Title IX, a provision of the Educational Amendment Act of 1972, applies to all institutions receiving federal funds. Title IX states that, "[n]o person in the United States shall, on the basis of sex, be excluded from participation in, be denied the benefits of, or be subjected to discrimination under any educational program or activity receiving federal financial assistance."

Both Title IV of the Higher Education Act concerning student aid and Title IX apply to men and women. Many people assume that both of these provisions, particularly Title IX, apply only to women. Since both social legislations were enacted, the number of men and women attending college has drastically changed (Mortenson, 2002b).

More women are attending college than ever before, and surprisingly, are now earning more college degrees than men. In fact, by 2000 the National Center for Education Statistics reported that the majority of associate, bachelor, and master's degrees was awarded to women (Knapp, Kelly, Whitmore, Wu, Gallego, Grau, & Broyles, 2001). Specifically, this report states that in 2000, "women earned 60% of all associate degrees, 57% of the bachelor's degrees, and 58% of the master's degrees" (Knapp et. al., 2001, p.6; see table 1). Doctorates and professional degrees are the only degrees in which men earn more diplomas than women, accounting for 56% of the doctorate degrees and 55% of first professional degrees (degrees such as law, medicine, pharmacy, and chiropractic). When comparing this percentage to the number of college-age men and women in society, the declining number seems even more astonishing since males remain a majority of the population in America through about age 24 (Mortenson, 2001). Mortenson (2001) reported that men constitute anywhere from 49.8 to 49.4% of the Gen X population, yet receive only 42% or fewer of all college degrees. And, by the year 2009, the National Center for Education Statistics has projected the number of males will increase by only 5.2%, whereas the projected number of females graduating with degrees is projected to increase 16.8% (Knapp et al., 2001).

TABLE 1	Number and percent of degrees by gender of 50 U.S. States and District of Columbia in the academic year of 1999–2000*			
	Male	Percent	Female	Percent
Total degrees	1,015,853	42.6%	1,368,310	57.4%
Associate degrees	224,721	39.8%	340,212	60.2%
Bachelor's degrees	530,367	42.8%	707,508	57.2%
Master's degrees	191,792	42.0%	265,264	58.0%
Doctoral degrees	25,028	55.9%	19,780	44.1%
First-professional degrees	43,945	55.3%	35,546	44.7%

*Data represents degrees conferred by Title IX participating, degree-granting, postsecondary institutions
SOURCE: U.S. Department of Education, National Center for Education Statistics, Fall 2000

Twenty-five years earlier, however, the majority of college degrees were awarded to men (Mortenson, 2002a). From these statistics, two very important trends in higher education are depicted: the progress of women in higher education and the lack of progress by men since the passage of Title IX and Title VII. To provide further statistics on this claim, the number of college degrees awarded in 1975 compared to 2000 can be examined. According to Postsecondary Education Opportunity, the number of bachelor's degrees that were awarded in those twenty-five years increased by a total of 314,942 (Mortenson, 2002a). Women have earned 91.9% of this increase, whereas men have earned only 8.1%. In addition, women have earned 81.6% of the increase in master's degrees, whereas men have earned 18.4%. Even though men still earn more doctorate degrees than women, a similar trend has also taken place within this terminal degree. Women have earned 116.7% of the increase in doctorate degrees and the number of men receiving doctorate degrees has actually decreased by 1,789 (Mortenson, 2002a).

By the year 2000, public institutions awarded 65.5% of the total degrees awarded for men and women (Knapp et al., 2001). When looking closer at the numbers of men and women who received degrees between 1970 and 2000, the private institutions showed the largest number of decrease in men's degrees. In public institutions, the bachelor's degrees awarded decreased from 55.1% to 43.2%, a decline of 11.9%. Whereas, private institutions, compared to public institutions, showed a decline of men's degrees by 16.2% from 58.3% to 42.1% (Mortenson, 2002a). Not surprisingly, the decrease in men's degrees awarded has been a concern among private institutions, in fact, "disappearing men" has been a topic at two national conferences held for private institutions. A conference at Goucher College in Baltimore took place in November 1999 and was titled *Fewer Men on Campus*. The second conference for private institutions took place at Morehouse College in Atlanta and was titled *Reconnecting Males to Liberal Education*.

CHANGE IN FAMILIES

Besides the increase of women and the decrease of men receiving college degrees, the change in family structure also influences Generation X's ability to return to college. With the broader definition and understanding of families (Ritchie, 1995), Gen Xers are experiencing different demands than generations before them. While growing up, Gen Xers experienced skyrocketing divorce rates (Kraus, 2000). In fact, Kruger (1994) reported that 40% of Gen Xers were raised by divorced or separated parents. Kraus (2000) concluded that on average "1 in 10 Gen Xers are already divorced or separated" (p. 28). Lankard (1995) contends that because Gen Xers were deprived of time with their parents when young, they are more committed to spending time with their own children. Moreover, Lankard (1995) and Yin (2002) both conclude that more Gen Xers that plan to have children desire to work part-time when their children are born so that they can spend time with them during their preschool years. The importance of family among Gen Xers can be seen by their emphasis on delaying marriage. Kraus (2000) provides evidence that thirty years ago women were typically getting married at the age of 21. Now, Generation X women are waiting until the age of 25. During the same period, men's marriage rates have been more difficult to "pin down" and average between 23 and 27 years old (Kraus, 2000, p.28).

As stated in chapter one, Gen Xers are not only waiting to get married – more are spending a longer time living with their parents. Ritchie (1995) argues that almost half of Gen Xers live at home through their late 20s. In a *Details* study Ritchie (1995) summarizes, "40% of Gen Xers said they still get money from parents in emergencies, 24% said their parents paid their doctor and dentist bills, 24% had parents who paid their insurance bills, 16% got help with the rent or mortgage, 16% with clothing or jewelry, 10% with car payments, and 7% with an allowance" (p. 36).

Issues for Gen X Women

BALANCING FAMILY

The delay of marriage compared to that of their parents indicates that Gen X women view family as important. A survey conducted by Catalyst of 1,263 Gen X professionals found that family is extremely important to this generation. Specifically, this study found that 84% of Gen Xers said that "having a loving family" was extremely important (Yin, 2002). In addition, Kraus (2000) reported that in 1998 over two-thirds of all Gen X women thought that having a child was important for every woman. Gen X women differ from the generation that preceded them given that fewer than half of Baby Boomers agreed that twenty years ago having a child was important. In addition, Ritchie (1995) reported that Baby "Boomers women were willing to sacrifice some of their family life … in a return for a chance at a career" (p. 38). Generation X women, on the other hand, are no longer willing to sacrifice their families and their personal lives for careers.

Yet, several pressures still loom for Gen X women. Women, even now, perform the majority of household chores and family responsibilities (Swanberg, Galinksky, & Bond, 1997), although more Gen X men are expected to share in household chores compared with Baby Boomer men (Ritchie, 1995). Noonan (2001) contends, however, that women still perform traditionally "feminine" tasks such as "getting children ready for school in the morning, preparing the evening meal, cleaning the home, and doing laundry", whereas the "male tasks" included "household repairs and automobile maintenance" which typically take place on the weekend (p.1135). Due to the amount of household labor that the women perform throughout the week instead of just on the weekend, Noonan (2001) concluded that household labor has had a negative effect on women's wages, contributing to the gender gap in salary between men and women since women have less time to "earn money."

In addition, the "soccer mom" mentality contributes to mothers expecting to be "everything" to their children and including their children in every possible opportunity. There is more pressure to provide young children with numerous opportunities for development, and women tend to bear the majority of this responsibility. Numerous studies have found that women have taken on the majority of the responsibility when their children are involved in after-school activities such as sports. Laundry, transportation, and cooking are the main responsibilities held by mothers, while fathers sit back and relax while enjoying the game (Chafetz & Kotarba, 1999; Thompson, 1999). If the mother is divorced and singly responsible for the child or children, this puts an even larger responsibility and burden on mothers. For example, The National Coalition for Women and Girls in Education (NCWGE, 1997) reported that "women who attend a postsecondary institution also are twice as likely as men to have dependents, and three times as likely to be single parents" (p. 6). Even though family and personal lives are important to Gen X women, over 72% of Gen Xers still believe their job interferes with their personal lives (Yin, 2002).

BALANCING WORK

In addition to viewing family as important, Generation X women are employed at a higher rate than women before them. Since 1950, the rates of females working have increased by 41.5% (Mortenson, 1999). Furthermore, the Bureau of Labor Statistics reported that women between the ages of 25 and 34 now put in more hours, and are more likely to hold more than one job, than in 1976 (DiNatale & Boraas, 2000). The Bureau of Labor Statistics also reports that women are earning more than the generation before them (DiNatale & Boraas, 2000). Generation X women are more likely to be raised by working mothers, and better educated than any generation in history (Kruger, 1994). Lankard (1995) contends that money, power, and status are motivators for the Generation X population and contributes to more of them becoming entrepreneurs than in any other generation.

DISCRIMINATION

Even though women are earning more than ever before, women in the Gen X age group are still earning only 82% of what men are earning (DiNatale & Boraas, 2000). In some professions, this gap becomes extraordinarily wide. For example, in the athletic coaching profession, male coaches earn almost double that of female coaches (Jacobsen, 2001). Many scholars speculate this gap exists because sports have traditionally been seen as a "man's world." Additional evidence supports the claim that women are still earning less than men. Sadker (1999) reported that among full-time workers, women with bachelor's degrees make only $4,708 more on average than men with high school diplomas. Women with bachelor's degrees make $20,000 less on average than men with bachelor's degrees. In addition, the Census Bureau reported that when comparing a bachelor's degree's worth over that of a high school diploma, a bachelor's degree adds about $1,266,000 to a male's lifetime income, and only $650,000 to a female's lifetime income (Mortenson, 2002b).

Moreover, women continue to have difficulty moving up the ladder, continuing to experience similar barriers as women of previous generations, commonly known as the "glass ceiling" effect. Frankly, women need to work harder than men to receive the same reward (Cheng, 2002). One study, for example, found that 42% of Gen X women say they have outperformed men to receive the same rewards (Yin, 2002). Another report found that husbands of Gen Xers still believe their careers are more important than the careers of their spouses (Cheng, 2002).

Women, in general, continue to experience discrimination and sexual harassment at work and in higher education. A recent study reported that the percentage of women who have experienced sexual harassment ranges from 19% for graduate students to 43% for administrators (Kelley & Parsons, 2000). Although much higher and less recent, Schneider (1987) indicated that 60% of female graduate students reported they had been sexually harassed by a male professor. The American Association of University Women's (AAUW) *Hostile Hallways* (1993) report suggests that at least 81% of students have been victims of sexual harassment before they enter college.

Additionally, the number of reported sexual offenses has increased on college campuses. The U.S. Department of Education (2001) confirmed that 2,469 sexual offenses were reported in 1999. This number represents an increased 6% from 1998. This statistic suggests that as Gen Xers are returning to college, the environment may be less safe. The Department of Education argues, however, that the number of sexual offenses has not increased on college campuses, but that the number of women reporting sexual offenses has increased. When college students are surveyed they report an even larger amount of sexual aggression. Perhaps the most cited study of sexual aggression is Koss, Gidycz, and Wisniewski (1987). Koss, et al. (1987) reported that almost 54% of women reported to have experienced some sort of sexual victimization (rape, attempted rape, or sexual coercion) since the age of fourteen. When the college men were surveyed, 25% admitted to engaging in some type of sexual aggression against women.

ALTERNATIVE PROFESSIONS AND MAJORS

Women continue to be concentrated in certain professions (see Table 2). For example, women make up 99% of kindergarten and preschool teachers, 85% of librarians, and 84% of legal assistants (DiNatale & Boraas, 2000). In addition, women graduate with 87.5% of elementary

TABLE 2	Ten largest programs of study of institutions in the 50 U.S. States and District of Columbia, academic year 1999–2000*

ASSOCIATE DEGREES		
Program of study	**Male Percent**	**Female Percent**
Liberal arts and sciences/liberal studies	37.0%	63.0%
Nursing (R.N. training)	10.7%	89.3%
Business administration and management, general	35.4%	64.6%
General studies	38.6%	61.4%
Business, general	35.2%	64.8%
Administrative assistant/secretarial science, general	4.0%	96.0%
Electrical, electronic and communication engineering technology	89.8%	10.2%
Liberal arts and science, general studies and humanities, other	38.6%	61.4%
Electrical and electronic engineering-related technology	90.2%	9.8%
Biological and physical science	40.8%	59.2%

BACHELOR'S DEGREES		
Program of study	**Male Percent**	**Female Percent**
Business administration and management, general	49.9%	50.1%
Psychology, general	23.6%	76.4%
Elementary teacher education	12.5%	87.5%
Biology, general	40.5%	59.5%
English language and literature, general	31.1%	68.9%
Accounting	39.6%	60.4%
Nursing (R.N. Training)	10.0%	90.0%
Communications, general	36.9%	63.1%
Political science, general	52.6%	47.4%
Sociology	29.8%	70.2%

*Data represents degrees conferred by Title IX participating, degree-granting postsecondary institutions
SOURCE: U.S. Department of Education, National Center for Education Statistics, Fall 2000

education bachelor's degrees, and 90% of nursing bachelor's degrees (Knapp et al., 2001). However, a greater percentage of women are venturing into new fields including agriculture, architecture, biology and life sciences, physical sciences, psychology, communications, social sciences and history, engineering, computer and information technology, and business. Since 1970 the percentage of women in these majors has increased by 40.8% in business, 39.3% in agriculture, 33.4% in architecture, 33.1% in psychology, 28.6% in biology and life sciences, 26.7% in physical sciences, 26.5% in communications, 19% in engineering, 14.5% in computer and information technology, and 14.4% in social sciences and history (Mortenson, 2002a). Furthermore, Long (2001) reported that there are now more women entering science and engineering professions. He reported a more than 350% increase from 1970 to 1995 in the number of new women Ph.D. graduates in science and engineering. Even though this increase

TABLE 2	Ten largest programs of study of institutions in the 50 U.S. States and District of Columbia, academic year 1999–2000*

MASTER'S DEGREES

Program of study	Male Percent	Female Percent
Business administration and management, general	62.1%	37.9%
Education, general	23.5%	76.5%
Social work	15.0%	85.0%
Elementary teacher education	12.8%	87.2%
Curriculum and instruction	20.5%	79.5%
Counselor education counseling and guidance services	19.9%	80.1%
Education administration and supervision, general	40.0%	60.0%
Business, general	63.3%	36.7%
Computer and information sciences, general	68.5%	31.5%
Special education, general	15.0%	85.0%

DOCTORAL DEGREES

Program of study	Male Percent	Female Percent
Chemistry, general	68.4%	31.6%
Clinical psychology	29.6%	70.4%
Education administration and supervision, general	40.1%	59.9%
Psychology, general	36.5%	63.5%
Electrical, electronics and communication engineering	87.8%	12.2%
Education, general	32.9%	67.1%
English language and literature, general	42.5%	57.5%
Physics, general	86.8%	13.2%
History, general	60.9%	39.1%
Economics, general	74.0%	26.0%

FIRST-PROFESSIONAL DEGREES

Program of study	Male Percent	Female Percent
Law	54.1%	45.9%
Medicine	57.3%	42.7%
Divinity and ministry	70.6%	29.4%
Pharmacy	34.3%	65.7%
Dentistry	59.9%	40.1%
Chiropractic	71.4%	29.6%
Veterinary medicine	31.5%	68.5%
Osteopathic medicine	62.6%	37.4%
Optometry	46.7%	53.3%
Podiatry	69.6%	30.4%

*Data represents degrees conferred by Title IX participating, degree-granting postsecondary institutions
SOURCE: U.S. Department of Education, National Center for Education Statistics, Fall 2000

is encouraging, women still account for only 31.6% of Ph.D.s in chemistry, and less than 15% of Ph.D.s in engineering and physics (Knapp et al., 2001; see table 2). The National Coalition for Women and Girls in Education (NCWGE) argue that these gender-segregated career patterns result in higher pay for men. For example, "in 1996 engineers had a median weekly earning of $949; in contrast, elementary education school teachers' median weekly earnings that year were $662, about 30% less" (NCWGE, 1997, p.7).

Issues for Men

BALANCING WORK

Several of the issues that women Gen Xers experience when returning to college are also prevalent for men including the need to balance work with life priorities. In the last fifty years, men's participation in the labor force has remained relatively stable with a total decrease of 4.8% (Mortenson, 1999). However, gender roles in Western society drastically influence the pressure that men experience to be the "breadwinner," or the primary income source in a heterosexual relationship. Although the male's need to be the breadwinner has decreased in recent years and is moving positively toward egalitarianism over time, many men still feel the need to be the breadwinner (Zuo, 1997). Furthermore, Zuo (1997) reported "younger men hold more egalitarian beliefs" (p. 9).

Few men, compared to women, stay at home with their children during the day while their spouse "brings home the dough" to support the family; however, more men are deciding to stay home with their children, a trend which started in the late 1970s. In fact, O'Connell (1993) reported that by 1991, 20% of preschool children were cared for by their fathers while their mothers worked. This was an increase of 5% since 1988. Even though more fathers are deciding to stay home with their children, the stay-at-home father needs additional social support from those around him because he may experience some social resistance by others in society. The stay-at-home father may experience comments from other men and women questioning the reason he, not the mother, is staying home. This gives societal messages that the stay-at-home father is not appropriate. For example, the popular term of programs for stay-at-home mothers where daycare is provided in order for the mother to have relaxing time by herself or with other women is called "mother's day out." There are rarely similar programs available for fathers who are staying home with their children while the mother works. In addition, this title itself, "mother's day out," is discriminating to men.

BALANCING FAMILY

Since fewer men than women are staying at home with their families, there is an additional need that men experience a balance of work, school, and family, especially since more and more men feel the need to be more connected to their families. As mentioned above, this can be seen by the increase of fathers staying at home with the children since the late 1970s (O'Connell, 1993). Since more women are involved in the workforce since 1960, men need to "pick up the slack" with housework. In general, Gen X men expect to share in household chores (Ritchie, 1995). There is also an increase in single fathers raising their children. For example, the number of fathers raising their children alone more than tripled between 1970 and 1990 (Greif, 1995). Being a single Gen X father going back to school, it is extremely difficult to maintain a balance between school, family, and work. Overall, Gen X men are taking on more household responsibilities, are staying at home with their children more often, and are more often single fathers. This change in the father's involvement with his family influences his ability to balance returning to school with other responsibilities.

ALTERNATIVE PROFESSIONS

As discussed above, there are now more women than men earning associate, bachelor, and master's degrees (Knapp et al., 2001). The number of these degrees has increased by 684,310 from 1975 to 2000, yet men represent only 13.1% of that increase (Mortenson, 2002a). Since 1970, the proportion of bachelor's degrees in historically popular majors for men has decreased. For example, the proportion of bachelor's degrees awarded to men declined 40.8% in business, 39.3% in agriculture, 33.4% in architecture, 33.1% in psychology, 28.6% in biology and life sciences, 26.7% in physical sciences, 26.5% in communications, 19% in engineering, 14.5% in computer and information technology, and 14.4% in social sciences and history (Mortenson, 2002a). There are only two bachelor's degrees in which men have experienced an increase since 1970. These include an increase of 3.9% in foreign language and literature and an increase of .5% in visual and performance arts from 1970 to 2000 (Mortenson, 2002a). Sometimes when males do express interest in careers that are thought of as "feminine" they may encounter social resistance. This may explain the decrease in males in elementary education teaching. Sadker (1999), for example, reported the percentage of males in elementary teaching is smaller today than when Title IX was enacted over twenty-five years ago.

CHANGE IN LABOR FORCE FOR MEN

Mortenson (1999) reported several trends that have influenced the participation of men in the American labor force by analyzing data from the Bureau of Labor Statistics. In his 1999 report described in Postsecondary Education OPPORTUNITY, Mortenson (1999) argued that men's future in the labor force looks bleak compared to that of women. Specifically, the problem for men in the labor force exists because men are hired for a majority of the manufacturing positions, and the number of these positions available has drastically decreased since the early 1980s. According to Mortenson (1999), the labor force is shifting toward a service-producing industrial employment base, which favors women over men. In addition, during the economic recessions of the 1980s and 1990s, men have experienced a higher unemployment rate than have women. Mortenson (1999) concluded from this data that women have become more successful than men at navigating the recessions over the past two decades. Additionally, he contends that men are not the only gender that are affected by these trends since "no one can think these changes reflect a healthy condition for the adult American male, nor for their mothers, wives, [partners], sisters, or their children – everyone whom their lives touch" (Mortenson, 1999, p.1).

Issues of Sexuality on Campus

In general, Gen Xers are reported to be more accepting of diversity (Ritchie, 1995), including accepting of all genders, racial and ethnic populations, and sexual orientations. Shugart (2001) reported the "members of Generation X are considered to be ... multiracial, and 'cool' about race, gender, and sexuality" (p. 133). In fact, GLBTQ issues are gaining momentum and more people are willing to be publicly identified as homosexuals (Ritchie, 1995). In general, Americans' attitudes towards homosexuals (or GLBTQ individuals) have changed over the past 30 years, especially over the past decade (Yang, 1997). This change in Americans' beliefs can certainly be reflected in the college population. According to the Census Bureau, there are more homosexual partners that are attending college than heterosexual married partners. Specifically, almost 40% of same-sex unmarried partners hold degrees compared to 18% of unmarried heterosexual partners, and 13% of married spouses in the United States (Ritchie, 1995). In addition, some experts estimate that about one in ten people are gay or lesbian, and one in five families have sexual minority members (Advocates for Youth, 2003). Shugart (2001) reported that Gen Xers are more diverse than generations before them including different members that represent various social classes, races, and sexual orientations.

According to the American Psychological Association, there are four components of sexuality, including: biological sex, gender identity, social sex role, and sexual orientation (Goodchilds, 1991). Biological sex includes physical attributes that compose men and women, whereas gender identity is the psychological sense of being male or female, and the social sex role is the cultural and sociological norms that make up feminine or masculine behavior (Goodchilds, 1991). Sexual orientation, the fourth component of sexuality, is the focus of this section. There are three commonly recognized sexual orientations including homosexual, heterosexual, and bisexual. Homosexuals are attracted to individuals of the same gender, heterosexuals are attracted to individuals of the other gender, and bisexuals are attracted to either gender (Scott, 1997). Many people view sexuality as a choice that people make, however, most scholars believe that sexual orientation is shaped for most people at an early age through a "complex interaction of biology, culture, history, and psychosocial influences" (Garnets & Kimmel, 1991, p. 148).

Many times people with a homosexual orientation are referred to as gay (a term used for both men or women), or as lesbian (a term used for women only). On the college campus, individuals who identify with the homosexual community are sometimes labeled as GLBTQ (gay, lesbian, bisexual, transgendered, and questioning) individuals. According to Scott (1997) in her *Dictionary of Queer Slang and Culture*, transgendered refers to individuals who blur the lines of traditional gender expression. This could include cross-dressers or transsexuals (a person whose birth sex is viewed as incorrect and steps are taken to change the physical, outer self). One's biological sex could be labeled as male, female, or intersexed (Sausa, 2002). The term questioning refers to individuals who are questioning their sexual orientation.

To completely understand how sexual orientation is manifested on college campuses, it is important to understand three other terms: heterosexism, homophobia, and sexual prejudice.

Heterosexism is the expectation that all people should be heterosexual, and that heterosexual is "normal", "natural", and "right" (Cramer, 2003). Many scholars also use Herek's (2000) definition of heterosexism, "an ideological system that denies, denigrates, and stigmatizes non-heterosexual forms of behavior, identity, relationship, or community" (p.19). In many ways, heterosexism parallels other types of prejudice including sexism and racism. The true essence of heterosexism and the belief that heterosexual is the norm is reflected in the following questions, "What do you think caused your heterosexuality? How did you learn what to do? When and how did you decide you were a heterosexual? Is your heterosexuality just a phase you will outgrow?" (Rochlin, 1982). Because of this heterosexism in America, many people, including students, staff, faculty, and administrators, develop homophobia – "an adverse reaction to homosexuals and homosexuality, and a fear and dislike of the sexual difference" (Fone, 2000, p.5). Homophobia can lead to sexual prejudice, which includes "all negative attitudes based on sexual orientation, whether the target is homosexual, bisexual, or heterosexual" (Herek, 2000, p.19); however, given the current social culture of homosexuals, sexual prejudice is almost always directed at gay, lesbian, or bisexual individuals (Herek, 2000). Like other forms of prejudice, sexual prejudice includes three features: 1) an attitude (i.e., an evaluation or judgment), 2) direction at a social group and its members, and 3) negativity, usually involving hostility or dislike.

Unfortunately, discrimination, sexual prejudice, and hate crimes are common in the U.S. today. In general, on college campuses between 40 and 75% of GLBTQ students reported verbal harassment, 16 to 26% have been threatened with violence, and almost 5% have been targets of physical assaults (Berrill, 1996). In addition, 75% of people committing hate crimes in the U.S. are under the age of 30 and some of the most pervasive anti-gay violence occurs in schools (Bitney, 2001). In the workforce, Schatz and O'Hanlan (1994) surveyed 191 employers. Their study revealed that 18% would fire, 27% would refuse to hire, and 26% would refuse to promote a person that was perceived to be gay, lesbian, or bisexual.

THE NEED FOR SAFE ZONES

As seen by some of the statistics reported above, Americans, in general, are not supportive of homosexual behavior. For example, according to the 1996 Gallup poll, 59% of the public believed homosexual behavior is morally wrong, compared to 34% who believed that it was not morally wrong. And even though Gen Xers seem to be more accepting of diversity and sexual preference (Ritchie, 1995), it is important that universities create a "Safe Zone" on campus, considering the number of students that face harassment, discrimination, and violence because of their sexual orientation (Franklin, 2001; Herek, 1993). In addition, GLBTQ students are more likely than heterosexual students to feel lonely and depressed (Westefeld, Maples, Buford, & Taylor, 2001), and more likely to have attempted suicide. One study concludes that 35.3% GLBTQ youth report having attempted suicide compared to only 9.9% of their heterosexual peers (Garafalo, Wolf, Kessel, Palfrey, & DuRant, 1999). Furthermore, studies have indicated that there is a "chilly climate" for many GLBTQ students on college campuses (Cotton-Huston & Waite, 2000; Herek, 1993).

Safe Zone programs have been created on college campuses to make *all* students feel "at home" and "safe." Generally, across college campuses, Safe Zone programs are maintained by a network of students, faculty, and staff who are in support of GLBTQ students. Members of the campus community that support GLBTQ students are known as "allies," in that they commonly display a Safe Zone sticker or sign in their offices or living spaces (Draugh, Elkins, & Roy, 2002). These signs or stickers display to the GLBTQ student(s) that the environment is safe and free of prejudice. The Safe Zone stickers or signs also indicate that the allies will work toward the confrontation of homophobia and heterosexism on their campus.

CAMPUS LEGISLATION

Besides developing a Safe Zone, administrators also must update university policies to make their campus accommodating to all Gen Xers. Each university should address sexual orientation in their sexual harassment, sexual assault, and nondiscrimination policies. Universities must be clear about how they will deal with sexual assault, harassment, or hate crimes against GLBTQ students. In addition, Sausa (2002) provides several tips on how to make universities more accommodating to GLBTQ students. Several of her suggestions can be applied to enrollment managers.

- Be gender inclusive on all applications, surveys, or administrative forms. Simply have a "gender identity" category where students could fill their gender in.
- Provide workshops or professional training to encourage staff and faculty to use gender-neutral language. For example, use parent or guardian instead of mother/father, or partner instead of girlfriend/boyfriend.
- Encourage staff and faculty to use students' preferred name instead of labeling them as a female or male.
- Create a safe zone and ally atmosphere in your enrollment services division. Provide Safe Zone training for your enrollment services staff.
- Hire openly gay, lesbian, bisexual, or transgender staff.

Current Issues in Higher Education

GENDER EQUITY

The issue of gender equity, a highly debated topic, has received a great deal of attention over the past two decades, to the extent that educators and administers in higher education may assume that it is no longer a problem. Recent reports, however, suggest that gender equity in higher education should still be a concern for all involved. For example, several studies suggest that gender equity should be a concern in higher education among administrators due to the amount of majors and careers that remain gender-specific. Sadker (1999) reported "the majority of females major in English, French, Spanish, music, drama, and dance, whereas males populate [into] computer science, physics, and engineering programs" (p. 23). The American Association of University Women (1999) found that women still cluster into a few traditional careers such as social sciences, health and allied careers, and teaching and education, whereas, men gravitate to business and engineering. In enrollment services, academic advisors and admissions counselors have a large impact on students' career choices. As an enrollment services leader, make it a priority that advisors understand the gender gap that is still taking place in careers.

The National Coalition for Women and Girls in Education (NCWGE) also suggests that gender equity should be a concern in higher education. The NCWGE (1997) gave higher education a grade of B– in gender equity in their recent report entitled *Title IX at 25: Report Card on Gender Equity*. They argue that "Title IX was intended to not only open the doors to educational opportunities formerly closed to women and girls, but also to provide avenues for enhancing their economic futures" (NCWGE, 1997, p.2). Twenty-five years after Title IX was enacted, there is room for improvement in higher education given the following statistics.

- Fewer than 20% of full professors in colleges and universities are women (NCWGE, 1997).
- Sexual harassment is pervasive in schools. The NCWGE (1997) reported that 81% of student surveyed have experienced sexual harassment.
- Overall, women still lag behind men in earning doctoral and professional degrees. Women still earn doctoral degrees that are in fields traditional to their gender. For example, in 1999 women earned 70.4% of clinical psychology doctorates, 67.1% of education doctorates, and 63.5% of general psychology doctorates. Men, however, earned 87.8% of engineering doctorates, 86.8% of physics doctorates, 74% of economics doctorates, and 68.4% of chemistry doctorates (Knapp et al., 2001).
- Some scholarships still exclude applications from women (NCWGE, 1997).
- According to the National Collegiate Athletic Association (NCAA), women athletes receive only 38% of scholarship dollars, 23% of athletic operating budgets, and 27% of money spent to recruit new athletes (NCWGE, 1997).

THE HIDDEN CURRICULUM

Since the 1970s, researchers have begun to look closely at the curriculum in higher education due to the increased attention to gender equity. Studies have found the written curriculum (i.e., books or readings assigned in class) as well as the unwritten curriculum (i.e., class discussions, examples and comments by professors) provides subtle forms of discrimination. This is important because students learn to understand norms, values, and beliefs through the classroom environment. Research has found that the written curriculum in higher education has focused almost solely on men and heterosexuals (Margolis, 2001).

An example of the unwritten curriculum in higher education can be seen by Draugh, Elkins, & Roy's (2002) example that begins the book *Addressing Homophobia and Heterosexism on College Campuses*. "A student responds to a comment in class by blurting out 'that's so gay'. The class, including the faculty member, laughs and continues the discussion . . . . A first-year student who intends to major in engineering is told by her student orientation advisor that the odds of finding a boyfriend will be in her favor. . . . An English professor fails to include sexual orientation in contextual conversations for literary works ....The Student Activities Office uses an image of a woman and a man kissing to advertise its healthy dating program" (Draugh, Elkins, & Roy, 2002, p.10). There are countless incidents of heterosexism and gender bias on the college campus every day. For example, the NCWGE (1997) reported that college women are more frequently interrupted and called on less often in higher education than men. In addition, female students typically receive less praise, criticism, or encouragement than male students. Professors can also support females' and homosexuals' invisibility in the classroom by using words such as "he" and "mankind", or making comments about students' sexuality. For example, just making a comment assuming that all students would be getting married, a professor could make some students feel marginalized. Margolis (2001) has recently published a book, *The Hidden Curriculum in Higher Education*, in which he provides several examples of the hidden curriculum in higher education. Chapters in his text include the hidden curriculum in professional schools, business education, pharmaceutical sciences, and engineering.

FEMINISM IN HIGHER EDUCATION

Feminism has gained momentum on college campuses worldwide and is now a focus in several academic courses. Even though most administrators, staff, and students have heard the word "feminism," there is widespread misunderstanding of feminism. Even though the meaning and interpretation of feminism is different around the globe, and no one universal understanding of feminism (Flew, Bagilhole, Carabine, Fenton, Kitzinger, Lister, & Wilkinson, 1999), the "waves" of feminism provides a good understanding of feminism in general. Feminism is thought to have three waves. The "first wave" and "second wave" include the right for women to vote, and was focused on middle class, white women. Many times the second and first wave of feminism is seen as "victim feminism" where women were "just knocking on the door" asking others to let them in (Heywood & Drake, 1997). The "third wave", which Shugart (2001) argues that Gen Xers relate to most, is classified as "power feminism" and is inclusive of *all* genders (men *and* women) and other social factors. For example, Boutilier and SanGiovanni (1994) define feminism as the "interaction between sexism and other social factors – classism, racism, ageism, heterosexism … formulating the problems and potential solutions of overcoming the oppression of *all* women [*and men*]" (p. 100).

So, why is feminism important for enrollment managers to understand? First, feminism is gaining momentum on the college campus, in particular with the Gen X population (Shugart, 2001). More men and women are demanding that universities accommodate them and their diversity. Second, there is often misunderstanding of feminism by students, faculty, and administrators. Two examples from a midsize public university in the southeast exemplify this misunderstanding of feminism. The first experience involved a female professor teaching an undergraduate class in which an entire class discussion was focused on feminism. When the professor started talking about feminism, there were a number of male students who wouldn't make eye contact with her. When she asked the class why they were so uncomfortable, they responded that they thought feminism meant "power of the women," or "men suck." When she explained the understanding of third-wave feminism which is inclusive of all genders and all social inequalities, their eyes were again focused on the professor and the students generally were much more relaxed. The second experience happened in an enrollment services office. A staff member was describing a recent interview that took place at his institution. The staff member described the interviewee and mentioned that she had a degree in women's studies and had discussed her research on feminism during the interview. The staff member abruptly stated that there is no way he'd recommend that she be hired because he thought she'd to be going around the office insisting "power to the women." Both examples provide anecdotal evidence that there is a misunderstanding about feminism, in particular third-wave feminism, on college campuses.

Why Does All of this Matter to Enrollment Services?

It is evident that higher education has discriminated against women and homosexuals in various ways. A connection between gender and sexuality to enrollment services staff and administrators can be made from this discussion. The following are recommendations enrollment services administrators should implement.

- Ensure that institutional policy is inclusive of all students, including GLBTQ students as well as women.
- Make sure publications are inclusive of *all* students. Shake up traditional gender roles by including an African American woman in a lab coat conducting experiments in a lab on the front of the catalog or recruitment flyer.
- Make sure admissions counselors and academic advisors avoid suggesting traditional careers for men and women.
- Ensure admissions standards as well as other policies in enrollment services are inclusive of *all* students.
- Establish guidelines on how to record, document, and handle harassment and abuse complaints in the division.
- Develop and implement procedures to ensure nondiscrimination in financial aid. Ensure that scholarship and financial aid awards do not favor either men or women.
- Educate staff by providing workshops and professional training to enrollment services staff about gender diversity and becoming advocates for themselves and others.
- Make gender equity a priority for staff to overcome bias and discrimination in their practice.
- Encourage staff to use neutral language and to call students by their first names instead of assuming the student is a "he" or a "she."
- Create a safe zone and ally atmosphere in the enrollment services division. Provide Safe Zone training specifically for enrollment services staff to truly understand sexual orientation on the campus.
- Ensure staff provides programming on campus for GLBTQ students. For example, ask the following questions: Does the institution have a center for GLBTQ students? Or does Multicultural Affairs cover GLBTQ issues on the campus?

- Make sure there is a group on campus joining GLBTQ students together. Since student organizations typically need a sponsor, encourage staff to get involved.
- Ensure that GLBTQ students feel accepted on campus by doing a few simple things. If magazines are available in a waiting room in enrollment services, include *Out* magazine, or *The Advocate*. Ensure that if husbands and wives of staff members get a discount in tuition, that gay and lesbian partners do as well.
- Designate a person in enrollment services to ensure the division is truly meeting the needs of women and GLBTQ students. Establish a uniform data collection procedure to ensure that each area in the division is complying with Title IX and Title IV standards.
- Serve as a role model by avoiding gender stereotypes and challenge negative comments about GLBTQ students or women heard on campus.

Conclusion

It is essential that enrollment services staff assume leadership roles in changing the culture in higher education to be inclusive of all students. The Gen X population provides additional support for this argument since Gen Xers are more accepting of diversity (Ritchie, 2000), and more diverse as a generation than generations before them (Shugart, 2001). Just by implementing small changes on campus, women and GLBTQ students are more likely to view their institution as safe and a place they will continue to attend.

The author would like to thank Dr. Kathy Jamieson, Dr. Mary Ellis Gibson, Bryant Hutson, Brittany Hanshaw, and Jeanne Irwin-Olson for their contributions to this chapter.

REFERENCES

Advocates for Youth (2003). I think I might be gay, now what do I do? [On-line]. Available: http://www.advocatesforyouth.org/publications/teenpamphlets/gay.pdf.

The American Association of University Women Educational Foundation. (1999). Hostile hallways: The AAUW survey on sexual harassment in America's schools. Washington, DC: American Association of University Women Educational Foundation.

Anderson, M. L. (1997). *Thinking about Women: Sociological Perspectives on Sex and Gender*. Needham Heights, MA: Allyn & Bacon.

Berrill, K. (1996). Organizing against hate. In C. F. Shepard, F. Yeskel, & C. Outcalt (Eds.), *LBGT Campus Organizing: A Comprehensive Manual* (175–190). Washington, DC: National Gay and Lesbian Task Force. [On-line]. Available: http://www.ngltf.org/downloads/campus/campusch8.pdf.

Bitney, C. (2001). Have a heart: Help prevent hate crimes. [On-line]. National Organization for Women. Available: http://www.now.org/nnt/spring-2001/hatecrimes.html.

Boutilier, M. A. & SanGiovanni, L. F. (1994). Politics, public policy, and Title IX: Some limitations of liberal feminism. In S. Birrell & C. L. Cole (Eds.) *Women, Sport, and Culture*. (97–109). Champaign, IL: Human Kinetics.

Chafetz, J. S., & Kotarba, J. A. (1999). Little league mothers and the reproduction of gender. In J. Coakley and P. Donnelly (Eds.), *Inside Sports*. New York, NY: Routledge. (46–54).

Cheng, B. (2002, June 25). Gen X women: Moving up. *BusinessWeek Online*.

Cotton-Huston, A., & Waite, B. (2000). Anti-homosexual attitudes in college students: Predictors and classroom interventions. *Journal of Homosexuality*. 38 (3): 117–133.

Cramer, E. (2003). Addressing homophobia and heterosexism on the UNCG campus. Presentation made at The University of North Carolina at Greensboro. Greensboro, NC.

DiNatale, M., & Boraas, S. (2001). The labor force experiences of women from 'Generation X'. *Monthly Labor Review Online*. 125(3). [On-line]. Available: http://stats.bls.gov/opub/mlr/2002/03/art1exc.htm.

Draugh, T., Elkins, B., & Roy, R. (2002). Allies in the struggle: Eradicating homophobia and heterosexism on campus. In E. P. Cramer (Eds.) *Addressing Homophobia and Heterosexism on College Campuses* (9–20). Binghamton, NY: Harrington Park.

Garnets, L., & Kimmel, D. (1991). Lesbian and gay male dimensions in the psychological study of human diversity. In J. D. Goodchilds, (Ed.), *Psychological Perspectives on Human Diversity in America*. Washington, DC: American Psychological Association.

Flew, F., Bagilhole, B., Carabine, J., Fenton, N., Kitzinger, C., Lister, R., and Wilkinson, S. (1999). Introduction: Local feminisms, global futures. *Women's Studies International Forum*. 22(4): 393–403.

Fone, B. (2000). *Homophobia: A History*. New York: Henry Holt and Company.

Franklin, K. (2001). Psychosocial motivations of hate prime perpetrators: Implications for prevention and policy. [On-line]. Available from American Psychological Association http://www.apa.org/ppo/issues/pfranklin.html.

Garafalo, R., Wolf, R., Kessel, S., Palfrey, J., & DuRant, R. (1998). The association between health risk behaviors and sexual orientation among a school-based sample of adolescents. *Pediatrics*, 101: 895–902.

Goodchilds, J. (Ed.). (1991). *Psychological Perspectives on Human Diversity in America*. Washington, DC: American Psychological Association.

Greif, G. (1995). Single fathers with custody following separation and divorce. *Marriage & Family Review*. 20(1–2): 213–226.

Herek, G. (1993). Documenting prejudice against lesbians and gay men on campus: The Yale sexual orientation survey. *Journal of Homosexuality*. 25: 15–30.

———. (2000). The psychology of sexual prejudice. *Current Directions in Psychological Science*. 9(1): 19–22.

Heywood, L. & Drake, J. (1997). Introduction. In L. Heywood & J. Drake (Eds.) *Third Wave Agenda: Being Feminist, Doing Feminism*. (1–20). Minneapolis, MN: University of Minnesota.

Jacobsen, J. (2001, June 8). Female coaches lag in pay and opportunities to oversee men's teams. *The Chronicle of Higher Education*. [On-line]. Available: http://www.chronicle.com.

Kelley, M. & Parsons, B. (2000). Sexual harassment in the 1990s. *Journal of Higher Education*. 71(5): 548–568.

Knapp, L., Kelly, J., Whitmore, R., Wu, S., Gallego, L., Grau, E., & Broyles, S. (2001). *Postsecondary institutions in the United States: Fall 2000 and degrees and other awards conferred: 1999–2000*. Washington, DC: National Center for Education Statistics.

Koss, M., Gidycz, C., & Wisniewski, N. (1987). The scope of rape: Incidence and prevalence of sexual aggression and victimization in a national sample of higher education students. *Journal of Consulting and Clinical Psychology*. 55: 162–170.

Kraus, S. (2000, June 5). Gen Xers' reinvented 'traditionalism'. *Brandweek*. 41: 28–30.

Kruger, P. (1994). Superwomen daughters. *Working Women*. 19: 60.

Lankard, B. (1995). *Career development in Generation X: Myths and realities*. (Report No., CE–070–190). Washington, DC: Office of Educational Research and Improvement. (ERIC Document Reproduction Service No. ED 388 801).

Long, J. (2001). *From scarcity to visibility: Gender differences in the careers of doctoral scientists and engineers*. Washington, D.C.: National Academy Press. (ERIC Document Reproduction Service No. ED 458 851).

Margolis, E. (Ed.) (2001). *The Hidden Curriculum in Higher Education*. New York: Routledge.

Mortenson, T. (1999, May). *Changing industrial employment effects on men and women: 1939 to 1998*. Number 83. [On-line]. Postsecondary Education OPPORTUNITY. Available: www.postsecondary.edu.

———. (2001, February) *Where the guys are not: The growing gender imbalance in college degrees awarded*. Number 104. [On-line]. Postsecondary Education OPPORTUNITY. Available: www.postsecondary.edu.

———. (2002a, February). *Earned degrees conferred by gender, 1870–2000*. Number 125. [On-line]. Postsecondary Education OPPORTUNITY. Available: www.postsecondary.edu.

———. (2002b, November). *What's wrong with the guys?* Number 125. [On-line]. Postsecondary Education OPPORTUNITY. Available: www.postsecondary.edu.

The National Coalition for Women and Girls in Education. (1997). *Title IX at 25: Report card on gender equity*. Washington, DC: National Women's Law Center.

Noonan, M. (2001). The impact of domestic work on men's and women's wages. *Journal of Marriage & Family*. 63(4): 1134–1145.

O'Connell, M. (1993). *Where's papa? Fathers' role in childcare. Population trends and public policy* (No. 20). Washington, D.C.: Population Reference Bureau. (ERIC Document Reproduction Service No. ED 365 434).

Ritchie, K. (1995). Marketing to generation X. *American Demographics*. 17(4): 34–40.

Rochlin, M. (1982). *A Heterosexual Questionnaire*. Boston: National Organization for Women, Lesbian Task Force.

Sadker, D. (1999). Gender equity: Still knocking at the classroom door. *Education Leadership*. 56(7): 22–26.

Sausa, L. (2002). Updating college and university campus policies: Meeting the needs of trans students, staff and faculty. In E. P. Cramer (Eds.) *Addressing Homophobia and Heterosexism on College Campuses*. (43–55). Binghamton, NY: Harrington Park.

Schneider, B. (1987). Graduate women, sexual harassment, and university policy. *Journal of Higher Education*. 58: 46–65.

Scott, R. (1997). *A brief dictionary of queer slang culture*. [On-line]. Available: http://www.geocities.com/WestHollywood/Stonewall/4219/.

Schatz & O'Hanlan (1994). *Anti-gay discrimination in medicine: Results of a national survey of lesbian, gay, and bisexual physicians*. San Francisco: Gay Lesbian Medical Association (formerly American Association of Physicians for Human Rights).

Shugart, H. (2001). Isn't it ironic? The intersection of third-wave feminism and generation X. *Women's Studies in Communication*. 24(2): 131–168.

Swanberg, J., Galinksky, E., Bond, J. (1997). *The national study of the changing workforce*. New York, NY: Families and Work Institute. (ERIC Document Reproduction Service No. ED 425 871).

Thompson, S. (1999). The game beings at home: Women's labor in the service of sport. In J. Coakley and P. Donnelly (Eds.), *Inside Sports*. New York, NY: Routledge. (111–120).

U.S. Department of Education (2001). *The Incidence of Crime on Campuses of U.S. Postsecondary Education Institutions: A Report to Congress*. [On-line]. http://www.ed.gov/offices/OPE/PPI/ReportToCongress.pdf .

Westefeld, J., Maples, M., Buford, B., & Taylor, S. (2001). Gay, lesbian, and bisexual college students: The relationship between sexual orientation and depression, loneliness, and suicide. *Journal of College Student Psychotherapy*. 15: 71–82.

Yang, A. (1997). Trends: Attitudes toward homosexuality. *Public Opinion Quarterly*. 61(3): 477–507.

Yin, S. (2002). Career matters. *American Demographics*. 24(4): 18.

Zinn, M., Hondagneau-Sotelo, P. & Messner, M. (2000). *Through the Prism of Difference*. Needham Heights, MA: Allyn & Bacon.

Zuo, J. (1997). The effect of men's breadwinner status on their changing gender beliefs. *Sex Roles*. 37(9–10): 799–816.

CHAPTER FOUR

Needs and Expectations of the Gen Xers

Pete Lindsey

Introduction

The *Random House Unabridged Dictionary* defines generation as, "a group of individuals, most of whom are the same approximate age, having similar ideas, problems and attitudes, etc." (Flexner, 1993, p. 1869). According to most authorities in the field, the age range of the current Gen Xer is from twenty-two to forty-two years of age. That age range represents some challenges as we try to identify the commonalities of this diverse generation. For example, does the unmarried twenty-two-year-old have the same educational needs and expectations as the forty-two-year-old who is married, has a family and four-figure mortgage to pay? Does this diverse generation see life through the same lens or have common experiences? Certainly they have some common experiences, but time has passed and life experiences change peoples' needs and expectations.

As we educate this generation we must avoid operating from stereotypes, or worse, prejudices. A stereotype is "a simplified and standardized conception or image invested with special meaning and held in common by members of a group" (Flexner, 1993, p. 1869). On the topic of stereotyping Generation X, Jennifer Grant Hawthorne writes, "The media's representation is largely a misrepresentation-and one that persisted despite a recent outpouring of empirical evidence to the contrary" (1997, p. 11). Even Sacks writes, "From my conversations with many people in their late teens and twenties, they often proved to be thoughtful, articulate people. No, we can't stereotype them, and we shouldn't" (1996, p. 139). When asked about the Generation X label, Coupland stated that he spoke for himself, and not for a generation (Hall, 1998). Some of the unflattering labels that have been assigned to this generation may even sound more like a prejudice, "an unfavorable opinion or feeling formed beforehand or without knowledge" (Flexner, 1993, p. 1525). The Gen Xers have even been called "The Doofus Generation" in a 1990 *Washington Post* headline and the "numb generation" by *New York Times* columnist Russell Baker.

Gen Xers who are returning to college are a diverse group that will warrant our personalized approaches to meeting their needs and anticipating their expectations. A one-size-fits-all concept of classroom teaching and student services will neither motivate, educate, nor satisfy this generation. Hawthorne cautions us of "two traps" that we must avoid as we educate the Xers. First, she warns against treating "them as indistinguishable members of a monolithic generational lot." Second, she contends that "when faculty and staff casually embrace media portrayals of college students, they not only readily dismiss the individuality of each student but also model for students (and others) lazy, stereotypical thinking rather than rigorous, critical thought" (1997, p. 14). Are her thoughts revolutionary or are they more akin to logical thinking as it applies to best practices in teaching and student services? There are commonalities among generations, and Generation X is no exception. These commonalities may provide starting points for planning educational strategies and the delivery of student services; however, truly dynamic teaching and exceptional student services are borne from a deep understanding of individual needs and expectations. And these needs and expectations are shaped by personal and global influencers.

Needs versus Expectations

Much has been written about caving in to the needs and expectations of Generation X. The advent of Total Quality Management and other customer service-focused theories have even prompted some in the academy to call students "customers." This way of thinking has clearly not been endorsed by all corners of the academy, most notably by faculty. A need is "a requirement ... an urgent want, as of something requisite" (Flexner, 1993, p. 1284), versus a want that is defined as looking forward to something with "a degree of probability that something will occur" (p. 680). Our responsibility as educators is to understand student needs and, at times, shape student expectations both inside and outside of the classroom. In the classroom, for instance, is it right for Xers to see themselves as consumers who purchase education (Sacks, 1996) and are "entitled to academic success" (Sacks, 1996, p. 118)? Perhaps a successful educational interchange requires attention to the whole person, both as student and as customer. As a student, the Xer must be an active participant who is engaged in learning, responsible for assignments and focused on meeting the academic expectations shaped by the professor. As "classroom consumer," money has been tendered for a course with the expectation of a comfortable classroom and a scholarly professor who is passionate about teaching and skilled at communicating and engaging students. Outside of the classroom the educational exchange continues, but it more closely mirrors that of a customer whose needs should be served. For example, this technologically savvy generation of students needs and expects convenient and ubiquitous student services. Processes such as admission, registration, financial aid, and housing are secondary processes that enable Xers to participate in the educational process. These outside-of-class activities are more transactional in nature and similar to business processes. However, even in these processes there is an element of education. It may occur when a student is denied admission to a university due to unacceptable academic performance. Or a current student may also become educated about following deadlines when he or she is dropped from classes for not paying his or her bill on time. In these instances it is clear that the customer is not always right!

Current Influencers – Personal

VARIED EDUCATIONAL BACKGROUNDS

Generation Xers returning to college are older now, and have experienced more of life in this rapidly changing society. They return to college with varied educational backgrounds. Some never applied to nor attended college, while most others have attended another two-year or four-year college, or a trade school. Many were successful academically, but others were academically dismissed or placed on probation at their last educational institution. Transfer students may have previously attended colleges with student populations of 500, or mega universities with student enrollments of 20,000 or 30,000 students. Their varied needs and expectations will be influenced, if not defined, by their previous educational experiences. With maturity and prior educational experiences, many have a better sense of their needs and even higher expectations both inside and outside of the classroom.

HOME AND FAMILY

Life has become more complex, and time more precious, for many Gen Xers. As described in chapters one and three, Xers have long been seen as the generation that delayed marriage and family but now approximately 44% are married and around half are parents (Kraus, 2000). In 1970 women usually married before the age of twenty-one, but now the median age at which they marry is twenty-five (Kraus, 2000). Similarly, the median age of marriage for men has moved from twenty-three to twenty-seven (Kraus, 2000). Gen Xers, who were previously responsible only to their biological families, may now have additional commitments to spouses and children. Colleges should be aware of the new forces that are reshaping the needs and expectations of these adults. For instance, engaging a twenty-five-year-old, unmarried Xer who lives with his parents may be quite different from involving an Xer who is thirty years old with two children and a spouse.

AGING PARENTS

In addition to their own family responsibilities, Gen Xers may also be concerned about the needs and expectations of their aging parents who are now in their fifties and sixties. Some generations may take lightly the needs and concerns of their parents, but that is unlikely for this generation of college-bound students. Many of this generation have lived at home throughout their late twenties and "continue to depend on an emotional and social connection with parents" (Ritchie, 1995, p. 36). Moreover, some will continue to feel an obligation to repay parents "taking on continued responsibilities for household chores, maintenance, and shopping" (Ritchie, 1995, p. 36). Many will feel the "tug-of-war" between divorced parents who are living in separate residences, often in different cities or states. These ties will weigh heavily on Generation Xers who are trying to finish the college education they may have started years ago. There will be a competition for their hearts, heads, time, and money. Colleges must be creative about the packaging and delivery of education and student services.

THOSE COLLEGE LOANS

Gen Xers are also likely to be concerned about debt. They may have enrolled in college just long enough to accumulate substantial debt, but not long enough to complete a degree. If they are working, it is unlikely they will be commanding the salaries of their college graduate counterparts. In fact, a need to improve their earning potential is likely to be the driving force behind their return to college. Now they may be faced with incurring additional debt as they pursue their dream of a college education.

"Thirty-nine percent (39%) of undergraduate student borrowers now graduate with unmanageable levels of debt, meaning that their monthly payments are more than 8% of their monthly incomes" (King and Bannon, 2002, p. 1). Further, "in 1999–2000, 64% of students graduated with student loan debt, and the average student loan debt has nearly doubled over the past eight years to $16,928" (King and Bannon, 2002, p. 1). What does this mean to colleges and universities that are planning to welcome Gen X back to college? The need is obvious: we must strive to constrain costs and build competitive financial aid budgets and packages. An even more compelling case for financial assistance can be made when we consider the ethnic diversity of this generation.

Current Influencers – Global

TECHNOLOGY AROUND EVERY CORNER

Cell phones, laptop computers, Palm Pilots, Game Boys, the Web, e-mail, CDs – the list of technology goes on and on. Growing up, no generation has been influenced more by technology than Generation X. And if that was true when Generation X went to college, it is most assuredly true as Generation X returns to college in this highly technological world. Many of the current educational needs and expectations of Xers are defined by these encounters with technology outside of the educational environment. As a result, when they return to campus they expect a technologically-enhanced educational experience that mirrors daily life. Automatic teller machines are available near their homes, why wouldn't they expect the same on the campus? And if they want to pay a bill or access personal account information, they do so at the touch of a few buttons on their home computer. Surely their university should offer them similar on-line services for paying tuition bills, accessing student accounts, and viewing their financial aid information. Access to the Web is expected in classrooms, the library, and in virtually every corner of campus, twenty-four hours a day and seven days a week. Remote services are expected to be available via the Web for those who are unable to travel to campus before offices close for the day.

In a way it is difficult to find the difference between the Xers' technological needs and their technological expectations. Technological advancements are creating student needs before there is an awareness of a need. And once met, today's need is likely to become tomorrow's expectation. Managing and meeting the technological needs and expectations of Gen Xers will require awareness of cutting-edge educational practices as well as those developed in the business sector. Moreover, many of these students are transfers and collectively they bring a smorgasbord of experiences with technological services from their previous colleges. Most are comfortable with technology and crave the information and convenience that it provides.

However, there exists Generation Xers who are less technologically sophisticated. At best, some are disinterested and at worst are intimidated by technology. The reasons for their indifference or fear are too varied to detail, but the need for technological assistance is real. For most, living in the technological world means "they excel at adapting to change easily and willingly" (Audibert and Jones, 2002, p. 20). Others change with difficulty — and avoid technology at all costs. We must understand these students and create educational approaches and student service delivery models that are personal and non-technical.

THE MEDIA GENERATION

It should come as no surprise that the impact of the media on Gen Xers has been and continues to be profound. Does it not dramatically impact all of our lives? A colleague of Sacks asserts that "the TV generation expects to be entertained. With an attention span equal to the interval between television commercials . . ." (Sacks, 1996, p. 144). He goes on to say that, "protestations about Generation X notwithstanding, corporate America knows that Xers are perhaps the most media savvy, image-conscious cohort, ever" (Sacks, 1996, p. 145). Ritchie offers a slightly different view. "If you want Generation X to adopt your product, it must be perceived as a useful product — not one to be purchased for reason of status or to make a statement, but one that fulfills a genuine need" (Ritchie, 1995, p. 36). But how does this apply to educating Generation X as they return to college?

The college educational process is not a product that is to be hyped without concern for substance or value. To be successful, colleges and universities must offer an education that takes into account Xers' expectations of utility and value. Should universities indiscriminately strive to satisfy capricious whims? No. But we must consider the relevance of the academic programs we provide and the services that we deliver. Xers are older now and they may have new responsibilities that compel them to make different, if not wiser, choices this time around. These educational choices need to improve their lives and the lives of their loved ones. More than before, time is of the essence and return on investment influences their educational choices. Although traditional-age students may have future career goals, the adult student generally has more pressing educational and career needs. As an example, a transfer credit evaluation for an adult student defines time-to-degree, and time is money. Further, as the adult students age their "employability" clocks tick. They need a marketable degree, and they need it now! And if there is any generation that understands speed, it's Generation X. From instant messaging to broadband Internet access, they are accustomed to and expect speed.

THE ECONOMY AND CORPORATE SCANDALS

The needs and expectations of Generation X have also been influenced by the current weak economy and the prevalence of corporate scandals. They may have been lulled into a false sense of security as they entered the welcoming workforce of the mid-1990s. But the economy has faltered and the confidence in corporate America has waned. The recession has been long lasting, and corporate scandals have fed the Xer's skeptical nature. They have "always been noto-riously anti-corporate and anti-government" (Sibliger and Brooks, 2002, p. 22), but now they have even greater reason for concern. Xers have also "watched as their hard-working, loyal-to-their-company parents were laid off" (Sibliger and Brooks, 2002, p. 22). Peter Sacks wrote of his concern that this generation delegitimized institutions and was skeptical of the knowledge and authority of professors (1996). How then do we connect with this skeptical generation as they return to college?

Trust grows from understanding and meeting needs, and keeping promises over time. So it is with the skeptical Generation X. The words of the financial firm Smith Barney seem to apply: "We make money the old fashioned way, we earn it." If we want students to choose our univer-sity and graduate as enthusiastic, supportive alumni, we must offer them a relevant education and personalized services. This generation has a more urgent need than ever to complete an education that will be the key to their future success. The first time around, some Xers departed from education as disenchanted students. Others completed an education and found themselves inadequately prepared for the workforce. Consequently, when the Xers return to college we will likely be held to higher standards of accountability for our promises both inside and outside of the classroom.

THE IMPACT OF SEPTEMBER 11, 2001

The terrifying events of 9/11 have had a significant impact on Generation Xers, and we are still assessing the long-term effects. Post-9/11, many Gen Xers "feel a newfound sense of impor-tance in spending quality time with friends and family" (Sibliger and Brooks, 2002, p. 23). And this is a generation that has been very hesitant to leave the protective confines of their parents' homes. Also many are "reevaluating their career paths, and are searching for more fulfilling professions or returning to school to change their careers" (Sibliger and Brooks, 2002, p. 23). The events of 9/11 caused Generation Xers, along with most Americans, to reflect on the priorities of life and future directions.

As educators we need to be sensitive to the post-9/11 personal and career struggles that are impacting this generation of young adults. They may need help sorting out the conflicting needs of family, friends, education, and career. This practical generation will expect practical and actionable advice on selecting a career that will allow them to integrate work and life (Audibert and Jones, 2002). They will also expect insights into careers that will provide financial security for themselves, their families, and even their aging parents. Their education must be relevant to the world of work and prepare them for career success.

Academic Needs and Expectations

In the classroom, Sacks characterized Generation Xers as students who expect to be entertained, and who believe they have a right to negotiate rather than work for good grades (1996). He saw them as a generation that needed extraordinary attention from faculty and that "handholding" was just part of getting their money's worth from education (Sacks, 1996). As pointed out above, others have seen this diverse generation differently. Even Coupland, who wrote extensively about the Xers, said that he spoke for himself and not for a generation (Hall, 1998). Is this generation a group of students with an extraordinary need for academic assistance? One educational trend suggests that there is a need. "In the fall of 1995, 81% of public 4-year colleges and 100% of public 2-year colleges offered remedial programs" (AAHE – Bulletin, 1998). Although many of these remedial services are targeted at students coming directly from high school, they may also benefit some Xers who were unsuccessful in their first attempts at higher education. Most Xers return to college without remedial needs. Perhaps, many years ago, extenuating circumstances interrupted their successful college careers. And now they return to college seasoned and influenced by life's events and responsibilities, exhibiting even greater determination to excel. In fact, many college professors are delighted to have these adults in their classrooms. Faculty appreciate the tone that Gen Xers set for some of the younger students as they stimulate classroom discussion by asking questions and sharing their work experiences.

Faculty and students alike would benefit from taking a fresh look at the education of Generation X. Both should reflect on the validity of their own needs and expectations. Both need to consider the behaviors and approaches that will best facilitate learning. Effective education is not a passive endeavor. It requires involvement and commitment from teacher and student. And these Xers have opinions regarding the characteristics of excellent professors and effective adult education.

The most frequently mentioned attributes adult learners expected of effective instructors were as follows (Donaldson, Flannery, & Ross-Gordon, 1993):

- to be knowledgeable
- to show concern for student learning
- to present material clearly
- to motivate
- to emphasize relevance of class material
- to be enthusiastic

By contrast, four teacher characteristics mentioned by adults were not cited among the top items for traditional-age undergraduates (Donaldson et al., 1993).

- creates a comfortable learning atmosphere
- uses a variety of techniques

- adapts to meet diverse needs
- dedicated to teaching

DIFFERENT LEARNING STYLES

Gen Xers possess varied learning styles that have been influenced by life experiences, both personal and global. Some personal influencers described earlier include marriage, family, career, college loan debt, and Xers' aging parents. Global influencers include technology, media, the economy, corporate scandals, and the impact of 9/11. The importance of these influencers alone should prompt us to reconsider the methods by which we engage this generation of learners. But understanding the learning styles of this generation is even more urgent and complex when we consider their ethnic diversity, current ages, and age range. Matching the appropriate teaching method to the corresponding learning style is indeed a challenge for faculty in the Generation X classroom. Furthermore, most classrooms are not limited to Generation X students. The added diversity of Millennials and Boomers exacerbates the challenge.

INDEPENDENT LEARNERS WITH A NEED FOR SPEED

Gen Xers have learned how to learn on their own and at their own fast pace. With both parents working or pursuing additional education, this generation received less guidance and instruction from their Baby Boomer, dual-career parents. When mom and dad were not around, they were left to their own devices and creativity to get through the challenges of the day. They became independent problem solvers who wanted support and feedback, but did not want to be controlled (Brown, 1997). They figured things out on their own, and when it came to finding out answers, technology was their closest friend. The Internet provided answers to almost any question or curiosity, and it did so immediately, without the constraints of time and space. E-mail offered immediate responses from and communication with teachers, friends, and family.

Throughout the educational process, Gen Xers will expect an environment that is familiar and similar to their life experiences. They will expect professors to be technologically proficient, presenting information via media such as CDs, the Internet, and Power Point presentations. They will assume that e-mails to professors will be answered in a timely and personal fashion. And the Xer's definition of timeliness may not fit that which is held by most educators.

Are all members of the X Generation independent, confident learners who are plugged in to the utility and speed of technology? Some of the adult students lack personal confidence, are unfamiliar with technology, and are intimidated by the advent of returning to college. After all, some of these adults have not stepped foot in a classroom of any kind for ten or more years. Dean Julian of the University of Pittsburgh, says that students who struggle academically look to professors for "motivation, inspiration and guidance" (Skorupa, 2002, p.2). Julian goes on to say that, "adults respond better to low pressure and that trust is very important in the relationship with their advisors."

LEARNING AT A DISTANCE

Educators are all aware, sometimes painfully so, that the world is becoming the classroom of today and tomorrow. Meeting the needs of today's Gen Xer does not mean business as usual. Today's classroom has no boundaries thanks to options such as video conferencing, self-paced modules, the World Wide Web, and Web-based teaching products like Blackboard, Web CT, and Top Class. Nearly all colleges today offer courses or complete degree programs via the Web. Others offer a blended model that combines instruction via the Web and face-to-face interaction. The Council for Adult and Experiential Learning, in a recent publication (2000), listed their "Educational Principles that Work for Adults that Work." One of the cornerstone principles is to "overcome barriers of time, place and tradition to create lifelong access" (Skorupa, 2002, p. 2). Distance learning is most assuredly a need of today's Gen Xers, many of whom are trying to balance work, family, and education. On the topic of technology and the Seven Principles of Education, Chickering and Ehrmann write, "electronic mail, computer conferencing, and the World Wide Web increase opportunities for students and faculty to converse and exchange work much more speedily than before, and more thoughtfully and 'safely' than when confronting each other in the classroom or faculty office" (Chickering & Ehrmann, 1996, p. 4). This speed and use of technology will appeal to the needs of the Gen Xer who is the independent, technologically sophisticated learner. But it may be the "safety" that most appeals to other Xers who are intimidated by their return to higher education.

DO I NEED TO LEARN THIS FOR THE TEST?

Who among us has not either said this to a professor or heard a reasonable facsimile uttered in class? A similar question that undoubtedly aggravates professors comes from the student who asks, "Is this material important?" This bit of "history" should remind us not to assign this attitude exclusively to Generation X. Disconcerting questions such as these have been around for a long time. In addition, many Xers have a skeptical view of society and its institutions. They "want their work to be meaningful", and to "know why they must learn something before they take time to learn how" (Caudron, 1997, p. 22). As they return to college, time is precious and in fact, time is money. For instance, credit for life experience and previous college work is the currency of the Gen Xer. They do not want to retake a course that they feel has already been completed. Moreover, Xers want to understand the pertinence and value of the courses within their chosen academic program. Janice Ford Freeman of the University of Alabama at Birmingham says that "she is less directive with adults" and she "explains things in greater detail" (Skorupa, 2002, p. 2).

Not only do Xers want to know the relevance and value of their courses, they will also search for the most convenient delivery method. For many Gen Xers, the best delivery method will maximize personal time and minimize time to degree. Xers either need or expect flexible class schedules. In response, higher education is offering this generation a plethora of options. For example, revamped class scheduling models provide a desirable degree of flexibility. Classes may meet only once per week rather than the traditional two or three times per week. Students may also be allowed to transition seamlessly from evening courses to day or weekend courses as their personal and professional circumstances dictate. Many colleges offer eight-week terms, mini-mesters, and weekend colleges. All of these options provide an accelerated education for this accelerated generation.

Services of value to students, of course! That seems like a simple goal with which no one could find fault. Provide a choice of student service delivery methods, and deliver what Xers want and need, as quickly as possible. Meeting student needs has been debated in the academy for some time. Some would say that this focus on student needs creates a customer-service provider relationship in which the customer (student) is always right. It is suggested this relationship undermines or replaces the academic integrity of the teacher-student relationship. Or is there a middle ground? That is, most student services interactions more closely approximate that of a customer-service provider relationship. Unlike the classroom where we challenge students with difficult material and exams, the student services goal is to make processes easy to understand, student-centered, and convenient to execute. For example, many financial aid offices facilitate the aid application process by offering access 24/7 to Web-based services, forms, and applications as well as face-to-face counseling at hours convenient to the student. The offices seek to provide answers and solutions rather than challenge students to become financial aid professionals.

Much has been written about the consumer orientation of Gen Xers. As such, this generation expects value for their educational dollar. This is especially important to them as they experience the increased cost of education since they last attended. Burnett offers some key ingredients to offering student services that are of value to today's service-oriented Xers (Burnett, 2002).

■ Student services should be designed from the perspective of the student, not the perspective of the institution. Truly student-centered processes are difficult to engineer and revise. Universities must have a tenacious commitment to student needs to foster breakthrough thinking and minimize the likelihood of convenient, "business as usual" solutions. For example, a Web page that lists student services by administrative office is institutionally focused. Students do not intuitively know the office that is most likely to serve their needs and answer their questions. Conversely, a Web page that lists processes in a sequence that mirrors the student's progression from applicant to graduate is student focused. This student-focused list would begin with processes like applying for admission and financial aid and end with processes related to graduation. Statements about the process would also be more helpful than listing the offices. For instance, "Get a campus job" is a very descriptive and intuitive phrase. By contrast, if the list were focused on offices, a confused student might chase needed assistance from three different offices (financial aid, career services, and business office) before their needs could finally be met.

■ "Consistency and excellence of the service experience must be developed at each touch point (in person, or via e-mail, telephone, or Web services)." (Burnett, 2002, p. 5) This generation expects student-centered services throughout their education, not occasionally or in one office and not the other. After all, in most cases, we are asking them to make a commitment to our university for four years. They expect the same commitment in return.

■ Networks and Internet services must be able to handle the volume of student traffic and demands. Again, speed is an essential component of valuable student services, especially when it is connected with the use of technology. The Gen Xers are accustomed to rapid responses from technology. For example, they will become frustrated or disillusioned with a university if on-line registration was slow because the university's Web site could not handle the traffic.

One-Stop Delivery of Student Services

One-stop Service Centers, either virtual or face-to-face, are expected by many Xers as they return to college. Both offer integrated and comprehensive information about student service processes, forms, and contacts. In varying degrees, each delivers student services through a blending of "high touch and high tech" approaches (Guvenoz, 2002, p. 26). The virtual approach has the advantage of being available 24/7 from almost any location, while the face-to-face offers a more personal connection. Xers have neither the time nor the inclination to walk from office to office in order to complete various student services processes. In fact, some colleges have found that "as more services are offered over the Web, the volume of business at the one-stop center decreases" (Burnett, 2002, p.8).

Career Services Needs and Expectations

Colleges offer a myriad of student services, but none is more important or deserves more attention than services related to careers. Some Gen Xers are returning to college for personal fulfillment, but most are returning to improve their career opportunities. They may have found their current career to be unrewarding and consequently want to retool for a new career direction. Others need additional education to advance more rapidly and to higher levels. Finally, a growing number have been casualties of corporate downsizing and desperately need additional education in order to reenter the workforce and find stable employment. Whatever the reasons are for returning to college, this diverse group of Xers is very concerned about career preparation and related career services.

A CAREER PROFILE OF THE GEN XERS

Career services offices are always faced with the challenge of understanding the needs and expectations of different generations as they pass through their years of college education. This knowledge enables career services professionals to better connect with each generation and to more effectively customize the services and delivery methods appropriate to that generation. This generation of Xers returning to college is particularly challenging for career services professionals. They are a diverse generation that has been influenced by a rapidly changing and sometimes confusing world. Descriptions of them have at times been equally confusing.

Patrick Montana and Janet Lenaghan compared earlier generations in the workforce to Generations X and Y. Their findings, appropriate to this chapter, came from a 1999 survey of 200 recent graduates (Generation X) and current undergraduates (Generation Y) of the Hofstra University Zarb School of Business. The survey participants "were asked to rank six (of twenty-five) factors they considered most important in motivating them to do their best work" (Montana and Lenaghan, 1999, p. 28). They found that rankings by Generation X and Y were identical to each other.

1. Steady employment
2. Respect me as a person
3. Good pay
4. Chance for promotion
5. Opportunity for self-development and improvement
6. Large amount of freedom on the job

Other authors provide insight, support, and variations on the findings of Montana and Leneghan. For example, Filipczak writes about the Xers' career needs, "they saw their parents laid off without cause and their perceptions of the working world were shaped in the time of economic turmoil. Consequently, they tend to see every job they take as temporary, and every company as a stepping stone to something better, or at least different" (Filipczak, 1994, p. 23). Wilkinson weighs in on the topics of steady employment and promotion by writing, "they believe that security nowadays comes from the transferability of one's skills to other jobs rather than from advancement in hierarchically managed organizations" (1995, p. 67). On the topic of good pay, Filipczak contends that money is a "top priority" (1994). And finally, in regard to personal respect and freedom on the job, Lankard states that Gen Xers are concerned with "having a balanced life," "time with their own children," and that "they are not workaholics" (1995).

EXPECTATIONS OF CAREER SERVICES OFFICES

The returning Gen Xer will have high expectations of career services offices. Many of their needs and expectations will be similar to those of other students; however, they will have special needs influenced by their past and current experiences with education and the workplace. Finding a new career or enhancing their marketability will likely take on greater urgency now than during their first trip to college. Successful outcomes and return on their tuition dollar will be heightened expectations.

Many Xers will need help finding their career direction. Some will need assistance finding career opportunities closely related to their current line of work. Others will require extensive counseling as they transition out of one field into a radically different career. Results of a survey conducted by the National Association of Colleges and Employers (NACE) on Generation X are informative and a bit disconcerting. One out of ten responded that "not knowing what they want to do in the world of work is the biggest obstacle they will face" (Collins, 1996, p. 42).

They lacked a goal around which to begin educational and career search plans. Regarding choice of academic program, a 1994 NACE student survey indicated "nearly 20 percent of the respondents said that they weren't sure what their college degree prepared them to do" (Collins, 1996, p. 42). A lack of career focus is often a leading cause of academic failure and poor choice of academic program. For example, when asked, 17 percent of students said "they chose their major by its earning potential" (Collins, 1996, p. 42), rather than considering their personal skills and interests.

Returning Gen Xers will likely be searching for colleges that offer opportunities for practical work experience to complement their classroom studies. They may have been unemployed or underemployed as a result of being deficient in work experience in their chosen field. When students were "asked what they think employers see as most important in job candidates, work experience in the field, communication skills, leadership roles, and teamwork topped their list" (Collins, 1996, p. 43). All of these skills could be enhanced by career-related work experience through internships and cooperative education. Employers make the case by stating that "they look for job candidates in their internship and cooperative programs first – then they look for candidates who participated in other employer's programs" (Collins, 1996, p. 43).

THE TECHNOLOGICAL WORLD OF CAREER SERVICES

Most Xers will return to college needing and expecting a technologically sophisticated career services office. Some, by contrast, will be more comfortable with face-to-face services rather than those delivered by technology. Type of service need and situation will also dictate the Xers' service delivery preferences. Consider the following results from the National Association of College and Employer's survey of recruiters and college students (Behrens and Altman, 1998).

- 70% of students said that they believe computers can help them find jobs much faster than traditional job-search methods. And recruiters add validity to this student belief. In fact, two-thirds of the respondents said they source candidates via corporate Web sites.

- By contrast, when it comes to a career consultation to discuss job-search frustrations, 75% of students would rather attend a personal session while 25% prefer their career consultation via video hookup.

- 90% of students would prefer to practice interviewing with a career counselor and get personal feedback; 10% would rather use a computer program to practice answering interview questions, with feedback provided in printout.

Many student services are important to the Gen Xers, but career services are likely to "take center stage" as Xers return to college. Before they apply for admission, pay their bills, or register for classes, Xers will want to have a plan for their future. That plan may need to take them from undecided to focused, or from underprepared to qualified. Regardless of the reason for returning to college, the outcome must be a better future. And career services will play an integral role in attracting, retaining, and graduating satisfied Gen Xers.

Conclusion

Generation Xers return to college having been influenced by the changes and challenges of adult life. Global realities and personal commitments have changed many of their educational needs and expectations since they were first referred to as the "slacker generation." Most are now adults in their twenties or thirties and they choose, or are compelled to return to college for a variety of serious reasons. They are one of the most diverse generations in history; so they challenge educators to avoid stereotypes as we look for customized ways to educate and serve them. As experienced consumers who are technologically savvy, they expect a lot from their education the second time around.

In the classroom they have different learning styles and expect Web-based and independent learning opportunities. Some continue to need career direction while they challenge us to provide an education that is relevant, marketable, and worthy of their tuition dollars. Faculty, many of whom are Baby Boomers, bristle at the notion that Xers could be seen as customers; however, much to their delight, they find these returning Xers to be more engaged and responsible learners than they were in their younger years.

When it comes to student and career services, the Xers expect them to be ubiquitous, valuable, and delivered with speed, with the convenience of high tech-high touch choices. Career services offices are challenged to meet needs for career counseling that will lead Xers to a career offering, security, advancement, and time for family. The Xers who return to college want a better life, and they want it the way they want it, and they want it now.

REFERENCES

Audibert, G., and Jones, M. (2002). The impact of a changing economy on Gen X job seekers. *USA Today Magazine*. 130(2682): 20–21.

Behrens, T., and Altman, B. Technology: Impact on and implications for college career centers. [Online]. Available: http://www.naceweb.org/pubs/journal/wi98/behrens.htm.

Brown, B. (1997). New learning strategies for Generation X. *Educational Resource Information Center*, ERIC Digest No. 184: 1–4.

Burnett, D. (2002). Innovations in student services best practices and process innovation models and trends. In *Planning for Student Services: Best Practices for the 21st Century*. Ann Arbor, Mich.: Society for College and University Planning.

Caudron, S. (March 1997). Can Generation Xers be trained? *Training and Development*. 51(3): 20–24.

Chickering, A., and Ehrmann, S. (October 1996). Implementing the seven principles: Technology as lever. *American Association of Higher Education*. 3–6.

Collins, M. (1996). Who are they and what do they want? *Journal of Career Planning & Employment*. 57(1): 41–43.

Coupland, D. (1991). *Generation X*. New York, NY: St. Martin's Press.

Donaldson, J., Flannery, D., and Ross-Gordon, J. (1993). A triangulated study comparing adult college student's perceptions of effective teaching with those of traditional students. *Continuing Higher Education Review*. 57(3): 147–165.

Essential demographics of today's college students. (1998). *American Association of Higher Education — Bulletin*. 51(3): 1–7.

Filipczak, B. (April 1994). It's just a job: Generation X at work. *Training*. 31: 21–27. (ERIC No. Ed. 480 564).

Flexnor, S. (1993). *Random House Unabridged Dictionary*. New York, NY: Random House, Inc., 2nd ed.

Guvenoz, A. (2002). Removing the barriers to education: creating a service model for the working adult student. In *Innovation in Student Services, Planning for Models Blending High Touch / High Tech*. Ann Arbor, Mich.: Society for College and University Planning.

Hall, S. (1998). Douglas Coupland, *Contemporary Literary Criticism*. 39(29): 1–3.

Hawthorne, J. (1997). The misrepresentation of Generation X, *About Campus*. 2(4): 10–15.

King, T., and Bannon, E. (2002). The State PIRGs' Higher Education Project. *The Burden of Borrowing: a Report on the Rising Rates of Student Loan Debt*. The State PIRG's Higher Education Project. Washington, D.C.

Kraus, S. (2000). Generation Xers reinvented 'traditionalism'. *Brandweek*. 41(23): 28–29.

Montana, P., and Lenghan, J. (1999). What motivates and matters most to Generations X and Y. *Journal of Career Planning and Employment*. 59(4): 27–30.

Ritchie, K. (1995). Marketing to Generation X (marketing to the post-baby boom generation). *American Demographics*. 17(4): 34–40.

———. (1995). *Marketing to Generation X*. New York, NY: Lexington Books.

Sacks, P. (1996). *Generation X Goes to College: An Eye Opening Account of Teaching in Postmodern America*. Chicago and LaSalle, Ill.: Open Court.

Schnaars, S. (1998). *Marketing Strategy: Customers and Competition*. New York, NY: The Free Press.

Sibliger, S. and Brooks, C. (2002). Generation DisconNext. *Brandweek*. 43(10): 22–24.

Skorupa, K. (2002). Adult Learners as Consumers. *National Academic Advising Association*. [On-line] Available: http://www.ncada.ksu.edu/Clearinghouse/Advising_Issues/adultlearners.htm.

Wilkinson, M. (May–June 1995). It's just a matter of time: twenty somethings view their jobs differently than Boomers. *Utne Reader*. 9(69): 66–67.

PART 2

Marketing
and
Recruitment

Marketing and Recruitment

CHAPTER FIVE

The Voice of the Customer

Brad Burch

Introduction

Each year Generation Xers who are not enrolled in college decide to return. Why is this so? One method of examining this phenomenon is by listening to the voice of the customer, Generation X students. Based on findings from interviews with Gen X students, their reasons can be grouped into four distinct categories: unfinished business, career enhancement/security, career change, and hopes and dreams. Examples of each category are described in this chapter and include qualitative research to illuminate the reasons. Combining the stories of the Generation X students with the published research on why they return to college provides interesting insights into the motivations and barriers behind their continued pursuit of educational goals.

The use of "voice" in qualitative, or narrative, research is significant. "Voice" is a person's retelling of his or her personal story (Reissman, 1993). The significance is that a person is allowed to speak, to give voice to that story. "Viewed 'against the background of bureaucratic, depersonalized institutions, storytelling seems pretty authentic, or at least expressive'" (Grumet, 1991, p. 68; in Casey, 1995, p. 9). The communal context from which our stories speak to life is critical (Bakhtin, 1981; Belch & Strange, 1995; Grumet, 1991). Reality is mediated through individual and community lenses (Vygotsky, 1962; in Miller, 1993). The hope of this narrative research is to listen to the specific individual stories of the Generation X students in order to detect the gateway to the whole population of Generation X students and illuminate reasons for this population's college enrollment as non-traditional students.

Methodology

The stories of the Generation X student experiences were gathered by examining the adult student profiles on the Web site of the Office of Adult Students (2003) at The University of North Carolina at Greensboro. The ages of students have been verified by searching their academic records to confirm that the participants are Generation Xers. The stories were examined to determine how the stories clarified and enhanced the published findings for Gen Xers returning to college. Permission for publication was granted from each participant in this study. Only first names are used to maintain some anonymity.

Unfinished Business

Generation X students may go to college to complete unfinished business (Fungaroli, 2000). The reasons underlying this unfinished college education include:

- only a few courses were completed each semester and the student is still persisting toward a degree
- the student was unfocused or unmotivated in college the first time around
- marriage at an early age
- the student went to work straight out of high school
- the student served in the military
- the student earned a GED after dropping out of high school
- the student finished a two-year degree and now wants to pursue a four-year degree

Some Generation X students show great persistence in completing their educations. Choosing healthy relationships and living with integrity seem to aid educational persistence while work commitments can have a negative effect on educational persistence (Kemp, 2002). Families committed to the same educational goal aid persistence of adult students (Hensley & Kinser, 2001). For some students, persistence is key:

> Stephanie has been enrolled in exactly as many colleges as she has children – six. Having the support of her family is crucial to her success. "My husband is really helpful," she says. "The kids know school is important to me. If I'm working on a paper, I tell them 'I need to get this done, you need to be helpful,' and they will do that."

> Diego and Leidy have shared many experiences in the six years they've been married. Together they moved from New York to North Carolina after Diego joined the marines. Together they enrolled in a community college, completed associate degrees, and then transferred to a four-year school. Together they celebrated the birth of their daughter. She was two when Leidy and Diego participated in the graduation ceremony, together.

Some students earn poor grades in college the first time they enroll. Reasons for poor academic performance range from inadequate preparation and an unbalanced daily schedule to lack of motivation (Rau & Durand, 2000). Poor academic preparation and focus may be overcome through academic support offered on college campuses, but this approach does not help all students (Amundsen, Kamphoff, & Ross, 2002). Why did many students succeed following an initial poor academic performance, working for a few years, and then returning to the college environment? "It's simple: they became adults" (Fungaroli, 2000).

> "I was not prepared for college," Hoge admits, of his experience as a traditional undergraduate student at UNC Wilmington in the early '90s. While he enjoyed playing varsity soccer, he found it hard to concentrate on his classes and dedicate himself to academics with no real sense of what to major in or what he'd do out of college.

> Eileen went to junior college and then attended a four-year school, but like many students fresh out of high school, Eileen had no clear idea of why she wanted to pursue a degree. She switched from major to major, never finding anything that held her interest. As she says, "I just really didn't know what I wanted to do." She decided to take a break from school until she truly felt motivated to return.

> Mary came to college as a traditional student. Some of her grades were As and Bs, but others were sabotaged by the distractions of personal issues, by skipped classes, and by too many hours spent working to maintain her off-campus apartment. When she left after eight semesters, she had a 1.7 GPA.

Marrying at an early age, dropping out of college to raise a family and then deciding to complete a degree was the choice of a few students. Though the number of students coming back to school after raising (or partially raising) a family is now few, more Gen Xers will probably come back to school as they and their families mature (Tinto, 1993; Aslanian, 2001).

> Stephanie began school as a traditional undergraduate with a major in computer science. Even though it was the wave of the future, it was not the major for her. "I hated it," she remembers. "I was glad to get married after two years [and drop out of college]." Now, being in school with six children at home means she has a lot to manage.

Working right after high school is beneficial for some. Reasons for working before attending college range from lack of financial resources and lack of motivation to poor academic preparation. And, although attending college had become quite popular in the U.S., some Generation X students' families did not encourage their children to go to college following high school. Some Gen Xers were the first in their families to attend college, which put them at a disadvantage for persisting through to graduation, as there was no example of a college-educated family member for them to emulate (Choy, 2001). Despite not attending college immediately after high school, many Generation X students appreciate the added maturity with which they are able to approach their academic work.

> Beth does not regret the time she spent away from school as a young woman. "You don't really know how much you need a degree until you get out there," Beth says. "You find out about yourself in the work world too [and] discover your real interests." [My] course work was so interesting throughout college "from a more mature perspective," she affirms. "And I would not have had such an interest in research as a younger student."

Some Generation X students served in the military right after high school. The Veterans Administration Educational Training Program makes it financially feasible for military veterans to return to school.

"I filled out my application sitting on my bunk in Bosnia," says Scot, a junior who is majoring in communication studies. After an eleven-year career in the army, he was ready for a new direction. "I sent the application to my wife. She gave it to the university and later mailed me the letter of acceptance," he recalls. At 29, he knew it was time to finish his college education.

Diane started college work when she was 21 at a branch campus of Penn State University, where she met her future husband Stephen, a veteran who had just returned from the Gulf War. Diane started her third semester at her third school in the fall of 2001 prepared to tackle the familiar challenges of succeeding as a student while also finding time for her husband and two preschool children and meeting her commitments to her army reserve unit. Now, after September 11, she faces the prospect that her reserve unit could be called into active duty at any time. Her life as a mother, wife, and student may change at any moment. [This interview was conducted before the Iraq War in 2003.]

Despite the fact that the vast majority of Americans currently complete and graduate from high school, some do drop out. Many of those students earn a General Educational Development (GED) certificate that is considered equivalent to the high school diploma. Earning a GED allows students to enroll at the community college level but is no guarantee of academic success and persistence in college (Perin, 2002).

Some students may decide to pursue a four-year degree after initially completing a two-year degree. Some students complete the associate in arts (AA) or associate in science (AS) degree. Since these degrees are designed for transfer to a four-year school, students may naturally progress and complete the degree. Some students complete the associate in applied science (AAS) degree and then wish to complete a four-year degree. Since these degrees are designed for students to enter the workforce following graduation, acceptance of these courses may be more problematic and usually necessitate specific agreements between the two- and four-year schools (Townsend, 2001).

Karen is a dietetics major. Since leaving high school in 1993, she finished an AA degree while working full-time, made a year-and-a-half mission trip for her church, returned to her home state where she again worked full-time, married and had a daughter, and then enrolled to finish her four-year degree.

Career Enhancement/Security

Generation X students are seeking career enhancement or increased job security because many cannot be promoted without a degree or they are unemployed or underemployed.

Many managerial-level positions require the minimum of a bachelor's degree. Still other positions require that employees receive additional training for advancement. There is a direct correlation between education and earnings (Pascarella & Terenzini, 1993). One reason Generation X students go to college is that they realize they cannot be promoted at work without a degree.

Curtis was a successful student taking one class at a time, his work responsibilities were expanding, and he and his wife Lisa had two young sons. But he had reached a crossroads – he had peaked in his job and gone as far as he could without a degree. And with one class per semester, he figured it would take over twenty years to finish. Curtis and his wife took a hard look at their priorities and their schedules. By splitting child care responsibilities with his wife and switching to part-time work, he could consolidate his classes and become a full-time student.

Some adults find themselves unemployed or underemployed. Many adults who began full-time employment right after high school work in minimum wage positions. The economic reality of trying to survive and not being qualified for better paying jobs is disappointing. These students believe that education can help them find a better job.

After high school graduation in 1993, Kineka spent two and a half years at East Carolina University as a traditional student. "There was no mom, no dad, no sisters ... just me, doing just as I pleased." She laughs. "I went from straight As in high school to Cs," she recalls. "I was surprised to find I wasn't ready for college." She withdrew from school and returned to Greensboro to work. Jobs in retail and fast food convinced her to give school another try.

Career Change

Generation X students return to college seeking a career change. Why is this so? Life changes precipitate most career changes (Aslanian, 2001). Life changes can include:

- an identity shift which prompts the pursuit of another career
- single again students who now need to support a family

An identity shift can motivate Generation X students to return to school. Some traditional-age students initially chose careers for the wrong reasons, including societal or parental pressures (Jacobsen, 2001). These former traditional age students, who are now Generation X non-traditional students, are seeking to do what they love for the rest of their lives (Griffiths, 2001).

"One thing about adult students is that they have thought about what they want to do," Angie notes. "They're not just interested in making money like some people are right out of high school."

Over the next few years, Teresa learned another thing – that money is not the only measure of a good job. While she had achieved job security with the U.S. Postal Service, she "saw people who made money but weren't happy and who hated work every day." She felt she "couldn't afford to spend [her] life like that."

Adults who come to college are "here to make the most of it," Dahron says. "They have specific interests and want to take specific classes. That was certainly my situation."

Some Gen X students are single again after either a divorce or the death of a spouse (White, 2001). Many women put their own careers on hold and follow the husband's career path. These women may then find themselves under-trained and underprepared to support themselves and, quite possibly, a family.

Bernadette's college career began with an Air Force scholarship to Indiana University Purdue University Indianapolis. After dropping out, she married, started her family, and moved to several states for her husband's career. When her husband did not join the family after the last move, Bernadette found herself with no money, no place to live, no significant work history, and no chance, without a college degree, to earn enough even to pay for childcare. As a single mother with three children aged four, six, and eight, suddenly thrown to her own resources to support her children financially as well as emotionally, she has come face-to-face with the public policy issues of homelessness and poverty that she studies in political science.

Hopes and Dreams

Gen Xers are searching to fulfill lifelong hopes and dreams. These are evidenced in several different ways:

- students are seeking hope for the future
- financial aid allows students to pursue the dream of a degree
- international students are seeking a college education in the United States

Generation X adults may seek hope for the future. Unfulfilled dreams lead Gen Xers to imagine a better life. Completing a college education can fulfill hopes and dreams and can transform lives (Sohn, 1999).

> Ram knew as a child he wanted a career in health care, a goal he set when visiting hospitals with his mother, a nurse. After a brief stint as an army medic, he found he could earn more money as a food service manager. After ten years in food service management positions in three states, he reentered school to become a nurse. After earning two- and four-year degrees in nursing, he is now enrolled in a combined MSN–MBA program.

Increased financial aid should assist Generation X students pursuing dreams of a college education (Pascarella & Terenzini, 1991; Wlodkowski, Mauldin & Campbell, 2002). The availability of financial aid itself prompts students to consider going to college. Grants and loans specifically for adults may be available, depending on the student's situation. The college or university advancement office may also be able to develop new monies aimed specifically at adult students. Several Generation X students reported that financial aid was instrumental in their ability to attend college.

> "If financial aid hadn't come through, I wouldn't be here," Angie admits. She was eligible for a Pell Grant initially, and after doing well academically she was awarded additional scholarship money, including a scholarship for adults without other support for their college work.

> It was difficult to quit his full-time job, but Ram decided to "go for it" – with the help of his wife (who worked full-time), his church, the financial aid officers at his community college, and a weekend job (7 A.M. to 7 P.M.) as a nurse's assistant at a local nursing home.

International students also comprise a population of the Generation X students attending college. These students could be traveling abroad or have recently gained U.S. citizenship or be part of a family that has permanent residency. With the expanding multiculturalism within the United States, as well as the increased use of on-line course selections offered worldwide, this population can profit from increased travel and technology.

> Kenny came to the U.S. from Nigeria in 1999 with a degree in chemistry and a plan to study pharmacy in America. When he learned he'd need credentials from a university in the States to supplement his degree from Yaba College of Technology in Lagos, he enrolled in a second degree program in biochemistry.

Conclusion

Why are Generation X students attending college as non-traditional students? Students have unfinished business to complete or they seek career enhancement and stability or they want to change careers or they have a desire to fulfill lifelong hopes and dreams. Pascarella & Terenzini concluded that college increases students' lifetime earnings and quality of life after graduation (1991). Changes in the Generation X students' careers and family lives precipitate the need to go to college (Aslanian, 2001). The Generation X voices shared in this chapter support the claim that college makes a difference in career opportunities and offers a better life for family.

What will motivate future adult students to continue their education? Meeting the needs for flexible scheduling that Generation X students can fit into already busy lives is the most important component to attract this population. "[Going to college] is a question of doing college in addition to many other things" (Tinto, 1993, p. 187). As described in chapter four, on-line education, eight week semesters, once-a-week course offerings, evening programs, off-campus programs – all of these can be structured around the Generation X student's already busy schedule. The increased flexibility of on-line coursework can especially enhance the marketability of higher education courses to Generation X students.

As this population continues to gray, other motives for attending college will include more parents attending school after the children are in college. Generation X students will also desire to continue learning after retirement. Gen Xers recognize the economic and intrinsic benefits to attending college. Some students go back to college in order to make a better living and others just want to be lifelong learners.

This study is a brief foray into the possible research for the Generation X population. The richness of each story reveals to higher education professionals that college makes a difference one student at a time. Future research should determine what on-line course offerings for Generation X students will meet the increased need for degree completion, career enhancement/ security, new careers, and the fulfillment of hopes and dreams. These four areas represent the main motivators for students returning to school. Discovering which programs and services meet their needs will allow the college or university that desires to enroll the Generation X population to tap into their motivators and barriers and thus, become more effective in marketing and recruitment.

REFERENCES

Amundsen, S., Kamphoff, C., & Ross, R. (October, 2002). *Strategies for Academic Success: An early intervention for students in academic difficulty.* Paper presented at the Annual Meeting of the National Academic Advising Association, Salt Lake City, UT.

Aslanian, C. (2001). You're never too old … excerpts from "Adult Students Today." *Community College Journal.* 71(5): 56–58.

Bakhtin, M. (1981). *The Dialogic Imagination.* Holquist, M., ed. Emerson, C., and Holquist, M., trans. Austin: University of Texas Press.

Belch, H., & Strange, C. (1995). Views from the bottleneck: Middle managers in student affairs. *NASPA Journal*. 32: 208–222.

Benshoff, J. (1993, November). *Educational Opportunities, Developmental Challenges: Understanding Nontraditional College Students.* Paper presented at the Annual Conference of the Association for Adult Development and Aging, New Orleans, LA.

Casey, K. (1995). The new narrative research in education. In M. Apple (Ed.), *Review of research in education.* Volume 21 (211–252). Washington, DC: American Educational Research Association.

Chickering, A., & Reisser, L. (1993). *Education and Identity* (2nd ed.). San Francisco: Jossey–Bass Publishers.

Choy, S. (2001). *Students Whose Parents Did Not Go to College: Postsecondary Access, Persistence, and Attainment. Findings from the Condition of Education, 2001.* (ERIC Document Reproduction Services No. 460 660).

Comprehensive Articulation Agreement between the University of North Carolina and the North Carolina community college system, revised. (2002).

Dinatale, M., & Borass, S. (2002). Labor force experience of women from "Generation X." *Monthly-Labor-Review.* 125(3): 3–15.

Dobie, A. (1992, March). *Back to school: adults in the freshman writing class.* Paper presented at the Annual Meeting of the Conference on College Composition and Communication, Cincinnati, OH.

Fungaroli, C. (2000). *Traditional Degrees for Nontraditional Students: How to Earn a Top Diploma from America's Great Colleges at Any Age.* New York: Farrar, Straus, and Giroux.

Griffiths, B. (2001). *Do What You Love for the Rest of Your Life: A Practical Guide to Career Change and Personal Renewal.* New York: The Random House Publishing Group.

Grumet, M. (1991). The politics of personal knowledge. In C. Witherell & N. Noddings (Eds.), *Stories lives tell; Narrative and dialogue in education.* (67–77). New York: Teachers College Press.

Jacobsen, M. (2001). *Hand-Me-Down Dreams: Integrating Family Perspectives into Career Counseling.* Focus on the Future: Achieving Balance in Career & Life Integration. International Career Development Conference 2000. (ERIC Document Reproduction Services No. 456 399).

Kemp, W. (2002). Persistence of adult learners in distance education. *American Journal of Distance Education(16).* 2: 65–81.

Knowles, M., Holton, E., and Swanson, R. (1998). *The Adult Learner: The Definitive Classic in Adult Education and Human Resource Development.* 5th ed. Woburn, MA: Butterworth-Heinemann.

Ludden, L. (1996). *Back to School: A College Guide for Adults.* Indianapolis: JIST Works, Inc.

Mellander, G., and Mellander, N. (1997, October). *Trends in community college education: a window of opportunity.* Paper presented at Seton Hall University Higher Education Conference, South Orange, NJ.

Miller, P. (1993). *Theories of Developmental Psychology.* 3rd ed. New York: W. H. Freeman and Company.

Office of Adult Students. [On-line]. Available: http://oas.dept.uncg.edu/.

Pascarella, E., & Terenzini, P. (1991). *How College Affects Students: Findings and Insights from Twenty Years of Research.* San Francisco: Jossey–Bass.

Perin, D. (2002). *Literacy Education After High School*. Washington, D.C.: Office of Educational Research and Improvement.

Rau, W., and Durand, A. (2000). The academic ethic and college grades: does hard work help students to "make the grade"? *Sociology of Education*. 73(1): 19–38.

Reissman, C. (1993). *Narrative Analysis*. Newbury Park: Sage Publications.

Sohn, K. (1999). *Whistlin' and Crowin' Women of Appalachia: Literacy Development Since College*. Dissertation, Indiana University of Pennsylvania.

Tinto, V. (1997). *Leaving College: Rethinking the Causes and Cures of Student Attrition*. Chicago: University of Chicago Press.

Townsend, B. (2001, Fall). Blurring the lines: transforming terminal education to transfer education. *New Directions for Community Colleges*. 115: 63–71.

Vygotsky, L. (1962). *Thought and Language*. in P. Miller's *Theories of Developmental Psychology*. 1993.

White, J. (2001). *Adult Women in Community Colleges*. (ERIC Document Reproduction Services No. 451 860).

CHAPTER 6
Marketing to the X Generation

Kara Mohre

The state of our present economy has placed colleges and universities throughout the country in a financial bind. Until recently, higher education has been able to rely heavily on expected funding from state appropriations, hefty endowments, along with alumni and corporate donations to help lessen the need to raise tuition. But as institutions of higher learning are feeling the pinch of what has been called the "perfect storm," many are clamoring to come up with new marketing methods and strategies to attract potential students to their hallowed halls, and some are specifically looking to Generation X students to relieve their financial burdens.

Colleges and universities influencing this generation's decision to attend one particular school over another must employ marketing strategies that are quite different from those used to attract previous generations. This is a "no nonsense" generation that values honesty, directness, and sincerity. Having an estimated $125 billion annual spending power in the U.S. alone, Generation X men and women can be convinced by the right marketing campaign to wear their college or university colors and write those tuition checks proudly (Marchetti, 1995).

Marketing Education to Gen Xers – What They Need and Want

Marketing education to Gen Xers can be tricky. To do it effectively, institutional marketers need to know what this generation really needs and wants and what they are willing to do without. Across the board, there are a few things to keep in mind as marketers encourage Gen Xers to jump on the educational bandwagon and to ensure that they hold on for the long haul. As emphasized in prior chapters, they all have different reasons for continuing their education. Gen Xers could be taking classes for the first time, returning to school, or making a complete career change. In any instance, they require and look for certain selling points in making a final decision about whether they will invest in their education. Important factors in this decision include affordability, convenience, reliability, and lasting value.

81

Even with all the hoopla and hype a university or college marketing team can muster, a major influence in a student's decision is affordability. Generation Xers are cautious and financially conservative. Because of today's economic state, this generation has seen the consequences of not having enough money to retire, the effects of corporate downsizing, and hold a fear that they may not "make it" (Furash, 1998). Due to the aforementioned, they become investors and they want backup plans to protect themselves. Many Gen Xers believe there is no better investment in their future than higher education.

Generation Xers may feel higher education will fix all the financial concerns they have about their future; even so, convincing these students to enroll is still a challenge. Institutions must be concise with the information they convey along with eliminating obstacles that could sway a potential student of this generation to enroll or may lead them to rethink their university choice. Today's students of Generation X are used to instant gratification whether it is from the local fast-food restaurant or the changing of channels with a remote control. Marketers should be quick to realize that this carries over into the university setting. Information needs to be provided in a timely manner. And as noted in chapter four, speed matters.

Even though Generation Xers do not enjoy the relatively robust economic times their parents did, they still have significant disposable income, either from their parents or their own jobs or both. They will part with their dollars if they readily see value in what they are purchasing. Individualized summaries of college costs are beneficial and help to create the student's trust of the university bureaucracy. They frown at any "surprise" costs that were not originally stated. Often, a student's first communication with a university is with financial services; therefore, strategic communications of financial assistance available must be revisited, evaluated, and continually refined to remain relevant and persuasive (Morrison, 1997).

Convenience is a word that carries a lot of weight in the lives of Generation Xers. Wasting time is not at the top of their lists because of loyalty to their families and other outside interests. Ideally, even class schedules should not interfere with their personal loyalties. As suggested in chapters four and five, convenient class times and delivery systems represent points of leverage that marketers can use to effectively position their institutions.

> This is a generation that grew up with both parents working and with the divorce rate at almost 50 percent. They were often latchkey kids so this group taught themselves responsibility and self-reliance at an early age, and it usually involved using technology as an information source when parents weren't around. Having grown up with computers and technology as part of their basic mental wiring, they assimilate many ideas quickly (Anatomy, 1998, on-line).

Questions generated by these students to various educational departments and student service offices must be answered at a click of a mouse via the Internet. Using this medium to disseminate information quickly not only offers convenience for the students but they feel comfortable because they are computer savvy.

Affordability and convenience are factors that impact a Gen Xer's decisions of whether or not to invest their time and money into an education. In addition, these students believe that "you get what you pay for!" An education gains value over time and Gen Xers appreciate the concept of return on investment.

Gen Xers need to trust that their acquired education will be as esteemed in the years to come as it is today. This generation can be somewhat insecure about tomorrow. Stamping a guarantee of success on education would be an ideal selling point for this generation. Many products sold today come with a warranty, which supports the idea that the product and services last a long time and that you are obtaining maximum value for one's possessions (Barrow, 1994). Colleges and universities can also sell a type of warranty. Promoting a school's national and/or international accreditation, percentage of teaching faculty holding advanced degrees, and high graduation, retention, and job placement rates enables Gen Xers to feel confident that they are buying into something that is reliable and enduring.

Efforts to Market Effectively to the X Generation

Colleges and universities continually think of innovative ideas for marketing effectively and efficiently to those they recruit. It is not an easy game, and much of it is trial and error. Today, many schools don't have room for error when it comes to spending money on new marketing initiatives; therefore, colleges and universities turn to the experts to learn what works before emptying their pockets. The following suggests a few ideas on how to target Generation X.

Universities and colleges must rely more on marketing strategy and less on the notion that we can sell higher education to "all" in the same way because it is an opportunity that cannot be turned down. How a college or university approaches this generation is of the utmost importance. No longer are the traditional methods of selling to the masses working. Gen Xers respond to being targeted as a valued customer with individual wants and needs.

With any marketing campaign, a high priority is to establish and nurture a relationship of trust between the university and the student. "Generation Xers are more easily identified by what they don't believe in than what they do. They laugh at unauthentic portrayals of themselves, possess a sixth sense for being talked down to, and their 'marketing-bullshit-o-meter' is usually turned on high" (Cloke, 1998).

A college or university marketing department must also remember that Xers

> … feel they've seen about everything and can spot the real from the dross from far off, so avoid the hard sell. They are hostile to marketing hype because they got it from the minute they were plopped down in front of the family electronic baby-sitter, the television. Gen Xers will ridicule and wisecrack their way through hype promotions (Furash, 1998, p. 88).

They want to be treated with more intelligence and respect than they ordinarily experience.

If you can't deliver, don't promise! This is an important message to remember when dealing with this generation. Fake promotional campaigns just do not work. These students respect bluntness and action over words. They dislike hyperbole, self-importance, and hypocrisy (Richie, 1995); therefore, an alumnus who just received his or her degree and immediately became a top executive, increased their salary by twenty thousand, and bought a Rolls Royce would not be a good student testimonial to sell education. These students realize that an education is a start to bettering their lives and not a "cure all" for personal and financial woes. Marketing an education as an investment in one's future will help in leading this generation to the prosperity they deserve along with hard work, experience, and a good work ethic. Depicting an alumnus being promoted in their job or a career change may resonate better with this generation in ads and commercials than the aforementioned.

In marketing, university personnel can fall into a convenient trap of pigeonholing and stereotyping members of this generation resulting in customer service being based and delivered on the misconception that all Gen Xers are the same. The word "joiners" cannot be used to characterize this group. Recruitment ads, publications, and other educational marketing materials must make individuality a selling point (Tieszen, 1996).

Gen Xers don't think of themselves as a market and resent it if those selling to them do. Being classified narrowly or lumped into another group stirs a lot of negative emotions. "They are 'market-of-one' devotees. They will respond well to providers that cater to their pride in being individuals" (Furash, 1998, p. 88).

Gen Xers are individuals, requiring and resulting in extraordinary growth in direct and database marketing techniques. One excellent definition states, "direct marketing is a system that uses precision database targeting, along with traditional advertising and sales promotion, to affect a measurable response and/or transaction" (Barrow, 1994, p. 24). This is an effective way to communicate with Generation X. Direct marketing allows you to customize the information to a specific group of students, which illustrates "outstanding value and a personal relationship of trust between themselves and the seller" (Barrow, 1994, p. 24). Combining technology and direct marketing can be quick, easy, and affordable given an available database of students. A student receiving an e-mail with her name listed conveys a message that she is valued as an individual and not viewed as only a number by the intended college or university.

Providing consumer service on an individual basis is quite an undertaking and particularly difficult in the university marketing arena. In any direct marketing campaign, an approach must be used that instills in each student a sense of personal value. Simple gestures of thanking them for inquiring about the school and requesting their suggestions in promotions make them feel special. Establishing an emotional connection also establishes trust and respect between the school and the student.

College and universities do not have to be cautious using technology as a marketing resource, because it has been part of this generation's everyday life and an avenue for quick answers and information. Advertising on-line is an easy way to target this group, but it needs to be interesting and eye-opening. By using graphics, color, sound, and video to hold their attention, the chances of their becoming intrigued enough to investigate the services and program offerings increase dramatically. Prospective students are drawn into college and university Web sites with photos, multimedia presentations, and intuitive navigation links (Brenner, 1998).

Generation Xers share many traits. Yet, college and university marketers cannot forget that this group takes pride in being identified as individuals and not joiners in today's society. Gen Xers challenge college and university marketers, because this generation has varied reactions to different marketing ploys. "The task for marketers is to target this group – or parts of it – with a relevant and heartfelt message. The ability to craft the message is the challenge. One solution: Speak to this group with candor and an edge" (Orgel, 1999, p. 12). Last, but not least … do not forget honesty.

Quick Tips for the "Xperts" Marketing to Gen Xers

Generation X cannot be easily assigned to a category, yet they share some common characteristics: an appreciation for honesty, integrity, and keeping promises, which should be at the core of every institutional marketing effort. Understanding a Gen Xer's unique needs, expectations, and ambitions is a prerequisite to establishing an enduring relationship. Employing vertical or relationship marketing strategies like those that follow will increase effectiveness, and consequently, yield with Generation X students:

- This generation knows what is real and what is hyperbole or deception. Market the truth to this generation with narrative copy and testimonials that are simple and straightforward.

- Diversity is important to Gen Xers, but avoid appearing too politically correct. They recognize when situations are staged or phony.

- Use bullet points and short phrases. Heavy text is not welcomed. Concise, informative, and to the point works!

- Illustrate convenience with flexible curricula schedules and Web-based courses. This generation has a life.

- Gen Xers are a four-color minimum generation. Black and white does not excite them. Use pictures and graphics in school publications to illustrate information. Remember, it needs to appear organized and not cluttered.

- Utilize catchy logos and brand recognition. Gen Xers are loyal to brands that equate to quality.

- Gear recruiting messages that focus on how an education can benefit the student now and in the future. This is a "me, me …" generation and they want to know what they can get from an investment.

- Illustrating that an education is well priced and attainable lowers any inhibitions that this generation may have about continuing their education.

- This generation thrives on feeling special. Make sure incentives are in place to market and attract this type of student. Free evening parking, a commuter deli, study lounges, and classes ONLY for adults are necessities. In addition, personalizing an e-mail or a letter really tells this audience they are valued as individuals.

- Gen Xers understand and trust technology. By leveraging technology, information is provided quickly and allows students to search efficiently and conveniently for answers to their questions.

REFERENCES

Anatomy of the "Generation X" consumer. (1998, April 27). *Denver Business Journal.* [On-line]. Available: http://www.bizjournals.com/denver/stories/1998/04/27/smallb4.html.

Barrow, P. (1994, Spring). Marketing to generation X. *Canadian Manager.* 19(1): 23–24.

Brenner, R. (1998). Selling to the generations, part 2. *Targeted Marketing.* [On-line]. Available: http://www.brennerbooks.com/sellgen2.html.

Cloke, S. (1998). X marks the shop. "Shoot The Messenger" Available: http://www.shootthemessenger.com.au/u_apr_98/infowism/i_xshop.html.

Furash, E. (1998, February). A mystery generation no longer. *The Journal of Lending & Credit Risk Management.* 80(6): 86–90.

Marchetti, M. (1995, December). Talkin' 'bout my generation. *Sales & Marketing Management.* 147(12): 64–69.

Morrison, D. (1997, March 17). Beyond the Gen X label. *Brandweek.* 38(11): 23–26.

Orgel, D. (1999, February 8). Generation X: marketing strategies for change. *Supermarket News.* 12.

Ritchie, K. (1995, April). Marketing to Generation X. *American Demographics.* 17(4): 34–40.

Tieszen, L. (1996, December 15). The X market. *Beverage World.* 115(1630): 98–101.

CHAPTER SEVEN

Recruitment Strategies and Communications for the X Generation

Jim Black

As described exhaustively in other chapters, the Generation X cohort has some unique characteristics. Consequently, Gen X recruitment strategies do not necessarily follow traditional patterns. For instance, many adults decide to apply late in the traditional admissions cycle. Within this more narrowly confined recruitment window, limited cultivation can occur. The Gen X recruitment window dictates that communications be compacted into fewer contacts or in shorter intervals than communications for high school students. Therefore, communications from the institution to this population, by necessity, must be practical, concise, and often process-oriented.

The messages conveyed in chapter six, affordability, convenience, reliability, and lasting value, while not limited to Gen Xers, certainly speak to this audience and influence their decision-making process. Recruitment strategies and communications need to reinforce these messages over and over again. More importantly, strategies and communications must be designed to promote how the institution delivers affordability, convenience, reliability, and lasting value in a way that is distinctive among its competitor set, typically local competitors for place-bound undergraduate students and local, regional, national, or international competitors for graduate students depending on the nature of the graduate program.

Even though the strategies and communications must be fashioned to appeal to the Generation X audience, many of the recruitment fundamentals are the same. Prospective students move from a state of institutional awareness or unawareness to varying levels of institutional commitment (e.g., apply, deposit, and enroll) based, to a degree, on interactions with the college or university. Communications should flow from general to specific, and customized communications are always more powerful than generic ones. Relationship building is central to the recruitment process, and as established in chapter six, this is particularly important to Gen Xers. Relationships that result in conversions are the ultimate goal. Incremental action steps (e.g., request information, visit the campus, send transcripts and test scores, apply for financial assistance) taken by the prospective student also influence conversion rates.

The Recruitment Funnel

Knowing how Generation X students choose a college is often more an art than a science (Litten, Sullivan, & Brodigan, 1983; Braxton, 1990). Influencing human behavior is never a simple matter. Nonetheless, recruitment strategies have evolved to a sophisticated level at many institutions. Using the recruitment funnel (Sevier, 2000; Low & Bryant, 2001–02), the process of student recruitment can be dissected and targeted with specific strategies. For example, prospective students who have not yet inquired about a college or university but may meet the institution's criteria and appear to be a "good fit" can be identified through data analysis tools such as geodemography, predictive modeling, testing service software, or mailing service filters (Low and Bryant, 2001–02). An institution's database can provide valuable data regarding enrollment trends by geographic area as well as by student population that can be used to target prospective students. Prior to engaging in prospecting, however, the institution should clearly define the kind of student it is seeking to enroll (Sevier, 2000).

Once a viable population of prospective students has been identified, communications designed to enhance institutional visibility or brand awareness are created. At this stage of the recruitment process, communications should have limited content and powerful visuals (Dennis, 1998; Noel-Levitz, 2002). In addition to providing information about the institution's academic programs and services, content should address "the personal needs and concerns of adults who are unaccustomed to viewing themselves in the role of student" (Council for Adult and Experimental Learning, 2000, p. 6). Inquiry generation strategies incorporating said communications might include: direct mail; point of sale posters; broadcast advertising such as radio, newspaper, or television; movie screen advertising; telephone directory advertisements; billboards; postcards; Web site; Web banners; and e-mail (Noel-Levitz, 2002). Other common inquiry generation strategies consist of visits to community colleges, businesses, and agencies; information sessions; workshops; area receptions; open houses; and daily campus visits (Breland, Maxey, Gernand, Cumming, & Trapani, 2000; Noel-Levitz, 2002). All of these contacts share one of two common "calls to action" – completion of an inquiry form or visit to the campus (Sevier, 2000).

Inquiry generation also occurs somewhat serendipitously by word-of-mouth. In fact, "positive word-of-mouth, often termed viral marketing, is very powerful, highly credible, but seldom orchestrated by the institution" (Black, 2002, p. 19). Finding ways to influence word-of-mouth is particularly important for institutions that draw adult students from a local market, where image is everything. While word-of-mouth can be influenced through recruitment strategies like training student volunteers for a calling campaign or to represent the school at an event, it can best be influenced by helping adults identify and overcome barriers to returning to college and make informed decisions regarding the match between the institution's offerings and their educational goals (Council for Adult and Experimental Learning, 2000). Furthermore, ensuring enrolled students have a positive experience, consistently exceeding the learning needs and service expectations described in chapter four, yields positive word-of-mouth with recruitment value far beyond any ad the institution could purchase or publication it could produce.

At the inquiry stage, the student has demonstrated some level of interest in the institution. Through a series of carefully designed communications, interest is ideally cultivated to the point that the student is ready to accept the next "call to action" – applying for admission (Sevier, 2000; Low and Bryant, 2001–02; Black, 2003). To achieve application goals for quantity, quality, and diversity, four processes must occur at the inquiry stage: (1) capture, (2) qualification, (3) grading, and (4) cultivation. Capture refers to the process for collecting personal information and entering it promptly into a database (Noel-Levitz, 2002). Personal information can be generated through referrals from current students, alumni, former teachers, employers, and others; self-initiated by means such as the submission of test scores or the Free Application for Federal Student Aid (FAFSA) data and Web, e-mail, written, phone, or walk-in inquiries; as well as through solicited inquiries like a response to a direct mail piece, community college visits, college guidebooks, Web college searches, and point of sale posters (Low and Bryant, 2001–02; Black, 2003). Of these sources of Gen X prospects, self-initiated inquiries tend to produce the highest rate of applications followed by solicited inquiries and then referrals.

Too often institutions miss opportunities to capture data from students who have expressed some level of interest in the school (Black, 2003). Lack of a functioning prospect database, poor collection and data entry procedures, failure to enter test scores and FAFSA data into the database, along with the absence of a data sharing mechanism or procedure when initial inquiries are made to administrative and academic units other than the admissions office, are among the most common reasons prospect data is not captured.

Once information is entered into a database, prospects can be qualified based on their expressed or perceived interest in the institution (Low and Bryant, 2001–02; Noel-Levitz, 2002; Black, 2003). Prospect qualification allows the institution to differentiate communication strategies thus saving money and time while improving effectiveness. Whether using sophisticated qualification systems such as predictive modeling, or simplistic approaches such as telecounseling qualifications or inquiry source ratings, recruiters can focus efforts on Gen X prospects whose decisions may be influenced rather than on those who are unlikely to enroll regardless of what the institution does. Conversely, those who already are prone to enroll will need minimal courting from the school (Low and Bryant, 2001–02; Black, 2003). The Gen X prospects whose decisions may be swayed represent the margin of success or failure in any recruitment effort (Black, 2003).

The grading of Gen X prospects relates to the institution's interest in the student (Low and Bryant, 2001–02). Institutional interest could be defined by academic criteria, special talent, or student characteristics such race, gender, or residency (Low and Bryant, 2001–02). Some institutions aggressively recruit finite populations of students such as community college graduates who have earned associate in arts or associate in science degrees or those who are eligible for employer reimbursements. Regarding the latter, estimates prepared by the National Center for Education Statistics indicated that during the decade of the '90s only 3% of all undergraduates and 7% of all graduate and first-professional degree students received employer reimbursements (Council for Adult and Experimental Learning, 1999). Whatever the selected population, admissions officers can use grading in combination with or instead of qualifying to target recruitment efforts.

Personal data collected during the capture process and differentiated in the qualification and grading processes is used for Gen X prospect cultivation. Effective cultivation requires frequent and relevant contact points (Sevier, 2000; Black, 2003). Contacts should convey information slightly more specific than at the inquiry generation stage, yet the primary purpose should be to develop a relationship (Peppers, Rogers, & Dorf, 1999; Williams, 2000; Black, 2001; Strauss & Frost, 2001; Black, 2003). Cultivation strategies might include campus visit events, area receptions, home visits, telecounseling calls, faculty calls, alumni contacts, instant messaging, Web chats, Web portals, personal notes or e-mails, digital publications, and interviews (Low and Bryant, 2001–02; Black, 2003). Regardless of the Gen X cultivation strategy, communication should be personalized and sequential – each one building synergistically upon the last (Noel-Levitz, 2002). It is the cumulative effect of these contacts that will yield an enduring and meaningful relationship between the student and the institution.

At the application stage, the institution must decide about the student's admissibility. Typically, admissions decisions are based on factors that have been correlated to student success and persistence at a particular institution (Bean, 1990; Black, 2003). Factors used to assess the potential for success of adult students might consist of objective measures such as previous academic performance or standardized test scores, but many institutions consider more subjective measures like information collected during an interview. Interviews are often used to evaluate intangibles: readiness, motivation, and life experiences. In addition to evaluating potential for student success, the interview process frequently is devoted to counseling and goal setting activities. Whether interview sessions are conducted in person, by phone, through video conferencing, or some other form of two-way communication, the focus should always be on the student in an attempt to include the adult learner as a partner in the admissions process (Council for Adult and Experimental Learning, 1999).

Though student success is a major driver in determining admissions criteria, it is not the only consideration. Mission, capacity, program viability, student diversity, student fit, institutional prestige, funding opportunities, faculty priorities, senior leadership aspirations, and political pressures are among the other factors that influence admissions policies at most colleges and universities.

From the point of admission to enrollment, yield strategies are designed to increase psychological, emotional, and financial commitment of the student to the institution (Black, 2003). Examples of yield strategies include admitted student open houses, admitted student receptions, orientation programs, calls from current adult students, personalized video or text messages, Web chats, on-line communities, Web diaries, vertical portals, financial aid leveraging, "vanity" awards, differential pricing, and tuition freeze plans (Abrahamson & Hossler, 1990; Hossler, 2000; St. John, 2000; Black, 2001; Black, 2003).

Four factors are of particular importance in the decision-making process at this stage: 1) perceived fit with the institution and academic program, 2) the affordability of tuition, fees, and other related expenses, 3) the transfer of credit, and 4) the degree to which school activities and related demands mesh with other life priorities such as family and work (Sevier, 2000). Although practical issues of "fit" are typically addressed earlier in the recruitment process (e.g., desired program, convenience of location, and admissibility), in this stage of the process, "fit" refers to more personal issues (e.g., comfort level, finding one's place, and self-confidence in one's ability to succeed). In some ways, determining personal "fit" with an institution is a journey of self-discovery. The journey, however, is influenced by interactions with faculty, staff, and peers. Colleges that are proactive and intentional about such interactions exponentially increase the likelihood of enrolling returning adults.

Affordability can certainly be determined within one's own resources but often is dependent upon the competitiveness of a financial aid offer or the flexibility of payment options. The Council for Adult and Experimental Learning (2000) cites several exemplary institutional practices for ensuring an affordable education to adult students:

- Provide information about convenient payment options.
- Offer deferred payment options when tuition reimbursement programs do not make funds available until the course is completed.
- Encourage employers to provide educational funds at the beginning of the student's academic process.
- Make financial aid and scholarships available to part-time students.
- Assess charges to adult learners incrementally throughout the duration of the program.
- Help adult learners develop strategies for locating external funding.

Transfer of credit should be evaluated no later than at the point of admission but much sooner if possible. Often, enrollment decisions are based on the student knowing the answer to two questions: 1) how much credit will transfer, and 2) how long it will take to complete a degree. Institutions that provide these answers early in the college selection process increase the probability that the student will enroll. A process for evaluating credit consistently and promptly is critical to the successful recruitment of adult learners, many of whom have multiple college transcripts complicating the expedient evaluation of credit. In addition to a fast turnaround, adult learners are also hoping for institutional flexibility in regard to the review of their formal as well as informal learning experiences. The Council for Adult and Experimental Learning (1999, p. 8) recommends that "learning acquired outside of formal settings" be valued, perhaps using Prior Learning Assessment (PLA) to define, document, and evaluate the learning experience. According to the Council for Adult and Experimental Learning (1999), such flexibility benefits adult learners by:

- Validating the worth of learning they have completed.
- Identifying what they need to learn in order to achieve personal, academic, and career goals.
- Reducing the time necessary to earn a college credential.

- Saving tuition costs by reducing the number of hours needed.
- Enhancing their appreciation of learning as a lifelong process.

Developing an educational plan "is a continuous process which begins with the initial inquiry and continues through graduation" (Council for Adult and Experimental Learning, 1999). At the point of admission, if not sooner, adult learners should receive assistance in effectively interfacing the demands of college with other *life priorities*. The exploration of life, career, and educational goals with an admissions officer, career counselor, or academic advisor is a prerequisite to a discussion of how best to integrate identified goals with the demands of life outside of college. The session concludes with the development of an education plan that fits within the context of the individual's life. Included in the educational plan are the steps needed to complete the enrollment process. For an adult student, particularly one who has not been enrolled in higher education recently, this approach lessens anxiety about returning to college while increasing confidence in the ability to succeed.

Regardless of the specific strategy or stage in the funnel, recruitment activities should be customized, relevant, and timely (Black, 2001; Low and Bryant, 2001–02; Black, 2003). Moreover, the arsenal of recruiting tools should be sufficient to sustain a level of frequency students welcome and consider as a sign of institutional interest in them (Noel-Levitz, 2002). Communications should emphasize benefits rather than mere institutional facts (Sevier, 1998; Low and Bryant, 2001–02). Every recruitment activity should be evaluated for effectiveness and cost/benefit (Sevier, 2000; Noel-Levitz, 2002). Evaluation measures, along with specific goals and objectives, action plans, responsibilities, implementation timelines, and budgets, should be incorporated into a recruitment plan (Noel-Levitz, 2002).

Institutional Applications

Applying the basic recruitment principles inherent in the funnel to specific institutional settings yields a variety of recruitment approaches and results. Effectiveness in attracting Generation X students can best be determined at the institutional level. This is definitely not a "one size fits all" or "quick fix" endeavor. Strategy effectiveness is largely determined by fit with and appeal to the target audience, alignment with the institution's mission and strengths, sufficiency of human and financial resources allocated for implementation, and the quality of execution. For the most part, the institution controls these variables and, therefore, the same recruitment strategy that is effective at one institution may be an unmitigated failure at another.

To better understand how institutions apply recruitment principles to the Gen X population, case studies from five very different but successful recruitment efforts follow. The authors of each are listed along with their case study.

VILLANOVA UNIVERSITY CASE STUDY

Suzanne Allen
Villanova University

Villanova University is an independent coeducational institution of higher learning founded in 1842 by the Augustinian Order of the Roman Catholic Church. For more than 80 years, the Division of Part-Time Studies has fulfilled the educational needs of thousands of men and women who were unable or did not wish to pursue a regular full-time day program. Part-Time Studies provides comprehensive advising services at registration time and throughout the year to assist students in planning their educational careers and academic schedules. The degrees pursued in Part-Time Studies are Villanova University degrees, in every respect commensurate with those offered by the full-time colleges of the University. Part-Time Studies students will range in age from 18 to 70, but the average age of this student population ranges from 33 to 37. Virtually all of these students live and/or work in the Philadelphia, Delaware Valley region. While the majority of students are interested in completing an undergraduate degree, approximately 36% are post-graduate students filling in prerequisites for a graduate degree program or taking courses to sharpen their professional skills and to advance their careers. Many of these students are also enrolled in one of two post-baccalaureate certificate programs in either accountancy or business administration.

Recruitment Strategy

While Part-Time Studies' recruiting efforts certainly benefit from Villanova's national reputation, at the same time, the division must work hard to get the message out to prospective students that it can provide an academic experience that meets the unique needs of the adult learner and compares favorably to the many other adult programs in the area. In a region where competition for that same student is unusually fierce, Part-Time Studies must continue to focus on two principles. The division must 1) develop good relationships with those area institutions that provide a continuous pool of qualified students (business, non-profit sectors, community colleges) and 2) initiate creative programs that will generate a steady new supply of applications throughout the year. The Part-Time Studies Villanova Days are an example of the latter. By providing individual attention in a convenient setting and addressing the two main concerns of adult students – academic and financial – not only do Part-Time Studies Villanova Days consistently produce new applications throughout the year; they also improve the chances of converting attendees to applicants and then to enrolled students. The most important service Villanova Days provide, however, is to make sure that at the beginning of the admissions process, the expectations of these potential new students are realistic and that no unpleasant surprises await them. The literature and the Part-Time Studies division data clearly indicate that this is an important factor in retention and student satisfaction.

Villanova Days are held ten months a year (exceptions are September and February). A postcard mailing goes out every month to all PTS prospects in the database for the past two years. Villanova Days offer personalized service to potential students that combine one-on-one, in-depth academic advising and financial counseling. By eliminating obstacles (lack of

Costs*	
Food	$1,186.25
Post Cards	$3,604.13
Mailing (Bulk Mail Rate + Handling)	$7,544.67
Total Costs	$12,335.05
Total Credit Hours Enrolled	1,739
Total Revenue (average $350/credit)	$608,650.00

*After 22 Villanova Days

information; fears about financial needs; fear of failing) that most adult students find overwhelming and can turn them away from completing their educational goals, the Villanova Days event consistently generates applications that convert to enrollments with comparatively high yields. Prospects are informed on the postcard that they can meet individually with a Part-Time Studies academic advisor, bring transcripts for an on-the-spot evaluation, find out about the Phi Theta Kappa Scholarship for part-time students, meet with a representative from the Bursar's Office who can answer questions regarding tuition and payment options, get information on the Villanova Tuition Employer Billing Plan as well as financial aid opportunities for part-time students. Additionally, if they submit their application at the program, the application fee will be waived. Students are asked to call and make an appointment and to bring their transcripts. Two appointments are scheduled for every half hour from 12:00 noon through 7:00 P.M. Two academic advisors and one financial counselor are available throughout the event. Appointments are encouraged, but all walk-ins are welcomed. There is generally significant walk-in activity. A room near the main Part-Time Studies office is reserved and is set up the day before. A table with light refreshments and another table with current publications and information for display along with conference tables and chairs are in the room. Every effort is made to create a welcoming environment and one conducive to private conversation.

Results

Below are data charts that show Villanova Days yield percentages by both overall totals and for the four most recent individual semesters. Also provided is a chart that makes it possible to compare the semester results with the same data for all of Part-Time Studies admissions during the same time frame.

Lessons Learned

- The successful development of Villanova Days begins and ends with an accurate prospect database.
- Yield percentages improve closer to start of each new semester.
- Program location should be as close to the office as possible to ensure fast access to student files, staff assistance, supplies, computer records, etc.
- Organize the programs a year in advance; reserve the space, order the year's supply of postcards, order refreshments for the entire year, communicate dates and arrange coverage with

Villanova Days

	OVERALL TOTALS*							
Dates	Total Attendance	Total Apps.	Yield %	Total Accepts	Yield %	Total Enrolled	Yield %	Total Enrolled Hours
4/10/01– 1/18/02	112	83	74%	58	70%	52	90%	
4/10/01– 9/11/02	199	149	75%	92	62%	77	84%	
4/10/01– 1/31/03	282	211	75%	143	68%	121	85%	
4/10/01– 7/2/03	367	260	71%	172	66%	138	80%	1739

*After 22 Villanova Days; data as of 7/2/03

FOUR SEMESTER TOTALS*					
Entry Term	Applications	Accepts	Yield %	Enrolled	Yield %
Spring 2003	56	45	80%	37	82%
Fall 2002	53	36	68%	27	75%
Spring 2002	49	31	63%	28	90%
Fall 2001	26	15	58%	13	87%

*Data as of 7/2/03; does not include summer semesters

Part-Time Studies Admissions Summary for Same Semesters

Semester	Applications	Accepts	Yield %	Enrolled	Yield %
Spring 2003	283	223	78%	155	70%
Fall 2002	385	303	77%	228	75%
Spring 2002	288	201	70%	139	69%
Fall 2001	373	228	61%	197	86%

the Bursar's Office and other key staff for the year, identify the postcard mailing dates and block out times to set up the mailing arrangements.

■ Maintain a good working relationship with the Bursar's Office.

■ The combination of academic and financial counseling in a one-stop shop and a one-on-one format makes the difference.

■ Take advantage of the benefits to be gained by linking promotional efforts for the specific Villanova Day event with the annual advertising plan for newspaper and radio.

DAYTONA BEACH COMMUNITY COLLEGE CASE STUDY

Joseph Roof
Dean of Enrollment Development
Daytona Beach Community College

On October 4, 1957, the Florida legislature established Daytona Beach Junior College (DBJC) and its black sister institution, Volusia County Community College, (VCCC). In 1965, after the passage of the 1964 Civil Rights Act, the two colleges merged, along with the local vocational school to form what is known today as Daytona Beach Community College (DBCC). For the next thirty-five years, the College remained committed to its mission of embracing diversity and providing open access to learning for all. In 1999, the DBCC Board of Trustees rededicated the student services building as the J. Griffen Greene Resource Center, in memory of the president of Volusia County Community College who served from 1957 to 1965. As part of this recognition, the Board established and funded the Daytona Beach Community College "Community Mentoring Project."

Four community mentors are assigned to the Admissions and Recruitment Office and are charged with increasing the enrollment of underrepresented populations, specifically African American and Hispanic adults. Each community mentor works in an assigned community or "territory" to build relationships with a variety of community agencies, churches, and employers who are able to provide access to the target population. The community mentors partner with the agencies in sponsoring events and activities within the communities that will target the adult population. Events and activities are held throughout the year. Activities range from visits to libraries, housing authorities, and job placement centers to visits to specific churches and community festivals.

For 2002–03, the Community Mentoring Project had expenditures of just over $150,000 including personnel costs. During this same period, over 550 inquiries were generated directly attributed to the Community Mentoring Project resulting in eighty-five students enrolling at the college. Inquiries are tracked by categories and specific agency/event. Three-quarters of these inquiries and 80% of the new students enrolled from these inquiries came from those activities associated with a community agency. The one agency that provided the most inquiries and yielded the most students was the One Stop Career Center, which also provides tuition assistance for short-term training programs. While many of the community events generated significant inquiries, fewer of these individuals were converted into students. Preliminary data indicates agencies that provide direct support to individuals result in more inquiries and a better yield rate from inquiry to enrollment.

Overall, the college has made significant improvements in the total enrollment of African American and Hispanic students. Since the implementation of the Community Mentoring

Project in 1999, the fall enrollment of African American students has increased by 21% and Hispanic students by 35%. The college's total enrollment increased 12.5% during this same three-year period. Even more impressive was the improvements in graduation rates, with African American graduates increasing by 49% and Hispanic graduates increasing by 62%. As a comparison, the college's overall graduation rate increased by 9% over the same period.

The college's commitment to access and diversity, combined with its willingness to invest significant resources in the community mentoring effort has resulted in positive enrollment and graduation gains for the college. The relationships that the community mentors have been able to develop with the various agencies in the community, as well as relationships with prospective students, have been a success for the students, the agencies, and the college.

PITTSBURG STATE UNIVERSITY CASE STUDY

Ange Peterson
Director of Admission and Enrollment Services
Pittsburg State University

Currently celebrating its centennial year, Pittsburg State University is a growing regional comprehensive university located in southeast Kansas. The university provides more than 100 academic programs with numerous accreditations and approval ratings and is home to the largest educational building in Kansas, the Kansas Technology Center. Serving a four-state area, the PSU mission continues to encompass the preparation of students for the challenges and opportunities of a changing world. Unlike the national trend analysis, Pittsburg State University has gone from 47% adult student learners in 1989 to 37% in fall of 2002. The university is a better fit for traditional residential students with 25 being the average age of the student body. Due to this changing demographic statistic, the strategic planning process, under the president's leadership, recommended the reallocation of resources to address adult students' needs in conjunction with needs of three distinctive communities. The three strategies are: the development of the PSU–KC Metro Center in Kansas City, a cooperative degree completion program in Wichita, and facilitation of a Department of Education grant to prepare paraprofessionals for teaching English as a second language in the southeast Kansas community. The planning process used demographic trends and needs analysis to set specific goals with objectives and strategies. The outcome-based reporting system in the planning model provides an assessment of the effectiveness of each program's initiatives. These initiatives are documented in the Pittsburg State University Strategic Planning document.

An environmental scan of the Southeast Kansas location of Pittsburg State University identifies the problematic issue of addressing and increasing the number of adult students. Southeast Kansas is the lowest socioeconomic area of the state and business and industry have been stagnant for many years and the situation is not likely to change. It became imperative that PSU would expand university services into areas currently needing very specific programs that PSU could offer and grow. Demographics indicated those programs needed to be located in two major metropolitan areas. After providing special education certification for teachers in the Kansas City area, it was obvious that the primary focus should be in the Kansas City area due to the demand for other cost effective graduate and degree completion programs. (UPC/SEM - *Objective 2 of Goal 4: Establish permanent presence in KC, KS for academic programs, recruitment for the Pittsburg campus and enhancement of alumni relations.*) The strategy was to locate an educational center in Kansas City. In the Wichita area, the strategy was to provide services to the aviation industry in the form of continuing education for full-time employees. Each of these initiatives has very specific goals and meets the needs of identifiable segments in each of the two communities. The third initiative was service to southeast Kansas through a grant written by Dr. Alice Sagehorn, C&I–Education, to fulfill a need for teachers to address the continuing increase of Hispanic immigrants and their children into the K–12 educational system. This synopsis will highlight the PSU–KC Metro Center development and progress in educating adult learners.

The offices of admission and enrollment services, continuing studies, alumni, and the president contributed the resources to establish the PSU–KC Metro Center in Johnson County, the fastest growing area in Kansas. Dr. Howard Smith, former chair of special services and leadership studies was selected as the director of the Center. Smith estimates that the Center serves about 50% Gen Xers and 50% Boomers. The programs offered are based on area demand and need. Two of the programs, Teaching Fellows (M.S. in Teaching) and Emergency Service Personnel Technology Management (B.S. in Technology Management) are partnerships. Each of the various programs are designed to accommodate the working student, take from two to four years to complete, and are offered in a cycle as indicated:

Program Offerings	College	Department	Cycle Ends
B.S. Technology Mmgt.	Technology	TED	Fall '04
B.S. Elementary Ed.	Education	C & I	Spring '04
District School Adm. Cert.	Education	SSLS	Summer '04
M.S. Educational Leadership	Education	SSLS	Summer '04
M.S. Educational Technology	Education	SSLS	Summer '04
M.S. Teaching: Cert.	Education	C & I	Summer '05
M.B.A.	Business	M & M	Summer '05

Smith indicated that the important lessons learned after three years include but are not limited to the following:

Students

1. People today shop for convenience, cost, and quality of programs, and in that order.
2. Varying delivery styles are necessary. Use of Web-enhanced classes, interactive learning situations, time of day, and frequency of class meetings are important to the student.

Within the University Organization

1. Make sure the key players are on board with the vision of the new strategy.
2. Find multiple ways to involve people in the process and leave the 'foot-draggers' dragging their feet.
3. You can never communicate enough.

After getting the PSU–KC Metro Center off the ground, a separate budget line was established for operating expenses and the combination of the original offices provided the continuation of resources for the Center.

PittState KC Metro Center

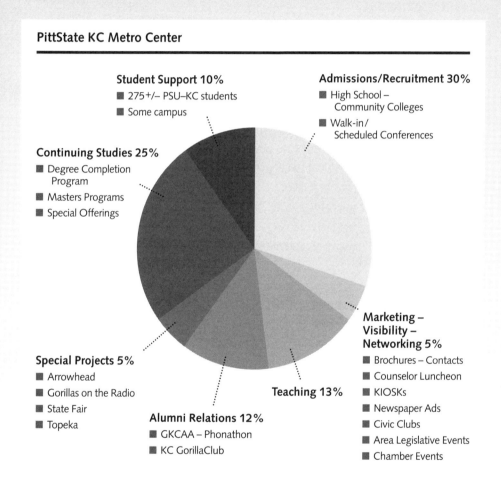

Student Support 10%
- 275+/– PSU–KC students
- Some campus

Admissions/Recruitment 30%
- High School – Community Colleges
- Walk-in/ Scheduled Conferences

Continuing Studies 25%
- Degree Completion Program
- Masters Programs
- Special Offerings

Marketing – Visibility – Networking 5%
- Brochures – Contacts
- Counselor Luncheon
- KIOSKs
- Newspaper Ads
- Civic Clubs
- Area Legislative Events
- Chamber Events

Special Projects 5%
- Arrowhead
- Gorillas on the Radio
- State Fair
- Topeka

Teaching 13%

Alumni Relations 12%
- GKCAA – Phonathon
- KC GorillaClub

The development of PSU–KC Metro Center has increased undergraduate and graduate enrollment consistently for the last three years. The allocation of resources to the center has provided a return on the monetary investment plus communicated a willingness to provide services to an area that is viable to the economic stability of the state, the community, and the university.

LESLEY UNIVERSITY CASE STUDY

Hugh Norwood
Vice President of Marketing and Dean of Enrollment Planning
Lesley University

Lesley University was a small, women's only college for nearly seventy years, when in the late 1970s it began to offer bachelor's and master's degrees off-campus in a unique, one weekend per month, "cohort" format. Through its outreach efforts, Lesley's enrollments grew rapidly through the '80s and early '90s, and the college began to specialize in offering accelerated cohort programs at a distance, including bachelor's degree programs in management, education, and human services.

The target population for these programs is adults – primarily women 30–49 – who wish to return to school. These students often have significant family and work commitments that prevent them from attending college during the day or on weeknights, or the students live in remote areas where getting to and from a university campus is difficult or impossible.

By the late 1990s, the bachelor's degree programs in education and human services had lost more than three-quarters of their enrollments in only four years. Increased competition from other, similarly convenient adult degree programs, rising operational costs, and lack of connection between the program and the marketing/admissions functions were some of the reasons cited for the precipitous drop.

The first step in this recruitment strategy was data gathering. Alumni, current students, and new prospects were surveyed, and data from the student information system was cut every way imaginable. Individual interviews were held with all of the core faculty members of the program, the program staff, and several adjuncts, asking about strengths and weaknesses. As the data was collected and analyzed, several trends became apparent:

■ More than 90% of alums in the last decade were suburban females, white, 35–49, with average household income (HHI) of more than $75k.

■ Retention in the cohort programs had fallen from 86% in the early '90s to 70% in 1999.

■ Yield on new inquiries (prospects) had dropped from nearly 20% to less than 8%.

■ Survey data from prospects indicated that price and the availability of financial aid were significant choice factors (more than any other single factor).

■ A scan of similarly positioned programs within the geographic area indicated that Lesley's was one of the highest-priced degree completion programs in the market.

With the primary enrollment objective being an increase in new students to these programs, increasing the yield on current prospects as well as increasing the prospective pool, became Lesley's focus. From the data, the university determined two strategic priorities:

1. *Diversify and broaden Lesley's target audience.* To achieve this, Lesley chose to target adult community college students as a new and more diverse source of degree completers.

2. *Reduce overall program cost and the "sticker shock" of prospective students.* To achieve this, Lesley relied on two key strategies: "freezing" tuition once a student started his or her degree program, and messaging Lesley's price and true tuition costs more effectively in the recruitment and financial aid advisement phases of the enrollment process.

Audience

An important component of the Lesley mission is "serving the underserved" and a commitment to a diverse learning community. The demographic data of Lesley alums and current students revealed that the bachelor's degree programs had targeted a primarily suburban, white popula-tion in the past. Marketing efforts were broadened to include a much wider set of demographics. The main reason was not so much sound marketing principles as a need to reconnect the programs and the students to the core mission of Lesley University.

Without a lot of resources to fund an expanded marketing effort, Lesley turned to community colleges as a source of qualified, prepared adult learners who needed to complete their bache-lor's degrees. The University originally thought of reaching community college populations directly, through direct mail and college publications and poster campaigns. The cost was too much, and as one of the recruiters pointed out in an early strategy meeting, "the adult students we want from the community colleges don't read or look at that stuff."

Instead, this audience was approached with a time-honored traditional-age recruitment strat-egy, an appeal directly to the counselors and the faculty of the community colleges for recommendations and referrals. In speaking with several of them, it became obvious that they were not only willing to talk about Lesley to their students, they were eager to form academic partnerships, "articulation agreements," between their programs and Lesley's (often described as a "2+2" program).

Operationalizing this strategy required the cooperation of Lesley's program faculties and the admissions/marketing units. Admissions identified a potential community college (through an alum referral, or a transcript review, et al.), and "qualified" the partnership through a series of conversations with the community college. The admissions office was looking for similarly focused associate degree programs, for instance, early childhood education, with a large enough enrollment at the two-year level to support a degree-completion program. The admis-sions office also identified an internal advocate at the community college who would work internally to break down barriers and reduce turf wars. With an advocate in place and the potential for enrollment identified, the admissions office liaised with the Lesley faculty from that program (i.e., early childhood education) to review the community college's catalog and course syllabi, and recommend articulations at the course level. Often, this required significant discussion between faculties, and sometimes changes to the course design.

With an articulation agreement in place, the admissions office would work with the commu-nity college faculty, the advocate (if different), and the alumni office of the community college to identify potential students for the degree completion program.

Results

Since 2000, Lesley has successfully entered into nearly a dozen articulation agreements with community colleges across Massachusetts, forming on-site cohort programs with five of those schools. The enrollment in Lesley bachelor's degree programs has grown significantly, from three new cohorts (approximately forty-five students) in 1999 to eighteen cohorts (approximately 300 students) in 2003. The student diversity has also improved, from less than 10% minority students to nearly 30%. Improved retention may also be a gain from this strategy, though it is too soon to know for certain.

What Was Learned

Getting an articulation agreement to work is hard. Good agreements benefit students by facilitating their transition from two-year to four-year programs, and by reducing the number of required courses they must take to complete the bachelor's degree. This is a significant benefit to the student, but it may not always outweigh alternatives (such as attending a public four-year, or "taking a break" from school after completing their associate degrees). Articulation agreements did not suddenly make Lesley degree programs cheaper (though it did make it more affordable by reducing the number of courses a student may need to take to receive his or her B.A.).

Another hurdle to completing an articulation agreement lies within the program faculty. At its essence, an articulation agreement is an academic contract between two faculties: the community college faculty agrees to provide a quality academic foundation within the discipline for the students; the four-year faculty agrees to accept those courses as part of a major or academic program (not just as electives). This agreement is not always reached easily, and at the four-year level, questions of student preparedness, academic quality, and the existential "is it really our degree" come at you early and often.

Yet the rewards of the strategy are both obvious – in the form of more and more diverse enrollment – and subtle. By forming lasting, meaningful articulation agreements with community colleges, Lesley is able to connect with the local community, and is seen as a viable option not just for affluent, suburban adults, but for the entire community.

Price

As a private institution, Lesley's tuition is determined by the Board of Trustees with recommendations from the president and CFO. Showing the pricing data to these decision-makers was an important first step in opening a dialog about price. While it was not feasible to lower tuition, the University leadership did argue successfully for a tuition freeze at the start of the cohort, thus allowing Lesley to tell prospective students that the tuition they started with would continue to be the tuition they paid for the remainder of time they were enrolled. The percentage of yearly tuition increase for the bachelor's degree programs over a three-year period was also reduced, in part by agreeing to more aggressive enrollment goals for the program, and thus employing economies of scale in the academic operations of the programs.

Another successful strategy was "facing up" to the tuition cost with prospective students, and finding ways to communicate options and solutions to students. The financial aid office was asked to train the recruitment staff to discuss financial aid options in much more detail than they ever had. The financial aid office helped produce a flowchart and list of frequently asked questions about student loans. The recruitment team was also trained by the academic advisors to discuss the Prior Learning Assessment (also known as Life Experience Portfolio) option. The PLA could help students earn valuable credit at a fraction of the tuition cost, and thus over the life of the degree program the "price" of a Lesley degree could be significantly less than that of Lesley competitors. A handout was made specifically for this discussion as a visual aid for recruiters at information meetings and career fairs.

MIDLANDS TECHNICAL COLLEGE CASE STUDY

Christopher H. Porter
Associate Director for High School Programs
Midlands Technical College

Midlands Technical College is a comprehensive, urban, public, two-year college serving the primary region of Richland, Lexington, and Fairfield counties of South Carolina. College programs and services provide accessible, affordable, high-quality post-secondary education that prepares traditional and non-traditional students to enter the job market, allows them to transfer to senior colleges and universities, and assists them in achieving their professional and personal goals. The college serves approximately 10,000 to 15,000 credit students and 30,000 continuing education students. In recent years, the college has developed two new strategies to recruit underemployed and under-trained non-traditional students.

In 1999, Midlands Technical College formed a partnership with six other institutions to form the Midlands Educational Learning Alliance (MELA). The alliance is composed of two-year, four-year, public, private, and for-profit institutions from the Midlands area of South Carolina that visit area businesses, factories, government agencies, and community organizations and provide a college fair for the respective employees/attendees. The seven institutions represent educational opportunities ranging from certificate programs to doctorate work. MELA members (as a whole) visit sites typically during the employees' lunchtime (11:00 A.M. to 2:00 P.M.) and disperse institution materials and answer questions. The partnership of institutions will visit an average of three sites per month. The goal of the programs is to inform employees of the many educational opportunities in the Midlands area.

Members of the college's recruitment and community outreach office also sit on various business alliances organized by the Central Midlands Career Partnership. "The purpose of the Partnership is to develop and implement a well-defined secondary and postsecondary curriculum, which prepares all students for further education or for the technological workforce and is supported by a complete career guidance program." The alliances developed by the Partnership include: business, management, and information systems; engineering and industrial technologies; health sciences and human services; manufacturing technology; and public services. "The main goal of the business alliances is to promote career awareness and opportunities in their respective clusters." College recruitment representatives aid alliance business members by providing education and career information for their respective employees and their families. In addition, similar to the MELA program, college recruitment representatives will hold college fairs at business alliance locations for the benefit of underemployed and under-trained employees.

Both initiatives have been successful for the college. In addition to providing information to non-traditional students, the MELA program has yielded additional benefits. First, the members of the alliance have become unofficial recruiters for other member institutions. MELA members will refer students to other institutions if they do not offer a program of study a prospective student is looking for. Secondly, the college continues to make new contacts in the community and develop relationships with area employers. Finally, while primarily non-traditional students attend the MELA college fairs, many of these participants will collect college materials for their high school age children. The same benefits occur when attending college fairs at business alliance locations.

As with any new initiative, trial and error must take place until things run smoothly. When first organized, members of the MELA organizations would schedule fairs wherever they were requested. It took about a year to realize that some fairs would yield 800 employees, while others might yield only ten interested employees. Over the past four years the organization now knows when, where, and who to speak with when scheduling college fairs.

Conclusion

To enroll Gen Xers, sound recruitment principles must be applied along with institutional flexibility. As described in these case studies, flexibility may include pricing or aid strategies, acceptance of transfer or life experience credit, instructional delivery, and even the curriculum. Successful Gen X recruitment also requires outreach. At the five institutions represented in this chapter, outreach took many forms: communications, events, visits, centers, programs, articulation agreements, and partnerships. Furthermore, outreach was not just the responsibility of the recruitment office. A variety of administrative and academic units, faculty, staff, and alumni were involved.

Bottom line, successful recruitment of Gen Xers requires a comprehensive approach along with a campus-wide commitment. Recruitment of the Generation X population must become an institutional priority. Leadership support, a clear vision, adequate resources, well-trained staff, and a detailed action plan combine with a new way of thinking toward the delivery of an education and related services to produce a recruitment effort that competitors will fear and strive to emulate.

REFERENCES

Abrahamson, T. & Hossler, D. (1990). Applying marketing strategies in student recruitment. In D. Hossler & J. P. Bean (Eds.), *The Strategic Management of College Enrollments* (100–118). San Francisco: Jossey–Bass.

Bean, J. (1990). Why students leave: Insights from research. In D. Hossler & J. Bean (Eds.), *The Strategic Management of College Enrollments* (147–169). San Francisco: Jossey–Bass.

Black, J. (2001, November). It's the student, not the software. *The Greentree Gazette.*

———. (2002, March). Are you ignoring a growing audience? *The Greentree Gazette.*

———. (2003). Enrollment management. In G. Kramer (Ed.), *Student Academic Services: A Comprehensive Handbook for the 21st Century.* San Francisco: Jossey–Bass.

Braxton, J. (1990). How students choose colleges. In D. Hossler & J. Bean (Eds.), *The Strategic Management of College Enrollments* (57–67). San Francisco: Jossey–Bass.

Breland, H., Maxey, J., Gernand, R. Cumming, T., & Trapani, C. (2000). *Trends in college admission 2000: A report of a national survey of undergraduate admission policies, practices, and procedures.* [On-line]. Available: http://airweb.org/images/trendssummary.pdf.

Council for Adult and Experimental Learning (1999). *Serving Adult Learners in Higher Education: Findings from CAEL's Benchmarking Study.* Chicago, IL: Council for Adult and Experimental Learning.

Council for Adult and Experimental Learning (2000). *Serving Adult Learners in Higher Education: Principles of Effectiveness.* Chicago, IL: Council for Adult and Experimental Learning.

Dennis, M. (1998). *A Practical Guide to Enrollment and Retention Management in Higher Education.* Connecticut: Bergin & Garvey.

Hossler, D. (2000, Spring). The role of financial aid in enrollment management. *New Directions for Student Services.* (89): 77–90.

Litten, L., Sullivan, D., & Brodigan, D. (1983). *Applying Market Research in College Admissions.* New York: College Entrance Examination Board.

Low, L. & Bryant, P. (2001–02). *Best Practices in Recruitment and Retention.* Iowa City, Iowa: USA Group Noel-Levitz [Producer and Distributor].

Noel-Levitz (2002, April). *How to Use Pertinent Decision Data in your Admissions Office to Enroll the Students You Want.* Littleton, CO: USA Group Noel-Levitz [Producer and Distributor].

Noel-Levitz (2002, June). *Marketing and Recruitment Self-inquiry.* Littleton, CO: USA Group Noel-Levitz [Producer and Distributor].

Peppers D., Rogers M., & Dorf, B. (1999). *The One to One Fieldbook.* New York: Doubleday.

St. John, E. (2000, Spring). The impact of student aid on recruitment and retention: What the research indicates. *New Directions for Student Services.* (89): 61–75.

Sevier, R. (1998). *Integrated Marketing for Colleges, Universities, and Schools.* Washington, DC: Council for the Advancement and Support of Education.

Sevier, R. A. (2000, Fall). Building an effective recruitment funnel. *Journal of College Admission.* (169): 10–19.

Strauss, J. & Frost, R. (2001). *E-marketing*. Upper Saddle River, New Jersey: Prentice Hall.

Williams, B. (2000, Winter). To the personalized go the prospects. *Journal of College Admission*. (166): 12–21.

PART 3

Advising and Retention

Advising and Retention

CHAPTER EIGHT

Back to the Future: The Reentry Transition

Micah Martin

With Gen Xers returning to college campuses in record numbers, many colleges and universities are undergoing major changes in how they serve students to better meet the needs and high expectations of this population. The reentry transition refers to the adjustment issues students experience as they return to a higher education setting. The transition period begins with the student's expression of initial interest in returning to school and lasts well into the first semester, if not longer. It is during this transition period that the expectations for services and information on demand must be met to ensure these students feel empowered to maintain their previously existing "professional and personal responsibilities" while pursuing new academic goals (Beede and Burnett, 1999). Colleges and universities that anticipate and examine the decisions Gen Xers face upon reentry will be well equipped for the task of convincing students that their school is the best fit. This chapter will examine the reentry transition process and some of the best strategies being used by many colleges and universities around the country to better serve this population and satisfy the needs and expectations they bring to campus.

The Reentry Process: A Student-Centered Model

For Gen Xers who decide to return to the classroom, the reentry experience is often the selling point for determining whether or not to continue at a particular institution. According to a study conducted by the University of New Mexico on the Gen X preference for workplace learning, this population values education as a component of their multifaceted lifestyles. Gen Xers commonly find a sense of security in continual learning that provides opportunities for personal growth and skill-set enhancement (Bova & Kroth, 2001). With the recent developments in global technology and an ever-changing economy, the once narrow path to a college education has grown into a freeway of options creating a whole new market of fast, affordable resources for reaching educational goals. The problem for many institutions lies in maintaining a tight grip on the educational markets they have traditionally held.

Historically, colleges and universities were designed to educate and support 18- to 22-year old full-time students living on or near campus (Guvenoz, 2002). Due in part to the enrollment growth of the Generation X population, many institutions are finding the support services currently offered and traditionally-styled educational methods being used to be increasingly ineffective. With a growing number of institutions beginning to view students as customers entitled to service, efforts are being made to ensure that they are provided with the products and services they desire. In many cases this will require a complete transformation of campus culture to reflect convenience and better satisfy student needs. It will also require large-scale initiatives to provide the services and educational options aimed at traditional students to all students all the time (Burnett, 2002).

The process of redesigning student services to reflect a highly marketable, student-centered philosophy can only begin with the student as customer. In many institutions this is being done with the implementation of entrance surveys and focus groups to find out what these customers want. These opportunities provide students with a sense of personal ownership in changes occurring at their schools. Though Gen Xers are characteristically accepting of change, opportunities like these, which allow student experience and opinion to influence changes that affect their education, appeal strongly to Gen Xers who possess a sense of entitlement and value personal opinions and the right to be heard (Wilton, 1999).

When Brigham Young University began developing a Web-based freshman advising and registration system in 1999, administrators offered opportunities for students and parents to tell them what they preferred and expected during the advising and registration process to ensure that the new system was developed with customer demands in mind (Burnett, 2002).

The University of Phoenix, which has had great success in marketing its programs and services to Gen Xers, surveys students when they enroll to better understand who they are and what they expect as customers. They also conduct end-of-course surveys to find out whether or not the student customer's expectations were met with the product they received (Guvenoz, 2002).

When the University of Minnesota decided to develop a new on-line enrollment process, student input was sought to learn student preferences for completing the enrollment process. The system that resulted provides students with a personalized on-line enrollment experience with a customized view of their semester schedule, classroom location, a list of books required for each course, campus map with suggested parking locations, and bill payment options (Beede, 1999).

The use of surveys and focus groups like these help institutions develop and implement the services and programs students want. They let the institution know where the customer feels dissatisfied as well as where they are most pleased so that changes are made in appropriate areas. Student-centered reentry processes begin with shaping the educational experience around the student.

So, where should institutions begin the overhaul of traditional college campus culture? Initially, they should start with an evaluation of the services already provided, or at least advertised as provided, for all students. A common problem many colleges and universities have is fulfilling the promise of equitable service for all students. As adult students who typically work during the day and attend class at night, on the weekends, or as distance learners, Gen Xers frequently find that on many campuses most services advertised as offered to all students are designed for the convenience of traditional students who attend on-campus classes that meet during the day. Services such as faculty office hours, business and advising services, tutoring, research facilities, and campus book stores are usually available during the 8:00 A.M. to 5:00 P.M. business day because of the institution's traditional hours of operation and are rarely offered in the evening or on the weekend. This creates a considerable inconvenience for working professionals trying to continue their education because the services designed to help meet their student needs are offered only while they are at work.

Many universities are beginning to offer on-line courses and on-line degree programs designed for distance learners that advertise a completely virtual campus education that appeals strongly to Gen Xers who see this as a convenient way to continue their education. The reality is that in many cases these programs still require students to physically come to campus to complete vital business transactions, meet with faculty members or advisors, complete research assignments, and receive enrichment or tutoring services (Volchok, 2003). Institutions need to understand the needs of all student populations whether traditional, nontraditional, on-campus students or distance learners and provide equitable and appropriate services to satisfy the needs of each (Kerr, 2003).

So, what services are most desired and expected by Gen Xers in this reentry transition? According to students surveyed by IBM's Education Consulting Team as part of its Best Practices Study, college students prefer direct access to their own information and the means to conduct institutionally required transactions themselves in an automated fashion with options for personal assistance available, if desired (Beede, 1999). These preferences compare closely with the Gen X appreciation for convenience and an entitlement to direct access to personalized information and customized service (O'Bannon, 2001).

When Seton Hall University began offering students an option for personalized customer service by phone, the demand for this convenient means of access became so great that a fully staffed call center had to be created within their student services center to handle the response. Once Web-based service options were introduced at Seton Hall, administrators soon found out, as many other institutions have since, that today's college students prefer getting information and completing transactions independently on-line as opposed to waiting in line to have someone else do it for them (Green, Jefferis & Kleinman, 2002).

Since examples like this from Seton Hall and IBM's Best Practices Study suggest answers to what students want, institutions attempting to meet these demands should evaluate all the services they provide from the student's external perspective instead of the traditional internal institutional perspective to ensure that any redesign of services appeals strongly to the expectations of the student customer (Burnett, 2002). Besides meeting student customer expectations, institutions should also take responsibility for providing services designed to meet students' needs as life-long learners to ensure their academic and career success and enhance their long-term relationships with the institution.

At most institutions there are similar entry requirements that all students must complete prior to attending. These usually include selection of appropriate learning environment, academic advising, course registration, financial aid assessment, fee payment, and purchasing books. These are the most basic student needs that should be met prior to reentering the classroom setting. Many adult students including Gen Xers need and desire additional specialized services such as separate orientation and registration sessions, optional parking services, child care, options for personalized assistance with required transactions, opportunities for social and professional networking, and access to personalized academic and career counseling (Steele & McDonald, 2000). Institutions should make sure new students are properly informed of these entry requirements and additional services as early as possible and develop ways to make sure students are completing them in a timely fashion to ensure their transition is a smooth one. Besides these basic services, many students will need and expect additional services to ensure that returning to school will be a convenient, satisfying experience.

Intuitive Steps to Enrolling

The reentry process is comprised of several required steps toward reenrollment that are similar at most institutions. Each of these steps must be designed from the students' perspective and with their convenience in mind. Students should find quick access to a list of steps for enrollment along with details describing what each of these steps require of them.

At The University of North Carolina at Greensboro, prospective students find a link from the UNCG home page to the admissions page that provides information links categorized by student populations. These categories include: high school students, adult & transfers students, returning students (former UNCG students), explorations (for non-degree seeking undergraduates), graduate students, international students, continual learning students (adult non-degree seeking students), and evening university students (evening degree programs). These categories are designed to capture the attention of each population and direct them to information specific to their needs at admission. At the top of this page is a prominently displayed link that reads "Consult our Steps to Enrolling site." This link directs students to a complete list of essential steps and prerequisites required for enrollment at UNCG. The list is arranged chronologically into four stages labeled: "Before You Apply," "Once You Apply," "After Admission" and "From Orientation to Classes." The "Before You Apply" section lists steps such as applying for admission and financial aid on-line, along with information options such as cost of attendance and course and degree information that conveniently provides answers to the questions most Gen Xers have at this stage of reentry. The next stage contains links that allow students to check their admission and financial aid application status on-line along with links to an on-line scholarship search engine and a direct link to a third party payment plan Web site. The third section, "After Admission," contains steps for confirming intent to enroll, information and applications for housing options, immunization requirements and deadlines, and additional information exclusively for admitted students. The fourth stage, "From Orientation to Classes," allows students to complete the enrollment process by applying and/or registering for both required and optional services over the Web at their convenience. This stage includes everything from orientation schedules and registering for classes to parking services, purchasing books, and final bill payment.

A comprehensive chronological list such as this works well for all student populations completing steps to admission, but should appeal strongly to Gen Xers who want to know exactly what they need to do to enroll as well as have the ability to complete these steps independently on a time frame that does not complicate their already busy lifestyles (Steele & McDonald, 2002).

One-Stop Shopping

Because of opportunities for customer feedback like those discussed previously, many institutions are becoming aware of the inconvenience these limitations on services create for the rather large population of Gen Xers they target. To remedy this problem, a number of institutions nationwide are implementing a service strategy that attempts to bundle services into a "one-stop shop" model designed to meet a variety of common student needs in one location in a single visit.

Many institutions have redesigned their physical student services processes based on this one-stop customer service model to give students a single location on campus to get information and answers to questions as well as complete required transactions, shifting the traditional design structure from the needs of the institution to the needs of the student. These customer services centers have made life more convenient for students on campus keeping them from having to go from building to building to take care of business and academic needs (Burnett & Pantel, 1999). These centers have significantly reduced student runaround and the need to make appointments with various offices to get things done. These one-stop service centers require employees trained to handle cross-functional tasks and provide general information on a variety of topics to ensure convenience is maintained.

The University of Delaware was one the first institutions to implement a physical one-stop model. Their initial design was based on a customer service model used in branch banking with cross-functional generalists handling the majority of student needs from a service counter, with area specialists available to handle more specific problems case by case in adjoining offices (Beede, 1999).

In 1996, Seton Hall University began to redesign its enrollment management services to fit a one-stop service model by merging the offices of admissions, registrar, financial aid, and bursar into one unit. This merger was followed by the creation of a one-stop student service center located in a prominent central location on campus to provide students the means for completing all enrollment service transactions at one time in one convenient location. As the demand for convenience grew the demand for in-person customer service began to decline at Seton Hall. University administrators soon realized that their innovative one-stop service center would have to be transformed into a more versatile service response center able to handle student customers over the phone and through the Web, as well as face-to-face on campus (Green, Jefferis, & Kleinman, 2002).

A few institutions with already developed student service centers also began to provide information telephone hot lines and/or e-mail services to allow students to obtain information and answers to questions without coming to an on-campus service counter. These types of services appeal to Gen Xers because they, like many other students, prefer a variety of options for getting needed information (Burnett, 2002). These high tech services allow students who prefer personalized attention to get just that without coming to campus. Many service centers like the one described at the University of Delaware also installed self-service computer stations to allow students an in-house self-service option using the Web, with generalists available for personal assistance if needed.

Transferring Credit

Many Gen Xers have already earned a two- or four-year degree while others have had at least some college education, which raises questions about how credits can be applied to their current educational goals. The speed and accuracy with which institutions respond to a student's request for a transfer evaluation directly affects enrollment decisions. Institutions responding promptly lower the anxiety level of prospective students and conversely, increase their commitment level to the institution. As stated in chapter seven, Gen X transfer enrollment decisions are also based on the flexibility with which the institution awards credit for hours earned and life experiences.

In an effort to answer questions about how previous course work from other institutions transfers into programs currently offered, and simultaneously lure former students entertaining the idea of reentry to their institution, Ball State University in Muncie, Indiana, developed an Automated Course Transfer System (ACTS) that allows students to access this information via the Web. Though their original vision for the development of such a program was for a more effective recruitment of undergraduate transfer students, the service is ideal for Gen Xers who have questions about using previously earned college credit to meet their current educational goals. Accessing this service through Ball State's home page, students can generate a report displaying exactly which courses transferred and the course equivalencies at that institution. Using the same program, a report can be generated that applies these transferable courses to the degree program of their choice to help give students a sense of how long it may take to reach their goals, and what a particular major or program will involve. This degree audit service also displays courses from the student's former institution, and the equivalencies provide students the option of enrolling in courses elsewhere that meet program requirements at Ball State, if necessary. Once all course work is entered, reports are generated in less than 30 seconds (McCauley, 1999). Currently, Ball State's ACTS database contains over 1,400 institutions with equivalencies for more than 30,000 courses. The site also offers e-mail support for students whose former institutions are not listed in the ACTS database. Since many Gen Xers return to school planning to take only a few classes before transferring elsewhere, services like ACTS combine practical resources with convenience to provide students with the comprehensive information they need to make informed decisions in a timely manner about when, where, and how to pursue their educational goals.

Financial Aid

Traditionally, federal student aid has been the primary source for most student financial aid. With over 70% of all student aid currently coming from federal aid programs, government-mandated methods for administering student aid have strongly influenced how most institutions manage and administer their financial aid packaging processes. These processes have traditionally required students to complete a number of paperbound transactions requiring frequent visits to the financial aid office, long lines and waiting periods to find out if they were eligible for financial aid (Phelps, 2003). Recently, federal requirements for financial aid have been altered to allow students to research and complete most application transactions for federal aid through a completely Web-based environment provided by the U.S. Department of Education. This service enables students to complete and submit the FAFSA, check loan balances, and communicate directly with loan aid officers to get answers and assistance throughout the application process. This site covers complete up-to-date information on all federal aid programs including Pell Grants, Stafford Loans, and PLUS loans (U.S. Department of Education, 2003). For students looking for other financial aid options or payment methods, a number of on-line resources are now available to help students locate and research the options that best meet their needs. The Electronic Signatures Act, passed in 2001, allows students, institutions, and aid providers to use electronic forms, records, and signatures in place of paper, dramatically decreasing the period of time students must wait for the results of their aid applications.

Though the technology and resources are available, few institutions have implemented completely automated financial aid services (Phelps, 2003). Brigham Young University has a highly developed on-line student aid service providing students with direct access to all required financial aid application forms as well as the ability to submit them for approval on-line. BYU requires all students applying for aid, traditional and nontraditional, to use their on-line student services process, called the Financial Path to Graduation, for completing all necessary transactions. Within this process, students must complete a financial aid educational session in which they are informed of the financial responsibility they are accepting by taking out a student loan or accepting a grant or scholarship.

Florida State University offers similar financial aid services including a guide to completing the FAFSA, with direct links to the FAFSA on-line and instructions for submitting on-line signatures.

The University of Southern California offers students a variety of on-line financial aid services that allow students to download all necessary application forms, monitor their application status through a dated checklist of required documents received, and view their current award status for the two most recent award periods over the Web. To access these services, undergraduates must complete the College Board's College Scholarship Service Profile application. Though all necessary forms are available for download directly from the USC Web site, students are required to fax or mail them to the campus financial aid office to complete the process (Phelps, 2003).

The University of Texas at Austin provides its students with a number of unique on-line financial aid services including an electronic aid notification service for accepted students who have applied for aid through their Web site. This service notifies students by e-mail of any awards they have been offered along with the option of accepting, reducing, or declining an award over the Web. The site also provides information on lenders, allowing students to compare options and select lenders directly from the site. UT also allows both students and parents to complete and sign required promissory notes on-line using a secure electronic signature service to expedite the loan process.

Services like these save time for both students and staff who traditionally have spent most of their time processing paper forms and completing transactions now available on-line. Changes in eligibility standards and the implementation of Web-based financial aid services has produced a fast and convenient way for Gen Xers to research and apply for financial aid and, therefore, make better decisions about which options for reentry best suit their current lifestyles.

Orientation

Once students have completed the admission and financial aid processes, the process of re-acclimatization to the educational environment really begins, as students have to be reequipped to succeed in the classroom. Traditionally, most institutions take an active role in this reequipping process by requiring students to attend orientation sessions that provide supervised completion of required steps toward reenrollment such as academic advising, placement tests, course registration, introductions to campus culture and routine processes, academic success workshops, student community building exercises, and parent/family information sessions (Volchok, 2003).

Orientation programs with these core components equip traditional college students and regular on-campus learners, but for many Gen Xers looking for a more convenient way to reach their educational goals, traditional college orientation programs may not be the most effective means. Since many Gen Xers are often working professionals who value what little time they have outside of work and/or personal responsibilities, they may find orientation programs in general to be inconvenient and an inefficient use of their time. For Gen Xers planning to enroll in on-line degree programs or distance learning courses, coming to campus to participate in a traditionally-styled orientation program makes little sense, when much of it will inevitably cover processes and information unrelated to their reentry and chosen learning environment (Volchok, 2003). If students perceive these programs to be of no benefit, they will not be an effective means for equipping them at entry or reentry (Daddona & Cooper, 2002). Many institutions are then faced with the question of how to best serve both traditional and nontraditional students during the entry/reentry stage while adhering to budgets designed to meet the needs of traditional populations. Just as with the admission and financial aid processes discussed above, using available Web technology is the best way to transform the traditional on-campus, in-person orientation session into a convenient virtual experience that can be completed anytime and anywhere by admitted students.

An on-line orientation program affords students who find it inconvenient to come to campus the same exposure to the information they need to prepare for reentry that traditional students receive. Virtual orientation gives institutions the ability to selectively release specific information to students based on their degree programs and chosen learning environment. Time-sensitive information, such as application and registration deadlines that may differ by population or program, can be sent to a specific student profile to ensure that students receive information pertinent only to them (Volchok, 2003). Virtual orientation should include all the information and opportunities students receive in traditional on-campus orientation including virtual campus tours, program information, placement tests that can be completed and submitted on-line, academic and career advising, course registration, additional opportunities to apply for financial aid, and information on additional services open to all students such as parking, tutoring, housing, and meal plans (Daddona & Cooper, 2002). Students using virtual orientation should be able to complete the same required transactions as students participating in traditional on-campus orientation, such as paying fees and purchasing books and parking permits, if needed. Traditionally, orientation for distance learners provided information about taking classes at a distance without really orienting students to the institution. While distance and on-line learners do often need specific initial instruction on the nature of their courses and the technology that will be used to deliver and complete assignments, many of these students would benefit from many of the social and cultural aspects of traditional orientation to help them feel a part of a wider community of students (Krauth, 2001). With many Gen Xers returning as distance learners, virtual orientation provides them with a convenient means for preparing to return without requiring them to come to campus.

Since orientation is the final stage of reentry for students and one of the initial points at which most retention efforts begin by the institution, customer satisfaction is extremely important (Volchok, 2003). Though many Gen Xers value an environment where they feel independent and empowered to complete the necessary steps for reentry on their own, their preference for interactions with students like themselves as well as social and professional networking opportunities can be satisfied by providing opportunities for nontraditional students to participate in virtual learning communities and student organizations. These opportunities benefit students and institutions alike because cultural connections to campus life and social networks increase retention among distance learners much like on-campus learning communities do with traditional students (Scagnoli, 2001).

The University of Central Florida has a comprehensive virtual orientation service designed to meet the needs of all new, transfer, and distance students. Students lead themselves through a series of informational pages that are followed by a quiz that requires them to earn a perfect score before allowing them to proceed to the next section. The service also requires students to complete the entire on-line orientation program before allowing them to register for classes.

Similarly, the University of Dayton's virtual orientation program is designed to serve all entering students by not only giving them an introduction to the institution but also by allowing them to complete steps to enrollment on-line such as taking math and language placement tests, reviewing degree and major requirements, as well as planning their schedules. Students can chat with an advisor over the Web if they have questions while completing orientation. They also offer a new student chat room feature that allows students to communicate with other students before taking classes.

The University of Utah has an elaborate orientation program with a variety of options to better suit the desires and expectations of all their students, including an on-line program designed for students who find it inconvenient to come to campus. This program is divided into nine components including campus resources, major requirements, schedule planning, and registration. Students can complete each component at different times or all at once. Utah's orientation home page also has a section to help students choose the orientation that would best meet their specific needs.

Portland Community College offers a somewhat unique on-line orientation program exclusively for students taking on-line courses through their institution. This service provides students with information about taking on-line courses, computer hardware and software requirements, required basic skills, and course platform information. The site also includes a variety of tutorials and quizzes to ensure that students understand the information they receive while completing various stages of the program.

Academic Advising

At most institutions a key component of the orientation process for all students is academic advising and course registration. Many colleges and universities nationwide are using some form of on-line registration but few have an on-line advising service that provides students with the same information and attention that students meeting personally with advisors receive. Academic advisors concerned with the needs of an ever-growing population of nontraditional students consisting largely of Gen Xers are challenged by a need to better serve these students who often feel that advising is either too inconvenient or unnecessary (Kerr, 2003).

Many institutions are now beginning to develop ways to use Web technology to provide virtual advising services designed specifically with nontraditional students and distance learners in mind. The challenge is then twofold with a need to take a traditionally high touch service and provide it in a high tech manner that students can be persuaded is convenient to use and worth their time (Wagner, 2001). Institutions developing and implementing Web sites to provide a more convenient means of advising nontraditional students and distance learners should make sure these high tech services provide both a "high touch" feel and quality equitable service to ensure customer satisfaction is maintained. Academic advising Web services should include a clear explanation of the core curriculum and specific program requirements. Since many students will be accessing and interpreting this information on their own, it should be concise and easy to understand with all key terms clearly defined (NACADA, 2001). Students must be able to understand what they need to do to reach the educational goals they have set. Since advising Web sites could potentially be used to meet the advising needs of all students by providing general academic information appropriate for all students at a given institution, links to information exclusively for populations such as nontraditional students and distance learners, or students pursuing specific majors, should be provided to ensure that students follow requirements and receive information that may be unique to their programs. Commuters, transfer students, freshmen, and students on probation are population samples with specific advising needs that could be met by providing this type of expanded on-line service (Wagner, 2001). To better serve students who expect information on demand and to produce less work for academic advisors, advising Web sites should include a list of frequently asked questions. Including FAQs on such sites benefits both students and staff and produces a quality advising service that students will use as a resource in future semesters (NACADA, 2001). These sites should also include links to other university services relative to academics to ensure that information used in a holistic advising approach available to students in face-to-face advising sessions is provided to students who cannot get to campus. These links should include information on tutoring, choosing a career or major, academic-standing policies, test taking and study skills, student organizations, personal health resources, and stress management (Wagoner, 2001).

One of the most important services advising Web sites should provide is direct access to academic advisors on-line. Several national institutions are beginning to implement such services using the same technology used to create Internet chat rooms allowing students to communicate with advisors via the Web in a "real-time" conversation. Such on-line advising services providing assistance on demand adds a sense of "high touch" to an otherwise high tech impersonal experience and should do well to satisfy the Gen X expectation for instant access to personal attention and information.

The University of Delaware offers a comprehensive on-line advisement program designed to cater to the needs of specific groups of nontraditional students. This site, called the ACCESS Advisement Center, offers advising information and options for all students with specific links for distance learners and personal assistance available on-line or by phone to help students with career counseling, schedule planning, course registration, and payment assistance. In promotion of the holistic advising philosophy, the site also has links to information on student success strategies and academic skills workshops.

The University of Arizona has an elaborate on-line advising center that provides students with up-to-date academic information, links to important dates and deadlines, on-line schedule planning, registration and fee payment, explanations of degree requirements, transcript evaluations, career services, and direct on-line access to academic advisors and faculty. UA's advising Web site also has specific links for special student populations and the university learning center, which provides tutoring and academic skills workshops. The University of Arizona also provides the Faculty Fellows Program, which is designed to build relationships and learning communities between students and faculty. Since many Gen Xers value relationships with faculty and peers, this type of service often goes beyond their academic needs to better satisfy their expectations.

Career Counseling

During reentry, many Gen Xers may feel the need for career counseling since many are either early in their careers or find themselves in a transition phase which has lead them back to school. Many of these students may return to school with one career/educational plan in mind, only to question or change it midstream. Institutions that recognize these questioning points as opportunities to gain and retain students, will adapt career services to meet the unique needs Gen Xers present. For many years, many colleges and universities have had career services centers that require students to make appointments with career counselors, which lead not only to an initial appointment where students receive face-to-face personal assistance, but often several subsequent visits to take various career-interest inventories and skills assessments. Upon completion of such instruments, the student and counselor discuss the results.

Since the 1970s, many institutions have also offered a variety of computerized career planning and job search tools. Though these services utilized the technology available when they were first implemented, they still required office visits designed for the convenience of traditional on-campus students (Ford, 2003). With the rise in distance education during the mid-1990s, many institutions have transformed their career counseling services by using Internet technology to provide up-to-date career exploration and job search tools available on-line to all students 24 hours a day. For Gen Xers, on-line career services should provide skills and interests assessments that can be taken over the Web, as well as those that can be evaluated and interpreted on-line to maintain the level of convenience expected. These sites should provide up-to-date information on majors and programs that prepare students for specific careers, as well as links to credible on-line job search and resumé posting Web sites and state employment agencies to ensure that students have the necessary tools to pursue the careers they desire (WCET, 2003).

On the practical side, many Gen Xers returning to school to change careers or look for new jobs may need to enhance their resumé-writing and interviewing skills to better prepare themselves for the job market. For these students, it is crucial for institutions to provide on-line tools they can use to build these skills at a comfortable pace and at convenient times. As with all on-line services offered by an institution, Gen Xers expect fast, convenient, personal assistance. Using the same technology many institutions are now using to enhance on-line academic advising centers, career services Web sites should provide students with direct access to a career services counselor through on-line chat, e-mail, and telephone services to ensure customer satisfaction is maintained throughout the experience (Ford, 2003). On-line services can always be used in conjunction with on-campus career fairs, counseling appointments, or classes.

For most institutions, providing these services on-line is cost effective because they no longer need to purchase hard copies of career resource data and job search tools that become outdated in weeks. These services should reduce career center traffic, allowing career counselors more time to provide career service options to a larger population of students who may have otherwise felt cut off from such a valuable resource (Ford, 2003).

The University of North Carolina at Wilmington offers a variety of career services on-line including assessments, workshops, links to job listing search engines, and information on specific careers and majors. UNCW also provides a service called E–LEADS, Employment Leads for Liberal Arts Students, that lists potential job opportunities and career information from organizations that typically hire liberal arts students. This service is unique in that it offers career leads listed in a specialized employment directory developed by eleven colleges and universities in North Carolina and available exclusively to students at those institutions.

The University of California at Berkeley's on-line career center provides students and alumni with an array of services including job search options, career exploration tools, employer spotlights, and links for specific careers of interest such as law and health-related fields. They also provide e-mail and phone contact options to allow students to communicate with their career center over the Internet.

North Carolina's Central Piedmont Community College has an extensive on-line career center providing not only career exploration options and Web-based assessment tools, but also a variety of practical career services such as a career portfolio service for curriculum students, resumé referral, mock interview service, and a comprehensive on-line career resource reference library. CPCC also provides career transition services designed to assist continuing education students with career development. Besides individualized career counseling, this service offers a small group career program that allows these students in transition to build relationships with other students like themselves to help each other in the career exploration process. This program is not only a great fit for many Gen Xers because of its academic ties, but also because it promotes relationships and networking skills that these student value.

Conclusion

For Gen Xers, convenience is essential during the reentry transition. As customers and as students, Gen Xers expect institutions to provide instant and personal information and assistance during transition from admissions and orientation to advising and career counseling. Institutions that view Gen Xers as a vital customer base will strive to learn exactly what services and features these students want and make the changes necessary to provide them.

Internet technology is and will continue to be the focus in developing more convenient and cost-efficient student services. For any institution serving adult students such as Gen Xers, there will inevitably be students who prefer, for a variety of reasons, the traditional "high touch" service process over a virtual experience. Students may not feel comfortable and familiar with the use of Web technology. Providing services at convenient times for Gen Xers who want an on-campus transition experience may be necessary. Minor provisions in accommodating services such as evening hours, reserved parking, child care, and refreshments may seem insignificant to the institution because they are often inexpensive to provide, but go a long way toward making the reentry process more convenient and enjoyable for these students.

REFERENCES

Beede, M. (1999) Student services trends and best practices. In M. Beede & D. Burnett (Eds.), *Planning for student services: Best practices for the 21ᵃ Century.* (5–11). Ann Arbor, MI: Society for College and University Planning.

Bova, B. & Kroth, M. Workplace learning and Generation X. *Journal of Workplace Learning.* 13(2): 57–65.

Burnett, D. (2002). Innovation in student services: Best practices and process innovation models and trends. In D. Burnett & D. Oblinger (Eds.), *Best practices in student services.* (3–14). Washington, DC: Society for College and University Planning.

Daddona, M. & Cooper, D. (2002). Comparison of freshmen perceived needs prior to and after participation in an orientation program. *NASAPA Journal.* 39(4): 300–318.

Ford. D. (n.d.). Career Planning. [On-line]. Available: http://www.wcet.info/projects/laap/resources/career_planning.asp

Green, T., Jefferis, N. & Kleinman, R. (2002). Change beyond change: The next iteration of enrollment services. In D. Burnett & D. Oblinger (Eds.), *Innovations in student services: Planning for models blending high touch/high tech.* (105–118). Ann Arbor, MI: Society for College and University Planning

Guvenoz, A. (2002). Removing the barriers to education: Creating a services model for the working adult. In D. Burnett & D. Oblinger (Eds.), *Best practices in student services.* (23–32). Washington, DC: Society for College and University Planning.

Kerr, T. (n.d.). Academic Advising. [On-line]. Available http://www.wcet.info/projects/laap/resources/ac_ad.asp

Krauth, B. (1999). Trends in support services for distance learners. In M. Beede & D. Burnett (Eds.), *Planning for student services: Best practices for the 21ᵃ Century.* (13–17). Ann Arbor, MI: Society for College and University Planning.

McCauley, M. (1999). Enhancing transfer student services through the web. In M. Beede & D. Burnette (Eds.), *Planning for student services: Best practices for the 21ᵃ Century.* (107–112). Ann Arbor, MI: Society for College and University Planning.

O'Bannon, G. (2001). Managing our future: The generation X factor. *Public Personnel Management.* 30(1): 95–109.

Phelps, M. (n.d.). Student Financial Assistance. [On-line]. Available http://www.wcet.info/projects/laap/resources/fin_aid.asp

Scagnoli, N. (2001). Student orientations for online programs. *Journal of Research on Technology in Education*. 34 (1): 19–27.

Steele, G. & McDonald, M. (2000). Advising students in transition. In V. Gordon & W. Habley (Eds.), *Academic Advising: A Comprehensive Handbook*. (144–161). San Francisco: Jossey–Bass.

Volchok, D. (n.d.). Orientation. [On-line]. Available http://www.wcet.info/projects/laap/resources/orientation.asp

Wagner, L. (2001). Virtual advising: Delivering student services. Online Journal of Distance Learning Administration. 4(3). [On-line]. Available http://www.westga.edu/~distnace/ojdla/fall43/wagner43.html

WCET Guide to Developing Online Student Services (n.d.). [On-line]. Available http://www.wcet.info/resources/publications/guide/guide.htm

Wilton, S. (1999). Class struggles: Teaching history in the post modern age. *The History Teacher*. 33(1): 25–32.

CHAPTER NINE
Advising

Scott Amundsen

Generation Xers are viewed as the children of inflation, political disenchantment, and workplace instability. Most are returning to college after a false start or long hiatus. They are dealing with a great deal of anxiety, and planning to take classes while juggling multiple responsibilities. As explained throughout this book, Gen Xers demand that their needs are met quickly and efficiently; and if they are not, they will leave (Mulligan, 2000).

They need the assistance of competent academic advisors and career counseling professionals. These advisors must meet the immediate needs of the Gen Xers, while assisting the student in personal development and critical thinking.

Academic Advising Models

Colleges and universities use several models of academic advising. The most common models utilize faculty and professional staff advisors. These models can be delivered through one-on-one advising, group advising, or virtual advising.

In the faculty or professional staff models, students are assigned a faculty or staff member well versed in their discipline. These advisors are experts in their fields and are most able to answer discipline-based questions and have a universal understanding of course content and curriculum rationale. It is essential that the faculty or staff advisor develop a rapport with the student both inside and outside of the classroom. These mentoring relationships are very important to student satisfaction and persistence (Gordon & Habley, 2000). When talking with Gen Xers, advisors should allow students to tell their story. Gen Xers are returning to school for reasons that are uniquely their own and often are of a personal nature. The advisor must listen actively and be aware of body language and other non-verbal cues. When asking students questions, paraphrase their thoughts to ensure mutual understanding (Gordon & Habley, 2000). Gen Xers want feedback and advice from the academic authorities. Authority is granted by Gen Xers to those who earn it by character and relationships, not by title alone (Codrington, 1998).

It is important that all Gen Xers have an opportunity to engage in one-on-one discussion with an academic advisor. As latchkey kids and children of divorce, Gen Xers crave one-on-one relationships. Since Gen Xers have often been deprived of intimacy, they place a stronger value on it than other generations. Developing a personal and meaningful relationship with an academic advisor is vital (Codrington, 1998).

Group advising is often used when the number of students far exceeds the number of available advisors. Group advising is particularly prevalent during college orientation programs when the number of advisees outstrips the limited supply of advisors during the winter break and summer months. The advantage of group advising is the relationship building with peers. When advised in groups, Gen Xers will be relieved to learn that other students have similar concerns and transition issues. Group acceptance and validation is very important to the Gen Xer. Gen Xers frequently work well in small groups and this advising format can offer a student a sense of belonging and family that is devoid in one-on-one advising.

The disadvantage to group advising is the lack of personal attention. Each Gen Xer has unique challenges in returning to college and successfully completing a degree program. Group advising can alienate students and discourage questions. As stated above, relationship building and individual attention are crucial for the Gen Xer returning to college.

Most Gen Xers are very comfortable with technology. Many are working full- or part-time and have difficulty getting to campus during general office hours. Research has shown that Gen Xers prefer to access general information on-line rather than meeting for a one-on-one appointment (Behrens and Altman, 1998).

Current best practices in virtual advising primarily utilize the World Wide Web. According to the WICHE and NACADA guidelines for virtual advising, an advising Web page should at a minimum provide:

- a description of general education and major requirements
- a Frequently Asked Questions page
- information for special populations (e.g., career information, study skills, academic good standing policies, and learning disability support)
- links to campus activity and event calendars
- direct access to an academic advisor through e-mail or virtual chat

(Wagner, 2001).

Although virtual advising is a great tool for the Gen Xer, it should not be viewed as a replacement for one-on-one or group advising. It provides instant gratification and should be viewed as a vehicle of convenience. The Gen Xers can get quick informational answers, but often will require a follow-up advising visit.

Developmental Advising

For academic advisors to be effective working with Generation Xers returning to college, they must use a developmental advising approach. Students and advisors should share responsibility for the advising relationship. Developmental advising should be a rational process. It employs environmental and interpersonal interactions, behavioral awareness, problem solving, decision-making, and evaluation skills. It is not the advisor's job to dictate to the learner how or what they should learn (Gordon & Habley, 2000).

The advisor must resist solving problems for the Gen Xer, even if the answers seem obvious. The process must be collaborative. Once the Gen Xers have stated their concerns, the role of the advisor is to provide direction, and ask the students questions that require them to develop their own answers. The Generation Xer will be less likely to succeed if a prescriptive method of advising is used. Gen X students will be much more successful if they feel invested in the development of an individualized learning plan (Crookston, 1973).

Prescriptive	vs. Developmental
Advisor has primary responsibility	Responsibility is shared between advisor and student
Focus is on limitations	Focus is on potentialities
Effort is problem oriented	Effort is growth oriented
Relationship is based on authority giving advice	Relationship is based on equal and shared problem solving
Evaluation is done by an advisor	Evaluation is a shared process

(Gordon & Habley, 2000).

Practical Strategies

In order to maximize advising effectiveness for the Gen Xer, Backes (1997) provides these proven approaches in adult learning:

- Establish a comfortable environment. Gen Xers need to feel wanted and appreciated. Greet them enthusiastically when they arrive for their advising appointment. Gen Xers are looking for a safe place, where they will be listened to and respected (Codrington, 1998).

- Identify commonalities and respect diversity. Make a personal connection with the student. Ask questions and demonstrate a genuine interest in their life experiences. Gen Xers need to feel respected and accepted. The advisor needs to meet the needs of Gen Xers at all developmental levels. All of these students have some positive life and work experiences. It is the job of the advisor to draw on these experiences and help the Gen Xer remain positive and confident.

- Use examples and anecdotes. Examples and anecdotes will help the adult learner retain information. The Gen Xer needs to be entertained, and stories are much more engaging and memorable than facts and figures.

- Establish flexible office hours and/or meeting times as noted in chapter eight. Many Gen Xers will be balancing work and family responsibilities when returning to school. It may be inconvenient for them to meet with an academic advisor during the hours of 8–5. Consider electronic forms of communication and flexible office hours. Advisors must be willing to meet students at times that fit their busy schedules. Night and weekend hours should be considered.

■ Do not treat Gen Xers like children. Operating as active independent, self-directed individuals, Gen Xers have a need to be involved in planning and directing their learning activities, and they want to accomplish things for themselves.

Accelerating the Degree Completion Process

Gen Xers are living in a fast-paced environment. Tom Cruise, in the Generation X classic *Top Gun*, summed up this generation's fast moving ideology when he said, "I feel the need, the need for speed" (Codrington, 1998).

The advisor should expect the Gen Xer to be efficiency-minded. Many will ask, "What is the cheapest, fastest, and easiest method for me to complete a degree?" (Zemke & Zemke, 2002).

Degree Requirements

Advisors need to provide the Gen Xer with a clear explanation of degree requirements. This should be in the form of a paper or electronic degree evaluation. Gen Xers should be encouraged to use this evaluation as a checklist. A realistic completion date should be set so that graduation is viewed as a concrete goal. The reality of graduation must be constantly reinforced.

Transfer Articulation

The advisor should be able to explain the transfer credit evaluation process. Whenever possible, the Gen Xer should be given credit for prior course work. Official copies of transcripts and course descriptions are typically required in the credit evaluation process. This process is time intensive and can be overwhelming to the Gen Xer. The advisor must point out the importance of this process. The student should set a realistic completion date for obtaining the documents, and arrange a follow-up appointment with the advisor. Gen Xers typically do not perform well in courses that are perceived as unnecessary. The transfer credit evaluation process is complex and labor intensive, but the student must understand the potential payoffs.

The advisor should provide the Gen Xer with information relating to opportunities that could accelerate the degree process. Credit-earning opportunities via challenge exams, independent study, distance education, and credit for life experience options should all be explored.

Alternative Credit	Examples and Web Links
Credit by Examination	**CLEP – College Level Examination Program** ACT PEP – Regents College Examinations DANTES – Defense Activity for Nontraditional Education Support
Challenge Exams	Many colleges and universities offer challenge exams for credit. If a student already has the knowledge or experience taught in an academic course he/she can "challenge" the course and earn college credit
Independent Study (Correspondence)	The institutions listed below offer a wide variety of independent study (correspondence) courses: The University of North Carolina – Friday Center http://www.fridaycenter.unc.edu/iscatalog/ Brigham Young University http://elearn.byu.edu Louisiana State University www.is.lsu.edu
Distance Education	Electronic campus – This site is a "one-stop" point of entry for distance learning opportunities http://www.electroniccampus.org/
Credit for Life Experience	Credit for life expertise enables colleges and universities to evaluate life experiences as being potentially equivalent to courses taught at the college level. In most cases, students must present a portfolio demonstrating their experiences and competency http://www.acenet.edu/calec/

Each institution handles the above opportunities differently, but all options should be explored. Adult degree programs must be flexible. Advisors should communicate problems with staff on campus who can remove barriers and facilitate change.

Developing a Learning Contract

Many Gen Xers are not where they want to be professionally or personally and are returning to school to develop new competencies. They are looking for practical approaches to academic success. It is the advisor's job to help clarify the steps in the learning process.

Adults, by nature, prefer self-directed learning (Knowles, 1995). It is the advisor's role to provide the Gen Xers with the necessary tools, support, and feedback to carry out self-directed learning.

The learning contract is a proven tool for adult learners. The advisor can facilitate the planning process, but students are setting the expectations and developing a contract for themselves. This approach allows Gen Xers to take a goal-oriented approach to their academic progress. By frequently completing short-term goals, the Gen Xer will move steadily toward the completion of a degree. The learning contract positions the Gen Xer for success.

Steps for Developing a Learning Contract

Step 1: Specify a learning objective. State the objective in a way that it is clear and meaningful.

Step 2: Specify learning resources and strategies. How will the student accomplish each objective? What resources will be needed?

Step 3: Specify a completion date. Choose a realistic deadline.

Step 4: Specify evidence of accomplishment.

Step 5: Specify how the evidence will be evaluated. By what criteria will the evidence be judged?

(Knowles, Holton, & Swanson, 1998).

Sample Learning Contract for the Gen Xer

Learning Objective	Learning Resources and Strategies	Complete Examples	Evidence of Accomplishments and Objectives	Criteria and Means for Validating Evidence
Increase my reading comprehension in elementary Spanish	**1.** Read and translate the Spanish newspaper for two hours each evening **2.** Spend three hours each week with Spanish tutors. **3.** Write a letter to a friend in Spanish each week	Four weeks	Weekly class meetings and feedback regarding homework assignments	**1.** Test grades will rise **2.** Translation speed will increase **3.** Feedback from instructor in the form of a mid-term grade

Career Counseling for the Gen Xer

Most Gen Xers returning to college have reevaluated their career paths and are well aware of the need to increase their education level and/or skills competencies. They have been working long hours and understand that many of the new jobs available in today's economy are temporary employment with no benefits and little security. Gen Xers are looking for steady employment and a chance for promotion (Montana & Lenaghan, 1999).

Career Advising Theory

The Self-Directed Search and the Strong Interest Inventory are a good place for Gen Xers to begin their career counseling. These assessments help guide students to a good career fit. The three-letter code gleaned from these inventories gives students a good starting point in career exploration (Gordon & Habley, 2000). Students should be encouraged to use the information gained in self-assessment to research different careers and evaluate their options. They should begin to narrow down their options, eliminate, and select occupations for further consideration. Whenever possible, Gen Xers should attempt to gain hands-on experience in their chosen field, perhaps by completing an internship or practicum. Some Gen Xers are having difficulty securing an internship or practicum due to lack of availability. Many cannot afford to take a summer off from their regular jobs to participate in internships. (Collins, 1996).

It is particularly important for Gen Xers to seek career advice in developing effective resumés, calling on potential employers, and networking. Ideally, these strategies will result in successful interviews and, eventually, a job offer. To ensure the interview is productive the student should prepare thoroughly by conducting extensive research on the potential employer and practicing mock interviews.

Technology has changed everything in the field of career services. Over 90% of career services offices surveyed stated that they relied heavily on Web resources (Behrens & Altman, 1998). Gen Xers have a strong preference for using the Web over speaking with a career counselor. Eighty percent of Gen X students prefer to gain information from the Internet than to speak with a counselor or look through a university catalog. Yet, Gen Xers still value the personal contact of a career counselor for mock interviews and to discuss job search frustrations (Behrens & Altman, 1998).

Three-fourths of companies surveyed post jobs on third-party Web sites. Students are becoming much more Web-savvy in regard to searching for employment. Students often post their resumés on campus and/or national Web sites like monster.com.

Conclusion

Frequently, Gen Xers are returning to college with a clear purpose or goal. Whether it is to earn a promotion that requires a degree or for personal fulfillment, the academic and career advisor plays a vital role in facilitating the degree completion process. The advisor must be willing to acknowledge that Gen Xers bring some positive past experiences and expertise to the college experience. It is not the advisor's job to prescribe or dictate the educational direction of the Gen Xer. The advisor exists to remove roadblocks and facilitate academic and career planning. One-on-one and virtual advising are effective for the Gen Xer. Both models allow for personalization, relationship building, and convenience. The advisor must understand that Gen Xers view themselves as free agents (Kizlik, 1998). If the barriers and obstacles are not identified and negotiated Gen Xers will "vote with their feet" and disappear.

REFERENCES

Backes, C. (1997). The do's and don'ts of working with adult learners. *Adult Learning.* 8(3): 29–31.

Behrens, T. and Altman, B. (1998, Winter). Technology: Impact on and implications for college career centers. *Journal of Career Planning & Employment.* 58: 19–22, 24.

Codrington, G. (1998). Generation X Papers: 25 sentences that define a generation. [On-line]. Available: http://tomorrowtoday.biz/generations/xpaper1010.htm.

Collins, M. (1996, Fall). Who are they and what do they want? *Journal of Career Planning and Employment.* 57(1): 41–43, 55–56.

Crookston, B. (1972) A developmental view of academic advising as teaching. *Journal of College Student Personnel.* 13: 12–17.

Gordon, V., Habley, W., & Associates. (2000). *Academic Advising.* San Francisco: Jossey Bass.

Kizlik, R. (1998) Generation X wants to teach. *International Journal of Instructional Media.* 26(2).

Knowles, M., Holton III, E., & Swanson, R. (1998). *The Adult Learner.* Woburn, MA: Butterworth-Heinemann.

Montana, P. & Lenaghan, J. (1999, Summer). What Motivates and Matters Most to Generations X and Y. *Journal of Career Planning and Employment.* 59(4): 27–30.

Mulligan, B. (2000, Summer). The Nature of Work. *Journal of Career Planning and Employment.* 60(4): 24–39.

Wagner, L. (2001). *Virtual Advising: Delivering Student Services.* [On-line]. Available: http://www.westga.edu/~distance/ojdla/fall43/wagner43.html.

Zemke, R. and Zemke, S. (2002). 30 Things We Know for Sure about Adult Learning. [On-line]. Available: www.hcc.hawaii.edu/intranet/committees/FacDevCom/guidebk/teachtip/adults3.htm.

CHAPTER TEN

Persistence and Graduation Characteristics

Stacy Fair

Introduction

The purpose of this chapter is threefold: 1) to review persistence rates and graduation characteristics while focusing on the impact of Generation X students returning to college; 2) to encourage further research in the area of graduation characteristics for Generation X students; and 3) to challenge higher education administrators to create a supportive educational environment – inviting and accessible to all who seek further knowledge, specializing in practices that assist Generation Xers in attaining their educational goals.

Educational Attainment

The attainment of a college degree has evolved from being a reality for only the elite of society to nearly a necessity in our service and information based economy. Since the late 1970s when Generation Xers first hit the college scene, educational attainment in the United States has maintained a relatively steady upward trend. From 1977 to 2002, the percentage of all 25–29 year olds who had at least four years of college increased from 24 to 29%. In 2002, 26.7% of the entire population age twenty-five or older had completed four years of college or more, which indicates that approximately one-fourth of the Generation X population has attended college for four years or more (Mortenson, 2003). In looking specifically at those who started college in 1992 through 2000, data reported by the U.S. Census Bureau shows that two-thirds of these students will earn an associate degree or bachelor's degree by the time they are 25 to 29 years old. Bachelor's degree completion rates as of March 2000 show that nearly half of the total 25- to 29-year-old population who had started college had completed an undergraduate degree. About 15% had earned an associate degree. Just over one-third of those who started college left before obtaining a degree by age twenty-nine (Mortenson, 2000). Those who have completed an associate degree and the one-third who left college without any degree may be part of the Gen X group seeking to return to college to complete their education.

Benefits of Higher Education for Generation X

When Gen Xers first hit the job market in the midst of economic prosperity, they were greeted with multiple job offers, flexible schedules, enticing salaries, bonuses, and perks. They were the cream of the crop: self-sufficient, energetic, technically proficient, and able to adapt to change with fierce determination. The mind-set was one of autonomy and independent success; however, they had seen their parents' generation devote years of their lives to companies who in turn laid off workers or forced them into early retirement. Due, in part, to having witnessed this phenomenon, Gen Xers expect to change jobs every five years. They are not as willing as previous generations to sacrifice everything for their careers; rather, they seek balance in their personal and professional lives. They seek more than financial gains, desiring opportunities to learn and have fun at work (Audibert & Jones, 2002).

Many of the jobs that offer great work environments with opportunities to learn and have fun require at least a bachelor's degree. Now, more than ever, as financial times continue to cripple the economy, millions of dedicated, ambitious, and highly motivated Generation Xers are turning to higher education to create their own opportunities, to increase their knowledge and skills, and to enrich their lives and the lives of others. Institutions of higher education are committed to shaping graduates who are well trained in critical thinking, problem solving, conflict resolution, collaborating with others, and communicating effectively in addition to teaching the hard skills required by each profession. Employers demand a workforce proficient in these skills. Those who have succeeded in higher education have greater opportunities to secure the most prestigious, rewarding, and well-paying jobs in America. Those who have not gained the necessary education and skills limit their options and may find themselves in jobs less fulfilling financially or personally.

Although Gen Xers expect more than financial rewards from their careers, the financial gains associated with higher education cannot be ignored given that Generation X has come to expect a lifestyle of convenience afforded only by those with some degree of financial stability. Generation Xers who began work immediately after high school and those with some college experience are finding themselves in need of additional training for personal development or to meet the demands of their continuously changing lives. Many of these individuals enter institutions of higher education with the hope of securing a meaningful and rewarding future for themselves and their families.

The Data

Due to the statistical nature of this chapter, a brief summary of relevant data sources is provided to encourage and support future research efforts in this area.

NATIONAL CENTER FOR EDUCATION STATISTICS (NCES)

NCES is the primary federal entity for collecting, analyzing, and reporting data related to education in the United States and other nations. It fulfills a congressional mandate to collect, collate, analyze, and report full and complete statistics on the condition of education in the United States. (www.nces.ed.gov)

POSTSECONDARY EDUCATION OPPORTUNITY: THE MORTENSON RESEARCH SEMINAR ON PUBLIC POLICY ANALYSIS OF OPPORTUNITY FOR POSTSECONDARY EDUCATION

Postsecondary Education OPPORTUNITY is a research letter founded on two fundamental beliefs. First, sound public social policy requires accurate, current, independent, and focused information on the human condition. Second, education is essential to the development of human potential and resources for both private and public benefit. The purpose of the research letter is to inform those who formulate, fund, and administer public policy and programs about the condition of and influences that affect postsecondary education opportunity for all Americans. (www.postsecondary.org)

ACT

ACT is an independent, not-for-profit organization that provides more than a hundred assessment, research, information, and program management services in the broad areas of education and workforce development. ACT gathers a variety of data from American colleges and universities on its Institutional Data Questionnaire (IDQ). The data is published in ACT's College Planning/Search Book, and is used in support of the ACT Assessment. (www.act.org)

UNITED STATES CENSUS BUREAU'S CURRENT POPULATION SURVEY

The CPS is a monthly survey of a national sample of about 50,000 U.S. households used to gather data on employment and unemployment. The survey is limited to the civilian, non-institutional population. (www.census.gov)

Shortcomings in Available Graduation Data

Most of the data collected in national surveys focuses on enrollment statistics as opposed to graduation statistics. Enrollment data is helpful from a marketing standpoint as institutions track numerous characteristics on students who are coming into their institutions based on their outreach initiatives, but graduation data would go one step further in providing a snapshot of what types of students persist and are successful in various degree programs. Future data to be collected should include information regarding the graduate's age, gender, race, ethnicity, socio-economic status, parental educational level, academic background including assessment test scores and high school GPA, transfer status, years to degree completion, number of major changes, average course load, degree programs, etc. A combination of these characteristics would provide a composite profile of who is successfully completing degrees, and is therefore reaching a higher level of opportunity in America.

Persistence Factors

Most students who enroll in college intend to graduate. In fall 2001, UCLA published a survey of American four-year-college freshmen that indicated 98.7% intended to earn a bachelor's degree or more from college. Most students plan to graduate from the college in which they first enroll. As many as 96.5% of freshmen indicated that they intended to earn a bachelor's degree or more from their current institution (Mortenson, 2002); however, many freshmen stop out, transfer, or simply withdraw from school, and slightly less than half will persist through the bachelor's degree. Many Gen Xers returning to college had originally planned to continue in higher education through completion of an undergraduate degree, but life can take a few unexpected turns.

Some factors used to predict persistence rates include academic preparedness indicated by college entrance exams or high school rank and GPA. Typically, institutions with more selective admission policies tend to have higher graduation or persistence rates compared to those with open or less selective admission policies. Graduation rates become an indicator of the quality of the institution, and institutions work vigorously to retain their students, but there are several factors negatively associated with persistence that may interfere with degree attainment. The characteristics as described by Horn (1996) and Horn and Premo (1995) are: delaying enrollment, attending part-time, financial independence, having dependents other than a spouse, working full-time while enrolled, having no high school diploma, and being a single parent. Generation Xers returning to campus or those as described in previous chapters from minority groups or from lower parental educational or socio-economic backgrounds may very well exhibit many of these factors, making their return to campus complicated from the start. Their success academically, socially, and personally during their first semester back on campus will have a significant impact on their persistence through degree attainment.

Persistence and Graduation by Gender

Much literature has been written on the progress of women in higher education. In 1975, a majority of the college degrees at every level were awarded to men. In chapter three, it was established that a majority of the associate, bachelor's, and master's degrees were awarded to women in 2000. Trends in degrees awarded show that 1978 was the first year in which more associate degrees were awarded to women than men. The first year in which women were awarded a higher percentage of bachelor's degrees was 1982.

Peculiar as it may seem, males are more likely than females (50.7% compared to 49.0%) to persist through completion of a bachelor's degree (Mortenson, 2000). As Generation X continues to enroll, it will be interesting to note whether the majority of Gen Xers returning to campus will be male or female. From the trends, it appears that the men may be coming back in higher numbers since they may not have begun college immediately after high school, although the greater numbers of women on campus may inspire more female Gen Xers to finish their degrees.

Persistence and Graduation by Racial and Ethnic Characteristics

In chapter one, persistence and graduation rates of individuals twenty-five and older are depicted for each racial and ethnic group. What follows is a closer look at the completion and persistence rates of specific ethnic and racial groups without restricting the age range. Of the Asians and Pacific Islanders who start college, over three quarters will earn a degree. At the other end of the spectrum, more than 50% of Hispanics who start college will leave without a degree by the time they are 25 to 29 years old. In looking at the degrees earned at the undergraduate level, American Indians are most likely to leave college with an associate degree, while Asians and Pacific Islanders are most likely to persist through the bachelor's degree. By breaking down this data further, completion trends from 1992 to 2000 remain relatively similar within the various racial or ethnic groups, but differ widely among these groups. By the year 2000, of the non-Hispanic whites who had started college, 53.1% had bachelor's degrees, and 15% had associate degrees by age 25–29, 33.9% of non-Hispanic blacks with college experience had earned bachelor's degrees, and 15.4% had associate degrees. Of the non-Hispanic Asians and Pacific Islanders who had begun college, 69.1% had completed a bachelor's degree, and 8.3% had completed an associate degree. Of the Hispanics from any race 29.4% had earned a bachelor's degree and 17.3% had completed an associate degree. For American Indians who had begun college, 34.1% had bachelor's degrees and 27.1% had associate degrees (Mortenson, 2000). Many of the Generation Xers most likely to return to campus to complete degrees may be from any of the various racial and ethnic groups who have some college experience or even an associate degree, but have not yet achieved their bachelor's degree. As these students return to campus, the diversity of their backgrounds and worldly experience will greatly enhance the classroom experience for all undergraduate students.

First-Generation College Student Persistence with Consideration of Socio-Economic Status

Compared to those whose parents had higher levels of education, first-generation students beginning college in 1989–90 were more likely to be 25 years or older, to be married, have dependents, be financially independent, and to start at public institutions. They were also less likely to have earned a degree or to still be enrolled by 1994 than their peers whose parents had attended college. As parental levels of education increased so did the secondary education persistence rates for their children (NCES, 1999). As noted previously, students from low-income families are less likely to attend college immediately after high school. It has also been documented that those who do make it to college are less likely to attain a degree. About one in twelve children born into low-income families with parents who are not college educated will achieve a bachelor's degree by age twenty-four (Mortenson, 2001). Many of the Gen Xers returning to campus may be first generation college students who had stopped out the first time they attempted college due to the many factors that affect the persistence rates of typical first-generation college students, or they may be students from lower economic backgrounds who are now able to pursue a college education. Now may be the second chance this generation needs to fulfill the dream of attaining a college degree.

The Next Step for Higher Education Administrators

It is important for administrators to continue to embrace traditional-age students immediately after high school when this group has the greatest opportunity to devote their time and energy to completing degrees. For those who enrolled in college after high school, but did not continue through degree completion, the road back to college may be more difficult. Gen Xers returning to school are in a different stage of life with more responsibilities and priorities competing for attention.

In the year 2000, the Generation X population (20–39 age group) totaled 78,547,000 people, slightly over 50% of whom had attended college. Of this group, 23.5% had some college experience, 8.1% had earned an associate degree, and 18.7% completed through the bachelor's degree. The group with some college experience combined with those who had an associate degree comprise the population of Gen Xers who may be returning to college: about 24,794,000 people (NCES, 2000).

The pool of potential Gen Xers returning to campus is plentiful, and the benefits of higher education for these students extend beyond personal and financial to the national and global level. As Generation X brings a lifetime of experience into the classroom and carries the knowledge of the classroom into the home and workforce, the positive outcomes for our nation will be felt both socially and economically.

Conclusion

According to Mortenson, "An undergraduate college degree has replaced the high school diploma as the minimum credential for the better paying jobs available in the American economy. Thus, who gets a college education decides who will prosper and who will be left out of life's opportunities" (2002, p. 1). Generation Xers who are returning to college do so for countless reasons. They have realized the need for education to improve their standard of living or for personal fulfillment, or simply for the joy of learning and the opportunity to meet other like-minded individuals. The persistence and graduation data collected on Generation X reveals the impact this population has had and will continue to have on institutions of higher education.

As noted, there are some shortcomings in data describing graduation characteristics. Research in this area is crucial to understanding the characteristics of students who are successful in college and are therefore able to take part in all of life's opportunities, as well as those who are not successful, so that progressive changes can occur in assisting these students.

Administrators who examine the data along with their current practices in an effort to see how to best serve this population of Generation Xers and who make the necessary changes will see the fruits of their labors as a new generation of adults enters the world with renewed vision, skills, and the motivation to succeed.

REFERENCES

Audibert, G. & Jones, M. (2002). The Impact of a Changing Economy on Gen X Job Seekers. *USA Today Magazine*. 130(2682): 20–22.

Horn, L. (1996). Nontraditional Undergraduates, Trends in Enrollment from 1986 to 1992 and Persistence and Attainment Among 1989–90 Beginning Postsecondary Students (NCES 97–578). U.S. Department of Education, NCES. Washington, DC: U.S. Government Printing Office.

Horn, L. and Premo, M. (1995). Profile of Undergraduates in U.S. Postsecondary Education Institutions: 1992–93, With Essay on Undergraduates at Risk (NCES 96–237). U.S. Department of Education, NCES. Washington, DC: U.S. Government Printing Office.

Mortenson, T. (2000, December). Undergraduate Degree Completion by Age 25 to 29 for Those Who Start College 1992 to 2000. *Postsecondary Education Opportunity*. 102. [On-line]. Available: http://www.postsecondary.org/last12/1021200DEGREE.pdf.

——. (2001, October). Family Income and Higher Education Opportunity, 1970 to 2000. *Postsecondary Education Opportunity*. 112. [On-line]. Available: http://www.postsecondary.org/last12/1121001FamilyIncome.pdf.

——. (2001, November). College Enrollment by Age 1950 to 2000. *Postsecondary Education Opportunity*. 113. [On-line]. Available: http://www.postsecondary.org/last12/1131101Age.pdf.

——. (2002, February). Earned degrees Conferred by Gender, 1870 to 2000. *Postsecondary Education Opportunity*. 116. [On-line]. Available: http://www.postsecondary.org/archives/previous/116202GENDER.pdf.

——. (2002, March). Institutional Graduation Rates by Control, Academic Selectivity and Degree Level 1983 to 2001. *Postsecondary Education Opportunity*. 117. [On-line]. Available: http://www.postsecondary.org/last12/117302IGR2001.pdf.

——. (2002, August). College Participation Rates by state for Students from Low Income Families FY1993 to FY2001. *Postsecondary Education Opportunity*. 122. [On-line]. Available: http://www.postsecondary.org/last12/122802CollegeParticipationRates.pdf.

——. (2002, November). What's Wrong with the Guys? *Postsecondary Education Opportunity*. 125. [On-line]. Available: http://www.postsecondary.org/archives/previous/1251102GuysFacts.pdf.

——. (2003, March). Educational Attainment, 1940–2002. *Postsecondary Education Opportunity*. 129. [On-line]. Available: http://www.postsecondary.org/last12/129303Attain.pdf.

National Center for Education Statistics, (1999). The Condition of Education 1999. Washington, DC: U.S. Department of Education. [On-line]. Available: http://www.nces.ed.gov/pubs99/condition99/indicator-56.html.

National Center for Education Statistics, (2000). Table 9. Washington, DC: U.S. Department of Education. [On-line]. Available: http://www.nces.ed.gov/pubs2002/digest2001/tables/dt009.asp.

CHAPTER ELEVEN

Retention Programs for At Risk Gen Xers

Bryant L. Hutson & Cindra S. Kamphoff

Introduction

Studies suggest that since Generation X students first entered college in the early 1980s, a significant number have left college without completing a degree. According to the American College Testing Program (ACT), institutional attrition across the nation has remained relatively stable since 1983 (Tinto, 1993). While this information suggests many Gen Xers have not had successful college experiences as traditional students, there is much evidence that they are returning to try again. Nontraditional students now make up at least 50% of higher education enrollments (MacKinnon-Slaney, 1994) and many of these are in the Gen X age cohort and have had previous academic experience. Clearly, it is critically important to understand the complex forces that put Gen X college students at risk for attrition and to develop appropriate intervention strategies. In this chapter, research regarding at risk Gen X college students and the reasons for at risk behavior among these students will be explored, along with some strategies for assisting these students, including effective programs that higher education institutions have implemented.

Increasingly, colleges and universities are making special efforts to identify and monitor at risk Gen X students. Once admitted, many institutions provide special student support programs in an attempt to retain these students and increase their graduation rates. Frequently, institutions monitor the enrollment of at risk students partly because high rates of noncompletion and declines in student enrollment have a direct effect on the increasing average cost per student (Jones & Watson, 1990). Demographic groups targeted as high risk by higher education institutions include: economically disadvantaged students, persons with disabilities, first-generation college students, women who are entering traditional male fields (see chapter three for a detailed discussion of this population), nontraditional-age students, and transfer students. Compared to previous or subsequent age cohorts, the Gen X student population has the highest number of students who fit into one or more of these categories (Saunders & Bauer, 2003).

DEFINITIONS

The term "student attrition" refers to students who leave a class before its completion. This includes students who enroll but stop working on the course without a formal withdrawal, as well as students who have completed an official withdrawal procedure (Bean, 1982). Conversely, student "success" or "retention," is defined as completing a course with a passing grade (Kember, 1995). The terms "at risk" or "high risk" describe those students whose probability of withdrawal from college is above average (Jones & Watson, 1990).

WHY BOTHER?

Why bother to discuss at risk Generation X college students at all? Are they somehow unique from previous generations of students who withdrew from college for academic reasons? A number of studies have appeared over the past decade that suggest Gen X students are uniquely at risk compared to previous generations of students.

College students born between 1961 and 1981 are highly diverse. Over thirty percent are minorities, twenty percent were born outside of the United States or have a foreign-born parent, and eleven percent spoke a language other than English while growing up (Choy, 2002). Traditionally, four-year-college students have enrolled full-time immediately after graduating from high school, were dependent on their parents to take care of most financial responsibilities, and worked part-time, if at all. Today, only forty percent of four-year-college students fit this traditional mold. Instead, about three-quarters of all four-year students now earn a paycheck, and about one-quarter work full-time (Choy, 2002).

A number of authors have discussed generational conflicts between Baby Boom college professors and Gen X students (Baker, 1998; McNamara, 1995; Sacks, 1996). Although descriptions vary as to the nature of these conflicts, there seems to be evidence that Gen X students frequently have learning styles that differ from those of previous generations. Kennedy (1996) contended that Baby Boomers and Gen Xers clash because of differences stemming from child-rearing philosophies that guided their upbringing. While Boomers were raised to be cooperative and competitive in a crowded generation of 78 million peers, Gen X grew up with computers and video games, becoming accustomed to learning alone through electronic media. Kennedy (1996) has discussed the significance of electronic media in Gen X students' early learning experiences, asserting that education became associated with entertainment among this age cohort. Perhaps the most well known study of Gen Xers in college was conducted by Sacks (1996). Sacks's case study of a western community college described students who refused to read their assignments, expected to be spoon-fed by the instructors, and accepted no responsibility for learning.

MODELS FOR RETENTION

Student retention research focuses on the forces that shape college student persistence. Tinto (1993) has categorized theories of student departure into five types: psychological, societal, economic, organizational, and interactional. Psychological models depict student departure as resulting from the personal attributes of the individual student. Societal theories of student departure are concerned with environmental perspectives, "… those attributes of individuals, institutions, and society, such as social status, race, institutional prestige, and opportunity structures, that describe the person's and the institution's place in the broader social hierarchy of society" (Tinto, 1993, p. 362). Economic theories of student departure share the view that "… individual decisions about persistence are not different in substance from any other economic decision that weighs the costs and benefits of alternative ways of investing one's scarce economic resources" (Tinto, 1993, p. 363). Organizational theories of student departure see attrition as reflecting the impact that the organization has on the socialization and satisfaction of students. Variables studied within organizational theories include bureaucratic structure, size, faculty-student ratios, and institutional resources and goals.

Organizational theories are especially appealing to administrators because they focus on institutional attributes that are directly alterable by college staff. Bean's *Industrial Model of Student Attrition* (1982) is perhaps the most well known of these organizational theories. Developed from an industrial model of work turnover, this study looked at the impact of organizational attributes (such as routinization, participation, and communication) and rewards (e.g., grades, practical value, and development) on retention. Bean (1982) asserted that rates of retention would be improved by institutional policies that increase student participation and enhance rewards they obtain for their "work" in the institution. In 1985, Bean and Metzner expanded the model to include nontraditional students. The adapted model does not emphasize the institution's social structure and the subsequent socialization associated with nontraditional students because they are firmly entrenched within adult lives outside the institution. Bean and Metzner (1985) assert that nontraditional students do not greatly change their social environment, and are not influenced by campus social pressures. Rather, nontraditional students are far more concerned with the external factors of a busy life outside of campus. Considering the increasing numbers of Gen Xers who are returning to college, this model may be particularly useful in developing programs for Gen X students who are in academic jeopardy.

Interactional theories of student departure currently dominate retention research. These theories reflect an interactive view of student experience where a student's leaving reflects his experience in the total culture of the institution, including both its formal and the informal aspects. Rather than focusing on formal organization alone, the role of informal social structures is stressed, such as student peer groups. Though individual attributes matter, their impact cannot be understood without reference to the perceptions that different students have of events within the institution (Tinto, 1993).

An example of an interactional theory is Astin's *Theory of Involvement* (1984). Astin suggests that students learn more from involvement in both the academic and social aspects of the collegiate experience. An involved student is one who devotes considerable energy to academics, spends much time on campus, participates actively in student organizations and activities, and interacts often with faculty (Astin, 1984). This theory posits that the student plays an integral role in determining his or her own degree of involvement in college classes, extracurricular activities, and social activities. Student interactions with faculty inside and outside the classroom, superior university programs, and policies reflective of commitment to student development are examples of efforts to support student growth.

Reasons for At Risk Behavior

THE UNIVERSITY OF NORTH CAROLINA AT GREENSBORO (UNCG) AS AN EXAMPLE

In Spring 2003, 247 students placed on academic probation after their first semester at UNCG were surveyed to identify causes that led to their probation. All students who completed the survey were in a probation program called Strategies for Academic Success. Of the 247 students, data was analyzed for the 211 students who completed the program and the survey process. Eighteen percent of the respondents were Gen Xers. The survey used Likert scale data, and t-tests were run to explore how Gen Xers differed from other age cohorts in their responses.

A number of statistically significant differences were found. For example, Gen X students were more likely to have decided on a major, were more likely to attend class regularly, were more comfortable contacting their professors outside of class, and more likely to ask for help from others. Yet, fewer Gen Xers felt connected to a staff member, faculty member, or advisor on campus and even fewer Gen Xers felt a part of the social network at UNCG. For instance, only 53.3% of the students strongly agreed or agreed to the statement "I feel there is at least one university employee on campus who cares about my welfare (i.e., instructor, advisor, staff member)" compared to 68.5% from other generational groups.

Gen Xer responses varied from those of other respondents in several areas. In this sample, Gen Xers worked more hours and spent more hours studying than students in other age groups. On average, Gen Xers worked between sixteen and twenty hours a week, while other students averaged between six and ten hours of work each week. In addition, the Gen X students studied between eleven and fifteen hours each week, whereas other students studied, on average, between six and ten hours each week.

Generally, Gen Xers were less likely to feel connected to campus. For example, Gen Xers described themselves as less likely to be involved in campus activities, less likely to have a network of friends on campus, and less likely to feel a part of the social network on campus. However, when comparing their academic study skills, Gen Xers felt they used their time more wisely, and were more likely to have good study skills. Overall, Gen Xers were more confident they would graduate from UNCG. Looking more closely at the reasons Gen Xers report for being placed on academic probation, they were more likely to attribute their probation status to classes being unavailable, and less likely than other age cohorts to report a poor study environment, missed class, inability to concentrate, and a lack of motivation as reasons for their poor performance.

In this case, the study supports both Tinto's (1993) and Bean and Metzner's (1985) contentions that Gen Xers feel less connected and have less involvement on campus. Since the student body at UNCG is diverse and over 20% are Gen Xers, this research was useful in identifying the needs of Gen Xers. Specifically, this data was used to explore the reasons students report being on academic probation in order to develop appropriate intervention programs. This research design is applicable to any campus with a program that identifies students on academic probation, and can be modified for any institution.

DISSATISFIED WITH THE INSTITUTION

Gen Xers return to college for specific reasons. For example, they may need a college degree to keep their current positions or to increase their salaries. Nevertheless, Gen Xers need to feel connected to the institution, which requires the need to develop relationships with professors, advisors, administration, and peers. In fact, Dehne (2003) argues that Gen Xers demand more attention from professors, administrators, and their peers than the generation before them.

Tinto (2003) outlines conditions for student retention that are applicable to Gen Xers. He suggests there are five conditions in which an institution can influence retention: expectations, advice, support, involvement, and learning. First, Tinto (2003) suggests that students are more likely to persist if the institution expects them to succeed. Too many institutions do not challenge their students, generally demanding too little in regard to learning. Second, students need to receive clear information about the institution and what is required of the student. Tinto suggests, "students need to understand the road map to [degree] completion and know how to use it to achieve personal goals" (2003, p. 2). Third, students need to feel that the environment of the institution provides academic, social, and personal support. Further research by Ashar and Skenes (1993) indicates that a supportive social environment relates positively to the retention of older adults. Reflecting this third principle, programs have been implemented for at risk students at various universities and colleges, including first-year experience courses, early alert programs, and early intervention programs (refer to the section *Programs Targeting Unique Generation X Populations* below). Fourth, students need to feel like a valued member of the institution to persist. Students must have frequent, quality interaction with faculty, staff, and peers. Other literature strongly supports the role of interaction with faculty in student persistence. Specifically, studies show that the frequency and quality of student discussions with faculty outside of the classroom are correlated positively and significantly with academic achievement (Cohorn & Guilliano, 1999; Pascarella, 1985; Terenzini & Pascarella, 1980). In addition, Pascarella (1980) concludes that informal student-faculty contact was associated with persistence in college. Finally, Tinto (2003) suggests that students are more likely to stay at an institution if the setting fosters their learning. If these five conditions do not take place, students may leave because they feel unsatisfied. In particular, Gen Xers may leave to find an institution that better meets their needs, and can provide them with the services they desire.

Tinto's model has been refined to apply to nontraditional students whose participation in college life is impacted by competing external factors such as jobs and family responsibilities. The linear life course of education, work, and retirement is rare among Gen X students, who frequently change jobs, often return to college for retraining, and reenter the workforce at various times in their lives. Since Gen Xers are at widely varying stages of the life cycle compared to the traditional 18- to 22-year-old cohort, they are perhaps at greater risk for attrition as returning students. Elaborating on Tinto's model, MacKinnon-Slaney (1994) developed the adult persistence in learning model, which combines personal issues (values, goals, interpersonal competence, mastery of life transitions), academic issues (ability, learning style, study skills), and social/environmental issues (environmental compatibility), based on the assumption that adult participation is a complicated response to a series of issues. As Gen X continues to return to college, the issues that puts this population at risk will likely be of increasing concern among faculty and staff, leading to further exploration of the applicability of Tinto's model to older students.

GEN X AS "NONTRADITIONAL STUDENTS"

Many Gen X students have been returning to college after previous negative academic experiences. The nature of attrition appears to be different for traditional and nontraditional students (Cleveland-Innes, 1994), since nontraditional students differ from their younger counterparts in many ways. For example, researchers have found that persistence rates were lower for older adults at four-year institutions who worked more hours and only attended part-time (Naretto, 1995), and nontraditional students generally report difficulty in integrating into student life and other campus activities (Graham & Donaldson, 1999). However, they also report a strong sense of commitment to the goal of obtaining a university degree (Bradley & Cleveland-Innes, 1992) and have better academic facility than their younger counterparts (Cleveland-Innes, 1994). In addition, adults have reported slightly higher levels of academic and intellectual growth than younger students (Graham & Donaldson, 1999). These studies suggest that returning Gen X students bring with them a set of concerns and advantages that make them unlike traditional-age students. Clearly, while not all Gen X nontraditional students are at risk, programs for at risk students should be designed keeping in mind that Gen X students have different needs from other age cohorts.

LACK OF INVOLVEMENT ON CAMPUS

As outlined above, Astin's (1984) theory of involvement contends that the more students are involved with campus life, the more likely they are to spend time and energy on studies. This involvement could include participation in student organizations and activities, or frequent interaction with faculty and staff. Students determine their level of involvement, yet they are more likely to become involved if the institution offers quality programs through which they can connect to campus. Although Gen Xers may live extremely busy lives outside of the classroom and be exceedingly occupied with work, family, and other responsibilities, they still need to feel involved on campus in order to be invested in the institution.

LACK OF TIME

Given the demands on Gen Xers' time (Kraus, 2000), it may be assumed that time management is a challenge to all Gen Xers in college. Recent surveys have suggested that more first-year students feel stressed for time. Between 1987 and 1997, the percentage of first-year students who reported being overwhelmed by "everything I have to do" increased from 16.4% to 29.4% (Astin, Parrott, Korn, & Sax, 1997). Two researchers at Brigham Young University recently conducted a study on why students fail (Roberts & Bell, 2002). In their sample, 57% of the students reported poor time management as a reason for at risk behavior. Poor time management was the number one self-reported reason for failing, followed by poor study habits (48%), money worries (46%), fear of failure (35%), ineffective study (34%), too much social life (33%), poor concentration (32%), the belief that they "must work to survive" (31%), poor study environment (28%), and inadequate study time (28%).

UNDERPREPAREDNESS

Another reason that students are at risk for failure is that they simply are academically underprepared for college. Gen Xers may have been out of school for as long as twenty years before deciding to return. Jones and Watson (1990) argue that not all students have received equal academic preparation for the college experience, even when elementary and secondary school preparation is taken into account; therefore, it certainly can be assumed that not all matriculating students are equally equipped to perform well in college.

The previously discussed Roberts and Bell (2002) study found poor study habits to be the number two rated reason students gave for academic failure. Effective study habits need to be taught throughout secondary school, but many students do not master them before enrolling in college. However, Levitz and Noel (2000) argue that academic preparedness does not equate to persistence, suggesting that just because a student is prepared does not mean that they will persist at your institution. In fact, over one-third of students who do not return to college had earned a first year GPA of 2.5 or greater. Levitz and Noel (2000) suggest that for institutions to counteract student underpreparation, they must provide students with support early in the college experience. "Front loading" during the first term of their college education by providing access to the right programs and people can be essential to student success.

LOW SELF-ESTEEM

Gen Xers may have anxiety about returning to college due to the unfamiliar environment. In fact, a growing body of evidence indicates that one of the most predictive factors of academic adjustment is self-esteem (Byrne, 1996). Some studies report that a sense of self-confidence can be a predictor for academic adjustment and persistence, and can be enhanced in part by informal contacts with faculty (Cohorn & Guiliano, 1999; Gerdes & Mallinckrodt, 1994). Similarly, self-esteem is negatively correlated with loneliness (Ginter & Dwinell, 1994), which is a predictor for student adjustment (McWhirter, 1997). In addition, Jones and Watson (1990) suggest that nonacademic factors such as an instructor's negative attitude can contribute to at risk students developing a sense of low self-esteem.

THE INFLUENCE OF FAMILY

Gen X families are drastically different from those of previous generations. First, smaller families are more predominant. Dehne (2003) reported that by the 1990s, 80% of couples have no more than two children. Second, the divorce rate is high, with one in ten Gen Xers already divorced or separated (Kraus, 2000). Third, as stated in earlier chapters, Gen Xers are waiting to get married later in life. In 1970, women were routinely married before age 21, while in 2000 women typically married around age 25. The average age that men marry increased from 23 to 27 in the same thirty-year period. In chapters one and four, we find that it is common for Gen Xers to delay moving away from home. In fact, nearly half of Gen Xers continue to live at home through their late 20s, and over 40% say they still get financial help from their parents in emergencies (Ritchie, 1995).

These family arrangements significantly influence Gen Xers as they return to college. For example, they may be divorced and solely responsible for their children; they may be married with children and their spouse is also a student; or they may still live with their parents and have responsibilities for household chores, maintenance of the house, or shopping for the family. These scenarios may be particularly applicable to women, since they tend to have greater family responsibilities (Eskilson & Wiley, 1999).

NEED TO WORK

The search for the "good life" has motivated Gen Xers to work. Gen Xers have been surrounded since birth by consumerism and televised images of financial success. When asked how they will compare to their parents financially, 75% of Gen X respondents thought they would be worse off (Eskilson & Wiley, 1999). This may influence Gen Xers' feelings of pressure regarding the need to work and earn a paycheck, while still perceiving themselves as having fallen short of their parents. Additionally, family needs may also reinforce the need to work since they may be the primary breadwinners. A majority of Gen Xers are children of working parents, so they are familiar with the need to work and the notion of working while in school (Ritchie, 1995). Roberts and Bell's (2002) study further supports the significance of the pressure to maintain a job while enrolled in school, finding that the need to work in order to survive was a contributing factor to failure described by almost one-third of the surveyed students.

UNDECIDED ABOUT CAREER

The student's intentions for returning to college, and the ability to set educational goals and make career decisions, have a large impact on the ability to persist. Although the majority of Gen Xers had a career before returning to school, a lack of direction may also have led them to pursue their college education after several years. Tinto (1987) identifies several factors that contribute to students dropping out, including a lack of clear academic and career goals. In addition, Tinto (1993) reviewed a number of studies and found that the higher the level of educational or occupational goals, the greater the probability that students will complete their college degrees.

Student Services and Interventions

Colleges and universities have focused considerable attention on developing appropriate strategies to increase the retention rates of Gen X students. Noel, Levitz, and Saluri (1985) identified a number of key programs and activities that support student retention, including financial aid, orientation programs, academic support programs, career planning and counseling, and appropriate student activities. Because Gen X students have unique needs and are unlike previous generations, consideration of life circumstances should inform a carefully planned series of strategies for supporting them. The following section describes some effective approaches for supporting Gen X students.

Scholarship recipients are slightly more likely to persist to graduation than other students, and college work-study awards and student employment contribute to student retention. Conversely, students who have difficulty securing adequate financial support are often at risk for attrition (Tinto, 1993). Since many Gen Xers are self-supporting, maintaining a strong flow of information between these students and the financial aid office is important to student retention. Effective strategies include distributing reminders via e-mail, posting notices on the school's Web site, and providing financial aid advising at convenient times and through innovative means such as Web chat.

Orientation programs can be powerful tools for heading off attrition among Gen Xers. The youngest members of this generation are several years beyond high school, and they often have previous college experience. Orientation sessions that emphasize resources for working adult students with families can be especially important. Further, these orientation sessions may be the best opportunity to get information to students about disability services, tutoring resources, and other beneficial programs (Kim, 2002). Orientation sessions can also be useful in collecting data to identify unmet student needs and for helping students connect to peers with similar interests and concerns.

Academic support programs can be the most important component of Gen X retention efforts. Included among the most effective programs are: personalized assessment and assistance to improve reading and math skills, required courses for students covering topics and skills necessary for academic success, support programs and required academic-skill classes for students on academic probation, workshops designed to sharpen and expand academic skills, and personalized tutoring (Schroeder, 2003). Having these services available during evening hours or on weekends may be vital for the academic success of Gen Xers, who frequently try to fit in work and family responsibilities alongside academics.

Developing appropriate student activities is essential for helping students feel connected to campus (Tinto, 1993); however, program planners should consider the needs of the Gen X students. Depending on Gen X student needs, appropriate programs may be as diverse as support groups for single Gen X mothers, programs such as "Brother2Brother" which matches African American men to on-campus mentors, or on-line discussion boards for evening students who are looking for peers with similar needs or interests. Establishing methods for collecting information from Gen X students can help in the development of strong student activity programs.

SPECIAL NEEDS STUDENTS

At risk "special needs" students can be described as falling into two groups: those with learning disabilities and those with physical disabilities. A number of colleges identify "at risk" students as "best fit" students. In North Carolina, for example, both Greensboro College and Louisburg College have implemented special programs for college students with learning disabilities and now target recruitment efforts to these populations. Similarly, Landmark College in Vermont was established specifically as an institution for students with learning disabilities.

LEARNING DISABILITIES

The estimated prevalence of learning disabilities (LDs) among students in two- and four-year U.S. colleges has increased to about three percent as of the mid-1990s (Henderson, 1995). This information suggests that the Gen X college population has the largest number of special needs learners of any previous generation. It also appears, however, that only a minority of college students with learning disabilities use the academic support services available to them. This is of concern, as college students with learning disabilities demonstrate significantly poorer academic adjustment to the college setting than their non-LD peers (Dunn, 1995). There is, however, evidence that these students benefit from academic services provided by postsec-ondary educational institutions.

Help-seeking behavior among students with learning disabilities is frequently influenced by their self-perceptions. These students frequently perceive more threat to their self-worth when considering asking peers for help, compared to students with higher perceptions of their own abilities. Students with higher global self-esteem are more likely to report willingness to seek academic help when necessary and less apt to report feeling threatened by having to seek help (Karabenick & Knapp, 1991).

PHYSICAL DISABILITIES

Several legislative acts have made public and university education available to individuals with disabilities. Gen X students are the first wave of college students for whom this legislation was beneficial, and consequently, this generation of college students contains the largest number of students whose disabilities were recognized and accommodated by educational institutions.

College has provided opportunities for professional development and the possibility of financial security and independence for physically disabled people. Disabled students have been reported to require more career support and guidance services, but are successful, given adequate services (Benshoff, Kroeger & Scalia, 1990).

Experiencing a disability has been shown to have an important impact on the sense of self (Toombs, 1994), and Blake and Rust (2002) found that disabled students ranked self-confidence as one of the major obstacles confronted while attending college. As this illustrates, appropriate support services for these students include both accommodations to improve their learning opportunities and programs to assist them in gaining self-confidence and a sense of connectedness to the institution.

Programs Targeting Unique Generation X Populations

A significant number of Generation X students with academic deficiencies are choosing to attend college (MacDonald, 1997). Unfortunately, many of these students have trouble because of the gap between the academic skills they possess and the academic demands of the college environment. These students are more likely to fail their college courses, and they graduate at lower rates than other students. Consequently, they tend to have lower earning potential and subsequently lower overall quality-of-life experiences. Thus, while the door to college is open for increasing numbers of underprepared students, many of these students leave college without the benefits associated with a degree and the skills necessary for future success (Dunn, 1995). Four programs that have been implemented on college campuses can be applied specifically to at risk Gen X students including first-year seminars, early alert programs, probation programs, and distance education programs.

FIRST-YEAR SEMINARS

The National Resource Center for The First-Year Experience and Students in Transition sent out a similar survey to over 2,500 colleges and universities and found that only about three-fourths of the universities had a special course for their first-year students called a first-year seminar, colloquium, or student success course (National Survey of First-Year Seminar Programming, 2003). Typically, these courses carry credit toward graduation and include topics such as orientation to the campus, developing essential academic skills, and easing transition to the college environment.

A successful first-year seminar can counteract several of the reasons Gen Xers are at risk. First-year seminars can influence retention rates, GPAs, and graduation rates. For example, Boudreau & Kromrey (1994) found that retention rates, academic achievement (which included academic standing, cumulative GPA, and total credits earned), and graduation rates increased for students who took a freshman seminar course compared to students who did not. In particular, Cuseo (1997) contends that first-year seminars have a dramatic effect on academically at risk students. In addition, these seminars should help students learn more about how to decide on a career, how to balance multiple responsibilities, and how to manage their time. If all of these essential competencies are covered well in the class, the seminar may influence their self-esteem levels, thereby shaping their desires to persist at the institution (McWhirter, 1997).

According to the First-Year Experience survey, nearly 90% of the seminars involve faculty in course instruction, over half of the seminars involve student affairs professionals in course instruction, and over one-third of the seminars involve campus administrators and other campus professionals in course instruction (National Survey of First-Year Seminar Programming, 2003). In addition, almost one-fourth of the schools offer seminars taught by the students' academic advisors. This option offers students a way to get to know a faculty or staff member with whom they will connect throughout their collegiate career. Several institutions are beginning to offer specific sections of the first-year seminar for at risk populations including transfer students, adult students, commuter students, and student–athletes. To address Gen Xers' concerns, it would be possible to offer a section specifically for students between the ages of twenty-two and forty-two.

EARLY ALERT PROGRAMS

Several institutions have developed early alert programs in order to provide students with grade feedback on or before the drop deadline. At the University of Missouri, for example, "Early Alert" notices were sent to students receiving a C-or below at the five-week point of the semester. Eimers (2000) reported that because of early alert notices, students took personal actions such as studying more (86% of students) and getting better organized (53% of students). In addition, students were more likely to talk to a parent or guardian (47% of students) or talk to their peers (45% of students) about their academic situation. However, Eimers (2000) concluded that frequent reminders of academic performance might have a larger impact on academic performance than only one notice at the fifth week of classes.

Cartnal and Hagen (1999) describe additional student behaviors resulting from early alert letters. They conducted the same study in 1998 and 1999, finding that a large proportion of students indicated they met with their instructors after they received the letters (43% in 1999 and 38% in 1998). Students also withdrew from the course for which they received the early alert letter (19% in 1998 and 34% in 1999), and indicated they "studied more" (20% in 1998 and 13% in 1999). Other actions reported by students included seeking tutoring, working less, accessing the library, or joining a study group.

Gen Xers would particularly benefit from early alert letters due to the need to feel connected to the institution and to professors, advisors, administrators, and peers. The letters provide Gen X students with more feedback on academic performance, allowing them to make better decisions about what is appropriate for them, whether it be to drop the course or to study more. In addition, given the demands on Gen Xers' time, it may be especially important for these students to receive more frequent grade feedback.

PROBATION PROGRAMS

Institutions are increasingly enrolling into probation programs students who have received poor grades. One program, which was recognized by LRP Publications in their Enrollment Manager's Report as one of the top forty-two retention programs, is The University of North

Carolina at Greensboro's *Strategies for Academic Success* program. The program focuses on the teaching of life skills and sections incorporated in the curriculum include personal responsibility, the difference between victim and creator language, interdependence, self-management, and goal setting/life planning. As Jones and Becker (2003) indicate, decision-making skills and self-advocacy are lacking in underprepared students. UNCG's program consists of a no-credit, half-semester course in which attendance is mandatory. The program is unique because of its "teeth" – any student who misses a class session is automatically suspended from the institution (Kamphoff & Amundsen, 2003). The results of the program appear extremely positive since the retention rate among these students increased by 17% from Spring 2000 to Spring 2003 and 19% from Fall 2000 to Fall 2002 (Kamphoff & Amundsen, 2003; Amundsen, Kamphoff & Ross, 2002). In addition, this program seems to be effective with the Gen X population. Gen Xers had a statistically significant change in their behaviors after the implementation of the program, specifically in Gen Xers' level of interdependence, time management, goal setting, connection to the campus, understanding of themselves, social support, academic preparedness, study skills, and confidence levels.

Shippensburg University, the University of Kentucky, and the University of Texas at Arlington have similar probation programs without the "teeth." Shippensburg University's Academic Improvement Program (AIM) consists of meeting over the course of seven weeks with a group of other probation students in which learning preferences, goal setting, time management, motivation, and taking charge of one's life is discussed (Whitfield & Aberman, 2002). The University of Kentucky, as part of their mandatory probation-advising program, piloted a three-credit course entitled "College Student Success" (Shanks, 2002). The course was designed for undeclared students on probation with study skills and career development as the primary focus. In addition, the University of Texas at Arlington offers a one-credit hour course that focuses on note taking, exam preparation, time management, concentration, and coping skills (Leach, 2002).

Courses that are available for probation students must take into account the new learning strategies that Gen Xers use compared to generations before them. Brown (1997) provides six ways that professors can be more accommodating in the classroom when teaching Gen Xers: 1) make learning experiential, 2) give students control over their own learning, 3) respect learners' abilities to engage in parallel thinking, 4) highlight key points, 5) motivate learning, and 6) provide challenges.

Generally, few courses are available to probation students nationally, although the programs discussed above drastically increase the retention rate of probation students (Kamphoff & Amundsen, 2002). A growing number of institutions, however, are implementing mandatory advising programs for probation students. These advising programs have been shown to be effective in improving retention, but to a lesser extent than courses that target probation students. Institutions that offer advising programs for probation students include the University of Kentucky and the University of Florida.

DISTANCE LEARNING PROGRAMS

Gen Xers have had greater access to higher education than any previous generation of students. Improved telecommunication and the subsequent growth of distance education have contributed significantly to this access. Gen Xers typically have a high level of technology savvy, and this fact has made distance learning appear to college administrators as an ideal method for increasing enrollments without requiring additional facilities. Further, Gen Xers frequently seek convenient course offerings since they often have work and family obligations. However, distance learning offers unique challenges as well as opportunities. Many colleges report extremely high attrition rates from distance courses, and the reasons for distance learning dropout are not fully understood. However, we do know that Gen Xers have a range of technology competency levels, and distance education courses require that students be able to use the technology before beginning to learn the course content. Further, distance learning also requires students to work independently and be self-motivated (Kember, 1995).

Increasingly, institutions are implementing programs to assist distance learners. These efforts include on-line counseling and advising services, 24-hour technology support via telephone and the Internet, and increasingly interactive Web-based instruction. NACADA (2003) has established standards for advising distance learners that require providers of distance education to offer a minimum set of core services which assist distance learners in identifying and achieving their education goals. In implementing standards for Washington State University Distance Degree Programs, it was found that the development of student services must be considered equally important to the development of courses, and must include services based on identified needs of distance learners as well as efforts to ensure that distance students feel connected to their institution (Kendall, Moore, Smith, & Oak, 2001).

Conclusion

Gen X college students have learning styles, life experiences, and personal challenges that are unique to their generation. Faculty and staff can harness these attributes to sustain quality educational encounters and student success. However, these students frequently have previous educational experiences, responsibilities outside of school, and other concerns that may put them at risk for leaving college. An integrated set of retention programs, developed with consideration for the characteristics and needs of the Gen X students being recruited, can make the difference between students leaving with degrees or with animosity.

A number of strategies can be implemented to assist in Gen X student success. Orientation sessions, financial aid information distribution methods, academic and social support programs, and other interventions that are already in place on college campuses can be modified to better serve Gen X students. Assessing these programs can be a challenge for Gen X students since they typically have work and family responsibilities. Consequently, careful planning should inform how and when these services are offered. Since the needs of Gen X students vary greatly, and most institutions have limited resources, retention staff may find it advantageous to assess the needs of the Gen X students they are enrolling and use this information to develop support programs.

REFERENCES

Amundsen, S., Kamphoff, C., & Ross, R. (2002). Aggressive intervention: Developing an academic success program for students in their first semester of probation. Paper presented at the National Academic Advising Association National Conference. Salt Lake City, Utah.

Ashar, H. & Skenes, R. (1993). Can Tinto's student departure model be applied to non-traditional students? *Adult Education Quarterly.* 43(2): 90–97.

Astin, A. (1984). Student Involvement: A developmental theory for higher education. *Journal of College Student Personnel.* 25: 297–308.

Astin, A., Parrott, S., Korn, W., & Sax, L. (1997). *The American Freshman: Thirty-Year Trends.* Los Angeles, CA: Higher Education Research Institute, UCLA.

Baker, G. (1998). Keeping all generations happy: The Xers, Boomers, and beyond. *Community College Journal.* 68(5): 10–16.

Bean, J. (1982). Conceptual Models of Student Attrition. In E.T. Pascarella (Ed.) *New Directions for Institutional Research: Studying Student Attrition.* No. 36 (17–28). San Francisco: Jossey–Bass.

Bean, J. & Metzner, B. (1985). A conceptual model of nontraditional undergraduate student attrition. *Review of Educational Research.* 55: 485–540.

Benshoff, J., Kroeger, S., & Scalia, V. (1990). Career maturity and academic achievement in college students with disabilities. *Journal of Rehabilitation.* 56(2): 40–44.

Blake, T. & Rust, J. (2002) Self-esteem and self-efficacy of college students with disabilities. *College Student Journal.* 36(2): 214–224.

Boudreau, C. & Kronrey, J. (1994). A longitudinal study of the retention and academic performance of participants in freshmen orientation course. *Journal of College Student Development.* 35: 444–449.

Bradley, M. & Cleveland-Innes, M. (1992). *Valuing diversity: Responding to the needs of adult students at the University of Calgary.* Calgary, AB: University of Calgary.

Brown, B. (1997). *New Learning Strategies for Generation X* (Report No., EDO–CE–97–184). East Lansing, MI: National Center for Research on Teacher Learning. (ERIC Document Reproduction Service No. ED 411 414).

Byrne, B. (1996). *Measuring Self Concept Across the Life Span: Issues and Instrumentation.* Washington, DC: American Psychological Association.

Cartnal, R. & Hagen, P. (1999). *Evaluation of the Early Alert Program* (Report No., CC_RR_98/99–06. San Luis Obispo, CA: Cuesta College. (ERIC Document Reproduction Service No. ED 441 541).

Choy, S. (2003). *Access & Persistence: Findings from 10 Years of Longitudinal Research on Students.* [On-line]. Available: http://www.eriche.org/digests/2002-2.html.

Cleveland-Innes, M. (1994). Adult student drop-out at post-secondary institutions. *The Review of Higher Education.* 17(4): 423–445.

Cohone, C. & Guiliano, T. (1999). Predictors of adjustment and institutional attachment in 1st-year college students. *Psi Chi Journal of Undergraduate Research*. 12: 33–37.

Cuseo, J. (1997). *Freshman Orientation Seminar at Community Colleges: A Research-Based Rationale for Its Value, Content, and Delivery* (Report No., JC 970 452). Marymount College (ERIC Document Reproduction Service No. ED 411 005).

Dehne, G. (2003). *The New Student Generation: Are We Ready? Do We Care?* [On-line]. Available: http://www.gdais.com/news_research/research_new_student.html.

Dunn, C. (1995). A comparison of three groups of academically at risk college students. *Journal of College Student Development*. 36: 270–279.

Eimers, M. (2000). *Assessing the Impact of the Early Alert Program* (Report No., HE 033–323). Paper presented at the Association of Institutional Research Annual Meeting in Cincinnati, Ohio. (ERIC Document Reproduction Service No. ED 446 511).

Eskilson, A., & Wiley, M. (1999). Solving for the X: Aspirations and expectations of college students. *Journal of Youth and Adolescence*. 28(1): 51–70.

Gerdes, H., & Mallinckrodt, B. (1994). Emotional, social, and academic adjustment of college students: A longitudinal study of retention. *Journal of Counseling and Development*. 72: 281–288.

Ginter, E. & Dwinell, P. (1994). The importance of perceived duration: Loneliness and its relationship to self-esteem and academic performance. *Journal of College Student Development*. 35: 456–460.

Graham, S. & Donaldson, J. (1999). Adult students' academic and intellectual development in college. *Adult Education Quarterly*. 49(3): 147–161.

Henderson, C. (1995). *College freshmen with disabilities: A statistical profile*. Washington, DC: HEATH Resource Center.

Jones, D. J. & Watson, B. C. (1990). *"High risk" students and higher education: Future trends*. (ASHE–ERIC Higher Education Report No. 3). Washington, DC: The George Washington University, School of Education and Human Development.

Jones, R. & Becker, K. (2003). Getting prepared for the underprepared. *The Mentor: An Academic Advising Journal*. [On-line]. Available: http://www.nacada.ksu.edu.

Kamphoff, C. & Amundsen, S. (2003). A probation program with "teeth": A workshop on empowering personal responsibility through a mandatory probation program. Paper presented National Academic Advising Association Regional Conference. Charleston, South Carolina.

Karabenick, S. & Knapp, J. (1991). Relationship of academic help-seeking to the use of learning strategies and other instrumental achievement behavior in college students. *Journal of Educational Psychology*. 83: 221–230.

Kember, D. (1995). *Open Learning Courses for Adults*. Englewood Cliffs, NJ: Educational Technology Publications.

Kendall, J., Moore, C., Smith, R., and Oaks. M. (2001, April 9) Student services for distance learners: A critical component. *Netresults: NASPA's E-Zine for Student Affairs Professionals* [On-line] Available: http://www.naspa.org/netresults/article.cfm?ID=229&category=Feature.

Kennedy, M. (1996). When a boomer meets a buster. *Across the Board*. 33(88): 53–54.

Kim, K. (2002) ERIC review: exploring the meaning of "nontraditional" at the community college. *Community College Review.* 30(1): 74–91.

Kraus, S. (2000, June 5). Gen Xers' reinvented 'traditionalism'. *Brandweek.* 66: 28–30.

Leach, L. (2002). Potential for academic success seminar: One advising center's strategy to help students PASS. Paper presented at the National Academic Advising Association National Conference. Salt Lake City, UT.

Levitz, R. & Noel, L. (2000). The earth-shaking but quiet revolution in retention management. [On-line]. Available: http://www.noellevitz.com.

MacDonald, R. (1997, April). Evaluation of an alternative solution for the assessment and retention of high-risk college students. Paper presented at the Annual Meeting of the American Educational Research Association, Washington, DC.

MacKinnon-Slaney, F. (1994) The adult persistence in learning model. *Journal of Counseling and Development.* 72(3): 268–275.

McNamara, P. (1995, April 21). All is not lost: Teaching Generation X. *Commonwealth.* 122: 12–15.

McWhirter, B. (1997). Loneliness, learned resourcefulness, and self-esteem in college students. *Journal of Counseling and Development.* 75: 460–469.

NACADA (2003). NACADA Standards for Advising Distance Learners [On-line] Available: http://www.nacada.ksu.edu/Clearinghouse/Research_Related/distance.htm.

Naretto, J. (1995). Adult student retention: The influence of internal and external communities. *NASPA Journal.* 32(2): 90–100.

National Survey of First-Year Programming. (2003). [On-line]. Available : http://www.sc.edu/fye/research/surveys/survey00.htm.

Noel, L., Levitz, R., & Saluri, D. (1985). *Increasing Student Retention.* San Francisco: Jossey–Bass.

Pascarella, E. (1980). Student-faculty informal contact and college outcomes. *Review of Educational Research.* 50: 545–595.

Pascarella, E. (1985). College environmental influences on learning and cognitive development: A critical review and synthesis. In J. Smart (Ed.), *Higher Education: Handbook of Theory and Research:* Vol. I, (1–56). New York, NY: Anathon Press.

Ritchie, K. (1995). Marketing to Generation X. *American Demographics.* 17(4): 34–40.

Roberts, N. & Bell, D. (2002). Why college students fail: Students' identification of obstacles. Paper presented at the National Academic Advising Association National Conference. Salt Lake City, Utah.

Sacks, P. (1996). *Generation X Goes to College.* Chicago: Open Court.

Saunders. L. & Bauer, K. (2003). Undergraduate Students Today: Who are they? [On-line]. Available: http://udel.edu/~kbauer/GenX.html.

Schroeder, C. (2003). Supporting the new students in higher education today. *Change.* 2: 55–59.

Shanks, M. (2002). Mandatory probation advising: A personal guide to the finish line. Paper presented at the National Academic Advising Association National Conference. Salt Lake City, Utah.

Terenzini, P. & Pascarella, E. (1980). Student/faculty relationships and freshman year educational outcomes: A further investigation. *Journal of College Student Personnel*. 21: 521–528.

Tinto, V. (1987). *Increasing Student Retention*. San Francisco, CA: Jossey–Bass.

———. (1993). *Leaving College: Rethinking the Causes and Cures of Student Attrition*. 2nd ed. Chicago: University of Chicago Press.

———. (2003). Taking student retention seriously. [On-line]. Available http://www.noellevitz.com.

Toombs, S. (1994). Disability and the Self. T. M. Brinthaupt & R. P. Lipka (Eds.) *In Changing the Self: Philosophies, Techniques and Experiences*. New York: SUNY Press.

Whitefield, H. & Aberman, K. (2002). AIM high! Paper presented at the National Academic Advising Association National Conference. Salt Lake City, Utah.

PART 4

Serving Gen Xers

PART IV
Serving Gen Xers

CHAPTER TWELVE
Preparing Staff to Serve This Population

Bob Roberts

Introduction

In any examination of methods and strategies of recruiting and serving a specific demographic, it is imperative to consider the associated staffing and human resource issues. Based upon his extensive research, Peter Senge developed the following conclusion: in the long run, the only sustainable source of competitive advantage is your organization's ability to learn faster than its competition (1990). Considering this assumption, it is of the utmost importance to recruit, retain, and develop quality employees if an organization wants to be successful in serving the Generation X student.

Recruiting and training quality employees is important, but an institution must know what competencies, knowledge, skills, and abilities are required for staff who serve Generation X students. First, and perhaps foremost, Generation X has a different perspective on the world from other generations. Students involved in a case study conducted by Carol Kasworm from North Carolina State University were attracted to academic programs that provided an "adult-friendly and supportive environment" (2003). Another study found that "nearly three-quarters of people age 18 to 24 and 65% of those age 25 to 34 say one can't be too careful in dealing with other people" (Mitchell, 2001, p. 9). This is just one shift in the demographic that shows a need for a different set of knowledge, skills, and abilities for employees who work with Gen Xers.

This, and volumes of additional research, implies a distinct difference in the needs and desires of Generation X from its successors and predecessors (Rosen, 2001). In order to successfully serve this population, faculty and staff must determine which of those differences are relevant to their institutional mission and prepare accordingly.

Aside from the differences in outlooks between traditional-age students and Generation X students, specific differences exist between recruitment and service needs for these populations.

Recruitment of Staff

One of the first steps in recruiting any new staff member is to analyze the competencies required for the particular position. Certain competencies are required for a position regardless of the student population worked with on a normal basis. For example, the American Association of Collegiate Registrars and Admissions Officers (AACRAO) lists human relations, administration, and technology skills as broad categories of competencies required for an admissions officer (Ancrum, Berson, Brink, Guerrero, Henderson, McKinney, Mills, Robinson, & Swann, 1991). Additionally, the following traits make for a smooth acquisition of basic skills that are required for an admissions officer:

- Ability to analyze quickly and make solid decisions
- Ability to maintain balance or centeredness (i.e., staying physically and mentally healthy)
- Dedication to purpose and mission; being flexible but confident
- Endless energy for erratic hours, changing schedules
- Friendly attitude with proclivity for automatic outreach and willingness to take the first step in conversations and in large groups, always employing kindness, sincerity, and honesty
- An innate capacity for public relations
- Keen self-discipline and mastery of motivating techniques
- Reliable sense of responsibility, undergirded with an obvious tendency toward unselfishness (Swann & Henderson, 1998)

In addition to the general competencies needed for any staff member, an institution should identify those competencies needed to work with the Generation X population. Perhaps the most obvious is work schedule; institutions that seek to serve this demographic cannot successfully attract or retain them on a conventional eight to five, weekday office schedule. They must provide a significant level of access in the evening and on weekends (Klein, Scott, & Clark, 2001). Thus, the institution must consider a staff member's ability to work a nontraditional work schedule.

Additionally, the Generation X cohort of students returning to college may need a more nurturing environment in order to build the confidence necessary to succeed. Adult students are often intimidated about their initial return to the classroom (Carlan, 2001). If thrown into an environment providing little emotional support and confidence building, an adult student's chances of developing the confidence necessary for long-term success are severely reduced (Carlan, 2001). Based upon these findings, it becomes obvious that student services staff at all levels must have an expanded level of counseling skills if they are to successfully work with the Generation X student.

Each institution must identify the specific competencies that it deems minimally necessary to work with the returning Generation X student in the context of the existing organizational structure. Each competency should be noted in detail in the position description and assessed of all applicants and potential employees. In addition to these specific requirements, subjective behavioral competencies essential to a job, such as flexibility, agility, and strategic insight should also be noted (Segal, 2002).

If current job descriptions do not provide adequate detail to complete this task effectively, the first step would be to create a new, more useful job description. The job description should explain all of the major facets of the position. This can be accomplished most effectively through the combined work of the hiring supervisor, incumbent (if there is one), or, if the position in question is currently vacant, an employee in a similar position (Milkovich & Newman, 1996).

Once the competencies are identified through a detailed and comprehensive job description, the supervisor or human resource professional should determine which of these would be required of an applicant and which could be taught to a new hire. As mentioned earlier, subjective behavior competencies should also be included (Segal, 2002). From these required competencies, interview questions can be created. The questions should ask for specific situations in which the candidate has demonstrated the competencies, rather than vague explanations of the theoretical application of the information.

The competencies are perhaps the most integral tool in evaluating candidates but an institution should also look for some of the intangibles. As mentioned above, the returning Generation X student may require additional service, emotional support, and confidence building. Thus, supervisors should identify employees who possess what has often been referred to as a servant's heart. Although the concept comes from religious ideology, it has been adapted by a variety of organizations to refer to the ideal customer service employee. The concept of the servant's heart refers to individuals who honor the needs of others before their own without seeking praise for themselves. Staff members with this level of commitment to customer service will prove to be excellent student services employees. To identify this characteristic, questions should be asked of applicants that gauge their commitment and attitudes toward customer service. The hiring committee should look for answers that reflect a selfless attitude toward serving students or customers.

Constant change in processes and environment are a reality in today's enrollment services environment. Dealing effectively with this change requires staff to regularly update their skills (Crosthwaite and Warner, 1995), thus, the most productive staff members are those willing to continually learn and grow within the context of their institution. Given this information, an institution would be wise to ask questions during the interview that gauge an applicant's proclivity to engage in lifelong learning (Senge, 1990). An employee who engages in continual personal and professional growth will likely be more successful in today's constantly changing environment.

Training

Once an employee is hired, he or she will experience a learning curve. Naturally, any new employee must learn some institution-specific information as well as compensate for other relevant deficiencies. Current staff members also need ongoing training and development in order to perform at their best (Doidge, Hardwick, and Wilkinson, 1998). The question becomes, who needs to know what?

The first area of training would be the institution-specific technical skills required for an employee's position. Once again, this depends heavily upon the institutional context. The major areas within an enrollment services operation affected by an emphasis on Generation X students are admission, transfer of credit, and advising functions. When dealing with traditional students, these areas can typically afford to operate with little understanding of one another. A high school student will ordinarily come to an institution with a blank slate or very few college credits earned through CLEP or Advanced Placement (AP). The Generation X demographic is much more likely to be transferring previous course work, often from multiple institutions, which adds a significant level of complexity to the process (Swann & Henderson, 1998).

The first categories of positions we will examine are those within the admissions office. Generation X students have many more questions about the transfer of credit and time until completion of degree. To be successful in serving these prospective students, managers must ensure that someone is available to answer the questions of these students (Swann & Henderson, 1998). One option is to train the admissions officers on how transfer credit is awarded and how degree audits are completed. The other is to expand the job of transfer credit staff and academic advisor's jobs to include advising of prospective students. Either option has advantages and disadvantages, but most importantly the institution must be prepared to answer more complicated questions from prospective students.

For those admissions staff members working in the application processing area, a heightened awareness of transfer issues must be learned. A traditional applicant will have a very predictable set of credentials to submit with the admissions application: a high school transcript, standardized test scores, and any additional institution-specific requirements (essays, letters of recommendation, etc.). The returning Generation X student could have a variety of additional credentials for the institution to handle. Examples may include, but are not limited to, continuing education transcripts, other college and university transcripts, military credentials, and other certifications of prior learning. Staff members responsible for application processing must be trained to deal with these additional documents, as well as to recognize the need for supplementary documents.

Should an institution decide to place an increased emphasis on the Generation X student, staff members responsible for transfer of credit will need counseling skills, communication skills, knowledge of institutional policy, and the ability to use effective questioning techniques. In addition to these areas of staff knowledge, another challenge will be to address the volume of activity that will be inherent in an increased focus on Generation X students. The institution must examine its procedures and staffing to ensure that it has the infrastructure and staff necessary to cope with the increase in workload.

Developmentally, a first-year student entering directly from high school is at a very different place in life from the Generation X student. All staff members must recognize this and alter their interactions accordingly. Employees new to working with this population will benefit from learning more about the developmental stages of a returning adult student in order to understand their actions and reactions.

Dealing with a greater variety of students will result in a larger number of students who lie outside of the norm. Employees should have a firm grasp of institutional policies that address outliers in order to handle the situations accordingly. Also, the Generation X student is more likely than a traditional student to inquire about the logic or rationale for decisions that affect their lives. This knowledge will help employees address such questions as they arise.

Communication skills necessary to serve the Gen X population encompass a wide array of topics. Almost all employees must have some level of speaking and writing skills. The type of position in question will dictate the level of proficiency required. An often-overlooked aspect of communication with students is the ability to translate the institutional jargon into the vernacular. Terms such as transfer equivalency worksheet, degree audit, registration windows, and advising codes often mean nothing to a returning student. Staff should learn to translate their terminology into layman's terms: a list of how courses transfer, a checklist of degree requirements, a timeframe for registering for classes, and computer password acquisition and use. This type of translation will create a much more effective line of communication between staff member and the Gen X student.

Another skill for staff to learn is the ability to answer a student's question, as well as to anticipate those questions a student does not know to ask. First, staff members should recognize gateway questions. A gateway question is one that indicates the student is engaged in a certain process. Often the student does not realize that he or she needs additional information to complete that process. Staff should be trained to be aware of these gateway questions, respond to them, and then detail the additional steps that a student should take.

An example of a gateway question and appropriate reaction follows. Many institutions require students to visit a central advising office in order to obtain a degree audit. If a student walks into such an office and asks for an audit, the most direct response is to provide the audit. However, a proactive employee will recognize that most students are using this information to register for next semester's classes; therefore, the staff member should also explain any important registration information to the student as well, thus addressing related issues before they become problems. This can be done verbally or by giving the student written instructions, but, in combination, they can be reinforcing.

Another aspect of answering the unasked question is to understand the motivation behind the question. Students will often ask questions that do not specifically answer the question that they have in mind. The most obvious example of this type of question appears from prospective students. A traditional student visiting a campus for the first time will likely have examined a variety of college guides. These publications often provide lists of questions to ask the admission officers when on campus – for example, "What is your student to faculty ratio?" The actual figure given to the student is largely irrelevant; the student should truly be interested in the level of faculty and student interaction. They may be operating under the mental model that the two items are correlated.

With an emphasis on the Generation X student, staff members are likely to encounter an entirely new group of questions of this nature. Generation X students are likely to have interests and expectations that vary greatly from those of a traditional student (Muchnick, 1996). A simple example could be a question about the length of time until completion of a degree. An incoming student may tell an advisor he or she is transferring 80 hours to the institution and wishes to know how many hours are required to complete a degree. The simple answer to the question may be 122, but a skilled advisor will recognize that the student is actually interested in the number of hours needed to finish his or her degree requirements. This number may be much higher than the 42 hours the above student's record translates. A staff member should be trained to identify the underlying questions and answer them, rather than answering the surface questions asked.

Finally, staff and faculty who handle academic advising may need to add knowledge and skills to their repertoire if their institution increases its emphasis on the Generation X student (Swann & Henderson, 1998). If advisors are to work with prospective students, they will obviously need a grasp of how courses transfer to the institution or easy access to this information. Regardless, advisors will need to understand how to translate a student's courses into their program in a sequence that may not match the lockstep method they are likely to have in place. These skills, along with the counseling skills, communication skills, and policy knowledge mentioned above will be imperative for advisors who are to work with the Generation X student.

Knowledge Management

The nature of Generation X students requires staff to work interdependently. Staff learning and training is imperative but an efficient and effective system of knowledge management must also be in place for staff to access.

Knowledge management is fundamentally about the discovery and capture of organizational knowledge, the filtering and arrangement of this knowledge, and the values derived from sharing and using this knowledge throughout the organization (Bernbom, 2001). To this end, an institution must have knowledge infrastructure conducive to demands that will be placed on it by the introduction of the Generation X student. Staff will require greater access to timely and accurate information if an institution commits to an emphasis on this demographic.

First and foremost, staff working with Generation X students need access to explicit knowledge. Explicit knowledge is documented information that can facilitate action, such as formulas, equations, rules, and best practices (Bernbom, 2001). An institution must ensure that it has effective and efficient knowledge management practices so that staff members will have access to information in a format that will enable them to answer questions in a timely and accurate fashion.

Implementation of effective knowledge management solutions can have a dramatic impact on an organization. Three fundamental categories of value propositions that can be derived from the application of knowledge management are innovation, customer (student) intimacy, and operational excellence (Bernbom, 2001). Using these three value propositions as drivers of business goals, an institution can develop knowledge strategies that have a resounding impact on the overall success of the organization.

An example of the bridging of innovation, business goals, and knowledge can be seen in the California Center for Teaching Careers (CalTeach) program. California demographics are such that its public schools see an increase of 150,000 students per year, requiring as many as 300,000 new teachers over the next decade. To meet this increased demand in teachers, the governor and the state legislature established CalTeach to create a one-stop information and referral recruitment center serving prospective teachers, counselors, and administrators. The program has created a Web site (www.calteach.com) that provides information about teacher recruitment programs, the teacher credentialing process, financial support and incentives, pathways into the teaching profession, on-line resumé and job postings, as well as a plethora of additional information for those interested in the teaching field (California State University Institute for Education Reform, 1998). This is an innovative example of how California has used knowledge strategy to meet its business goal of recruiting more teachers.

Another example of knowledge management exists at The University of North Carolina at Greensboro. The enrollment services division developed a student services intranet (ShareNet) for all student service providers. Among the features of ShareNet are a lexicon of enrollment-related terms, how-to steps for every enrollment process, any form a student or staff member may need, searchable contact information for every student services provider, and up-to-date references for policies, procedures, and deadlines. ShareNet exists inconspicuously as an icon on the computer desktop of student service providers – ready to be accessed when needed but otherwise invisible. This just-in-time approach to knowledge management relies more on maintaining accurate information within ShareNet than institutional memory or the residual effects of training, thus improving the accuracy and reliability of information provided to students.

Community Building

In order for enrollment service areas to work interdependently to best serve the Gen X student, an environment of open communication and community must be maintained. By building a strong sense of community, the staff members of the institution will function as an interconnected team working to serve their students. Staff should be trained to think outside of their current office or responsibilities. They should be trained to understand the entire enrollment process and how their primary responsibilities fit into it. This may seem like a subtle difference at first but it should be the first step in developing a sense of community.

When staff members understand their roles within the larger context, they are more likely to see themselves as part of a team. This team has the larger goal of serving their students in the most effective manner possible. Also, a community environment leads to greater staff satisfaction, which is observable by students in the actions and attitudes of staff.

Who should be involved in this community? Ideally, everyone on campus should feel some level of connectivity to the campus community. For the purposes of serving the Generation X student, specific emphasis should be placed on recruitment, transfer of credit, and advising, as these are the areas with the most obvious need for increased understanding and communication.

A sense of community must be a conscious goal, as it rarely happens naturally. An often-unacknowledged barrier to building community is that many of these staff members communicate only when there are problems. Given the frequent differences of agendas and goals, this communication is often conflict oriented. Changes in the manner and occurrence of cross-departmental communication can be a major step in improving the sense of community.

The first step in effectively creating a sense of community is to engage staff members in interactions that do not involve their direct responsibilities. Encouraging people to interact in social settings, larger information-sharing meetings, and during training sessions begins to create a personal bond among staff members from different areas. This relationship building will translate into more effective and collegial interactions when problems arise.

Another proactive measure that can be used to encourage team building is the creation of cross-functional teams to analyze a variety of work-related issues (Poe, 2002). Once again, this helps to foster communication before it has the opportunity to become negative conflict. It will also encourage staff members to learn other areas of responsibility and the interactions among the various functions. Understanding other functions will enable staff to appreciate the agendas of other offices, helping them to work together for more collaborative solutions to problems.

In addition to these formal opportunities to create a sense of community, informal and social interactions should be designed for staff to engage in situations outside of the stresses of the workplace. Events like the traditional office picnic, holiday party, or Friday luncheons are great opportunities to encourage positive interaction among employees. Positive interaction will result in more effective communication and a more pleasant work environment.

Conclusion

Research in the area of student recruitment and retention shows a need for additional and varying skills when dealing with the Generation X student (Richardson, 1998). To do this effectively, an institution must closely examine the competencies required for each of its positions. These competencies should be derived from a careful consideration of institutional characteristics as well as the unique attributes of the Generation X students being served. In addition to this detailed analysis, the institution should work diligently to create an environment that fosters staff learning, knowledge management, open communication, and a feeling of community.

REFERENCES

Ancrum, R., Berson, G., Brink, K., Guerrero, D., Henderson, S., McKinney, M., Mills, G., Robinson, L., & Swann, C. (1991). *The Admissions Profession: A Guide For Staff Development and Program Management*. Washington, DC: American Association of Collegiate Registrars and Admissions Officers & Alexandria, VA: National Association of College Admission Counselors.

Bernbom, G. (Ed.). (2001). *Information Alchemy: The Art and Science of Knowledge Management*. San Francisco: Jossey–Bass.

California State University Institute for Education Reform. CalTeach. [On-line]. Available: www.csus.edu/ier/calteach.html.

Carlan, P. (2001). Adult students and community college beginnings: Examining the efficacy of performance stereotypes on a university campus. *College Student Journal*. 35(2): 169–81.

Crosthwaite, E. & Warner, D. (Eds.) (1995). *Human Resource Management in Higher and Further Education*. Buckingham: The Society for Research into Higher Education.

Doidge, J., Hardwick, B., & Wilkinson, J. (1998). *Developing Support and Allied Staff in Higher Education*. London: Kogan Page Limited.

Kasworm, C. (2003) From the adult student's perspective: accelerated degree programs. *New Directions for Adult and Continuing Education*. 97: 17–27.

Klein, T., Scott, P., & Clark, J. (2001). A fresh look at market segments in higher education. *Planning for Higher Education*. 30(1): 4–19.

Milkovich, G. & Newman, J. (1996). *Compensation*. Chicago, IL: Times Mirror Higher Education Group, Inc.

Mitchell, S. (2001). *Generation X: Americans Aged 18 to 34* (3rd ed.). Ithaca, NY: New Strategist Publications, Inc.

Muchnick, M., (1996). *Naked Management: The Bare Essentials for Motivating the X-Generation at Work*. Delray Beach, FL: St. Lucie Press.

Poe, A. (2002). Family-friendly university: Helping people blend work and personal lives makes UC Davis a top employer. *HRMagazine*. 47(5): 91.

Richardson, J. (1998). Adult Students in Higher Education: Burden or Boon? *The Journal of Higher Education*. 69: 65–88.

Rosen, B. (2001). *Masks and Mirrors*. Westport, CT: Praeger Publishers.

Segal, J. (2002). Hiring days are (almost) here again! Before rushing out to add scads of new staff members, take a moment to review your hiring practices. *HRMagazine*. 47(6): 125.

Senge, P. (1990). *The Fifth Discipline*. New York, NY: Doubleday.

Swann, C. (Sr. Ed.) & Henderson, S. (1998). *Handbook for the College Admissions Profession*. Westport, CT: Greenwood Press.

CHAPTER THIRTEEN
Mega Trends and Implications for Enrollment Managers

Jim Black

While there are many issues that enrollment managers will encounter in the next ten to twenty years, there are three mega trends that will impact Generation X students directly. The first, affordability and accessibility, threatens an American ideal – that higher education is not only an available privilege, but as the gateway to living the American dream, it is an inalienable right of the citizens of this country. Second is higher education's responsiveness to returning Gen Xers while gearing up to meet the service expectations of a new generation of students, the Millennials. The final mega trend relates to the Information Age. Higher education served a vital role in American society's transformation from an agricultural economy and an industrial economy to a service economy. Still unclear, however, is the role of postsecondary education in the shift to a knowledge economy. How will the academy prepare Gen X students to contribute to and lead the knowledge economy?

These mega trends, along with several others, are expected to shape the face of higher education in the decades to come. More specific to this book, however, is how the impact of these mega trends on Generation X students can be affected by enrollment managers. Whether it is providing a voice in making campus-based decisions or shaping federal policy, enrollment managers possess expertise and knowledge that is invaluable to the discussion. Silence is not a viable option, nor is relegating the voice of the enrollment manager to one that generates discrete pieces of data for others to digest and interpret. Indeed, the role of the enrollment manager in the coming decades must be more influential and visible than ever before. For Generation Xers to succeed in their educational quests and expand their contributions to the country, enrollment managers must play an integral role in developing higher education policy and practice.

PART 4 CHAPTER THIRTEEN

171

A Defining Moment in U.S. Higher Education History: Affordability and Access

From its modest beginning, serving a small proportion of a fledgling colony's elite in hopes of producing learned clergy and lettered gentlemen (Rudolph, 1962; Brubacher & Rudy, 1976), U.S. higher education has become the world leader, serving over fifteen million students (U.S. Department of Education, 2001) through a seemingly infinite number of programs – each with its own purpose. According to Clara Lovett (2002), access for large numbers of students regardless of age, social class, institutional pluralism, and the convergence of excellence in teaching and research – the hallmarks of American higher education – are in jeopardy. She fears that the rising cost of preparing skilled personnel, the need to develop and maintain expensive infrastructure, and the increasing expectations of the consumers of higher education (students) will result in higher tuition, lower academic quality, and diminished access for economically disadvantaged students.

State support for higher education reached a peak in the early 1980s but has been declining ever since – dipping sharply in response to the recent downward spiral in the economy – and over the past twenty years, tuition and fee levels have risen inversely proportional to the decline in state appropriations (Mortenson, 2002). Though the future is uncertain, few economists are predicting an imminent resurgence in the economy, and hence, many college and university administrators are anticipating further reductions in state support (Arnone, Hebel, & Schmidt, 2003). The sustained decline in the stock market, and thus, on institutional endowments, along with the escalating costs of recruiting and retaining top faculty, employee benefits, insurance premiums, utilities, facility upkeep and construction, technology, student recruitment, and institutional aid have further compelled colleges and universities to increase tuition and fees (Nelson, Flood, & Goodman, 2002). Other than a few institutions and state systems that have invoked tuition freezes or reductions as part of an enrollment strategy (a response to public accountability, or legislative pressures) there is no evidence that this trend will reverse itself.

Since the late '90s, enrollments have burgeoned at many institutions. Estimates of high school graduates for the next seven years suggest continued growth in college enrollments (U.S. Department of Education, 2000) even though college participation rates have remained relatively stagnant in recent years. The participation rate for low-income students, however, has declined for two consecutive years – a trend that is expected to continue (Mortenson, 2002). This raises serious concerns about affordability and access for economically disadvantaged students of all ages.

While college costs have been increasing by double digits since 1999, the net worth of families, as measured by household corporate equities and mutual funds, has declined by 36% during the same period (Federal Reserve, 2002). Similarly, the rate of return on savings accounts and stock portfolios of families planning to send their sons and daughters to college has declined, and the rate of unemployment rose nationally to 6% in November 2002

(Nelson, Flood, & Goodman, 2002). The combination of these factors hits Gen Xers who want to return to school particularly hard because they may have lost jobs or are employed but economically disadvantaged.

The affordability and accessibility conundrum becomes more difficult to solve in light of the fact that federal financial aid has not kept pace with the rise in college costs, some states are considering cuts to state financial aid programs, and many institutions (particularly private colleges with small endowments) have reached a diminishing point of return regarding the amount of institutional aid dollars they can invest (Nelson, Flood, & Goodman, 2002). Though families have substantially increased borrowing to pay for college over the last decade by means of increased access to federal loan programs as well as favorable home equity loan rates, this too has its limits (Nelson, Flood, & Goodman, 2002). A family's ability to take on debt and their willingness to do so are entirely separate matters. The combination of these variables has led to a growing affordability gap.

For the colleges and universities, the convergence of costs associated with increased enroll-ments, the general costs of doing business, and the decline in state funding are largely responsible for the increases in tuition and fees (Goral, 2002). If tuition increases are prohibited or are otherwise restricted and/or state funding for enrollment growth diminishes, institutions may be forced to turn qualified students away — further limiting access, at least to the institu-tion of choice. Student enrollments will continue to shift from expensive four-year privates and moderate cost four-year publics to the less costly community colleges. Over the next two decades, a number of private institutions may merge or close their doors (Nelson, Flood, & Goodman, 2002).

During this time of "belt tightening" and balancing affordability and access with financial viabil-ity, administrators will be forced to make difficult decisions. Many will be required to choose between preserving short-term financial strength while risking competitive position, which could affect long-term financial viability (Nelson, Flood, & Goodman, 2002). Some will elect to improve their institution's competitive position by investing in faculty salaries, facilities, technology, and the like, while sacrificing short-term financial health or borrowing against an uncertain future. Still others will play it safe and attempt to weather the storm. Regardless of the path they choose, the world of higher education administrators, including enrollment managers, for the foreseeable future will be fraught with ambiguity and risk. Especially during these difficult times, "adult learning focused institutions must make continuous and deliberate efforts to simultaneously ensure the affordability, accessibility and quality of educational degrees and programs" (Council for Adult and Experimental Learning, 1999, p. 13).

The Millennial and Generation X Students

The affordability and accessibility phenomenon could not come at a worse time in the history of American higher education. It coincides with the emergence of the most ethnically diverse population the United States has ever experienced. According to the U.S. Department of Education (2002), the number of Hispanics from birth to age twenty-four is expected to increase from 14.5 million in 2000 to 22.3 million in 2020, and the number of black, non-Hispanics is expected to increase from 14.6 million to 17.4 million during the same time period. Many of these individuals are disproportionately from economically disadvantaged families and, hence, will be disproportionately impacted by the affordability and access crisis.

Based on the research of Howe and Strauss (2000), the Millennial Generation, like no other in America's history, is more affluent, better educated, and more abundant (76 million strong). They also exhibit positive social habits like good behavior, modesty, teamwork, and an achievement-orientation. They strive for perfection in everything they do. They have a positive, upbeat attitude and are actively engaged – doers more than talkers. They are civic-minded individuals who represent a highly effective social force. Today's kids believe in the future and their ability to change it for the better. Howe and Strauss believe the Millennials represent the next generation of American heroes.

Like their Generation X predecessors, the Millennials are technologically sophisticated, far more so than the usual faculty member who will teach them. After all, they have grown up digital. Having cut their "techno teeth" on Nintendo or Game Boys, Millennials are undaunted by new technology (Black, 2001). According to Diana Oblinger (2002), executive director of higher education for Microsoft, 94% of students they surveyed indicated that the Internet is used for school-related research; 73% used the Internet more than the library for research; 79% said the Internet had a positive impact on their academic experience; 60% felt that the Internet had improved relationships with classmates; and 56% believed the Internet had improved their relationships with professors. Oblinger conveyed that e-mail has become a powerful educational and communications tool as well among Millennials: 72% checked their e-mail daily; 89% have received class announcements via e-mail; 75% used e-mail to get clarifications on assignments; 46% believed e-mail allowed them to express ideas that they would not have expressed in class; and although only 19% communicated with professors more via e-mail than face-to-face, 55% said they used e-mail to arrange face-to-face interactions with instructors.

Frand (2000) found that Millennials do not consider computers to be technology. Computers are just another appliance, much like a television, only more interactive and entertaining. He also discovered that for many Millennials the line between reality and imagination is increasingly blurry. Virtual worlds and multitasking have become a way of life. Somewhat contradictory to the findings by Howe and Strauss (2000), Frand observed that Millennials practice what he calls, "Nintendo over logic," or trial and error. They experiment until they get it right but never resort to reading the owner's manual. Like the Gen Xers, staying connected is essential to Millennials. The Internet, e-mail, and instant messaging are their links to the world as well as to their peers.

Faculty and staff interacting with Millennials will see great promise in them; however, Millennials do present challenges as well. They have zero tolerance for delays or bureaucracy (Frand, 2000). According to Howe and Strauss (2000), their expectations are high for themselves as well as for others. Unlike the Gen Xers, the Millennials follow rules and accept authority, particularly from principle-centered leaders. Furthermore, they heed moral exemplars.

Therefore, faculty and staff who will be effective with this generation will be those who demonstrate moral and ethical principles and engender trust. Not unlike Gen Xers, creating trust with the Millennium Generation means developing relationships, taking action, and consistently delivering on promises.

As one might expect, the differences between the two generations form interesting challenges in the classroom as well as in the student service areas. Often with competing needs and expectations, the Millennial and Generation X students do share some common service expectations. They expect, even demand, unlimited access to information, decision-making tools, and business transactions. Among the most precious possessions in today's world, and more so in tomorrow's world, is time. There is never enough of it. Busy students do not want to waste valuable time navigating a physical campus to obtain a form or conduct routine business. How they learn, transact business, communicate, and initiate and sustain relationships changed forever with the popularization of the Internet and e-mail (Black, 2001). They have come to expect immediate, reliable service available 24/7 from anywhere.

Convenience and reliability are increasingly the way to win students' hearts and build brand loyalty. Students want the ability to choose between face-to-face and Web-enabled student services. Consequently, the emerging trend in higher education student services is a blended model that combines high touch with high tech approaches (Burnett & Oblinger, 2002). With choice comes a feeling of control. When students control their time and, to a degree, the outcome, they are generally satisfied with the student service experience. That satisfaction translates into a positive image of the institution, improved student retention, and powerful, word-of-mouth promotion.

Higher education tends to lag behind business by three to four years. An advantage of changing at a slower pace is that we can see trends long before they become a reality in the academy. One interesting trend, already deeply ensconced in the business culture, is the one-to-one, customized approach to marketing, communications, and customer service (Peppers, Rogers, & Dorf, 1999). The higher education forerunners in this movement utilize customer relationship management (CRM) software that allows them to learn more about each student with every interaction, and use the information collected to create a profile, so that communications as well as program and service offerings can be tailored to the individual. To illustrate the CRM model, consider how amazon.com learns from every purchase a customer makes and then follows up with book or music offers in a similar genre. Do not be surprised to see student relationship managers on college campuses in the near future.

Jafari (2002) provides a high tech example of the CRM concept applied to an academic setting. He describes the use of intelligent agents within a course management environment such as Blackboard or Web CT. The intelligent agent is a software tool linked with other applications and databases running within one or multiple computer environments. Jafari illustrates three possible roles for intelligent agents: a digital teaching assistant, a digital tutor, and a digital secretary. Digital teaching assistants would monitor inactivity by students and make faculty aware of student participation levels, send notices to students of overdue assignments, and provide assistance with grading. The digital tutors would utilize a smart search engine to find specific resources to facilitate learning needs of students and create a learning profile through interactions (e.g., learning styles, learning preferences, study habits, problem areas) and deliver related pedagogical packages suited to the individual learner. Acting as a digital secretary, the intelligent agent could schedule appointments or find peers with similar research or content interests.

The convergence of data, voice, and video on the Internet coupled with the expansion of residential broadband, wireless connectivity, along with the integration of cell phones, PDAs (personal data assistants), and laptops will only further escalate the demand for on-line services (Weigel, 2000; Frand, 2000). The integration of technology will change the nature of student services. We will be able to reach out and touch students more easily—sending e-mails, voice messages, Web forms, video clips, and much more to a single device. Usually, the device will be on the student's person (e.g., cell phone, PDA, or even an article of clothing such as eyeglasses). They will be able to respond to requests or access information instantaneously and almost effortlessly.

Other advances in technology that have application for student services include biometrics – the use of thumbprints, retina or facial scans, or voice recognition to identify a student rather than traditional identification cards, one cards, or personal identification numbers (PINs). Such technology would reduce existing security risks, simplify compliance with the Family Educational Rights and Privacy Act as well as the Social Security Act, and reduce student frustration with forgotten PINs or lost cards. Authentication for phone, video, or Web chat services also would be simplified, creating an opportunity to provide confidential admissions, financial aid, academic, career, wellness, or personal counseling remotely.

An infusion of high tech services alone will not yield satisfied students. The real gains come from changing mindsets. As staff begin to view their work through the eyes of the students, attitudes change and new possibilities emerge. They develop a servant's heart as described in chapter twelve. Through hiring practices, setting clear expectations for behavior and performance, rewarding desired behavior, and holding staff accountable, a student-centered culture can be created (Black, 2002).

To meet or exceed ever-changing Gen X student expectations, enrollment managers must leverage technology to provide mass customization and real-time responses. Not only must responses be immediate at any time of day or night, but they also must be tailored to a single individual. Magic. Perhaps, but this kind of response is possible. The technology already exists. But it requires more than technology. It requires a new way of thinking. Enrollment managers must help staff move outside of the traditional student services box and imagine new possibilities.

The Information Age

Some, including Lovett (2002), believe that the academy has been slow to respond to the Information Age that these Gen Xers and, to a greater degree, the Millennials have embraced. Arthur Levine, for example, was recently quoted as saying,

> We are faced with a New World, and educational institutions that were created for an industrial society don't match the needs of an Information Age. The challenge today is not about fixing educational institutions that are broken, but about radically redesigning our whole educational system for a dramatically different world than it was created for originally (Page, 2000, p. 49).

In the Information Age, "how we access information, how we learn, how we conduct business, how we communicate, how we are entertained, and even how we initiate and maintain relationships" has changed dramatically (Black, 2001).

Colleges and universities must become increasingly nimble and responsive to be competitive with emerging educational providers like the University of Phoenix, already the largest private university in the world – primarily serving Generation X students. Gen Xers who have grown up with personal computers will be more likely than their predecessors to enroll in on-line programs. They will increasingly be associated concurrently with multiple providers and modes of instruction rather than limiting themselves to a single institution or learning modality. Wallhaus predicts that

> ... educational services will become unbundled, with different providers carrying out various functions: curricular development, delivery of instructional modules, provision of student services, student evaluation, and awarding of credentials. Students will assume greater control over their educational experience.... Program completion will be defined increasingly by the knowledge gained and skills mastered rather than credit hours earned (2000, pp. 22–23).

As Wallhaus (2000) points out, it is possible to utilize e-learning to transform instruction from faculty-centered to learner-centered. That, indeed, will be one of the great challenges for educators over the next twenty years. Though technology has dramatically enhanced instruction both on-line as well as in traditional classrooms, we are still searching for better ways to incorporate it into the curriculum. In a recent article in the *New York Times*, professors lamented that computers in their classrooms had become a distraction rather than an enhancement to learning. Students were surfing the Web or e-mailing friends instead of listening to the instructor (Schwartz, 2003).

Administrators and faculty in the Information Age must grapple with the best and most economical ways to infuse technology into instruction. In the e-learning arena, for example, the costs of creating entire programs in-house are high compared to contracting with an external vendor or partnering with other institutions to share capital, infrastructure, and services costs (Graves, 2001). Hard decisions regarding spending for instructional purposes must be made. Should the institution invest in technology in the classroom, the development of e-learning courses, other forms of distance learning such as two-way video, faculty development, faculty salaries, or traditional pedagogical enhancements? Few institutions have "deep enough pockets" to do it all. Clear priorities must be identified and a course of action charted. The lure of technological advances and the budding interests and enthusiasm of faculty will undoubtedly be tempting. For an institution to thrive in this new era, however, senior leadership must focus more on when and what subjects students want to take. Enrollment managers can provide market and student demand data to inform such decisions and help institutions stay the course.

Aligning with the Internal and External Environment

Understanding trends that impact higher education and the students we serve is imperative. Indeed, the success of any enrollment management enterprise depends on the enrollment manager's ability to assess the internal and external environment and then align strategies with the environment (Johnson, 2000; Massa, 2001). Even the organization itself should be realigned with the environment (Dolence & Norris, 1995). Inherent in such a realignment is adjusting the institution's products and services to meet the needs of learners within the environment (Dolence, 1997) – in this case, Gen X learners. According to Dolence (1997), alignment is a primary function within the enrollment management enterprise and extends far beyond recruitment and retention alone.

An analysis of the internal environment may consist of an assessment of the institution's core competencies: the degree to which its mission is met, faculty and staff commitment, the work environment, internal communications, academic and cocurricular programs, facilities, capacity, the student profile, student satisfaction, discount rates, and net revenue (Bryson, 1995; Black, 2001; Massa, 2001). "Through this process, an institution's strengths and weaknesses are delineated as enabling or preventing a successful response to the external environment" (Massa, 2001, p. 159). An external analysis often includes a study of demographic trends, competitors, the economy, local conditions, price, and consumer attitudes (Black, 2001; Massa, 2001).

The analysis of the internal and external environment informs strategies to attract, serve, retain, and graduate Generation X students. Enrollment managers have an obligation to conduct such an analysis and use related findings to enlighten strategic planning, influence policy, and guide the development of services and instructional strategies. Armed with this information, we must creatively overcome issues of affordability and accessibility for Generation X students. We must effectively serve and educate a diverse student body of Millennials and Gen Xers. And, we must exploit the opportunities inherent in the Information Age in order to prepare our students for the world in which they live and work. Indeed, the task before us is daunting, yet exhilarating at the same time.

REFERENCES

Arnone, M., Hebel, S., & Schmidt, P. (2003, January 3). Another bleak budget year. *The Chronicle of Higher Education.* 49(17): A21.

Black, J. (Ed.). (2001). Garnering resources and building infrastructure. In J. Black (Ed.), *The Strategic Enrollment Management Revolution* (173–183). Washington, DC: American Association of Collegiate Registrars and Admissions Officers.

——. (2001). Students in the dot-com world. In J. Black (Ed.), *The Strategic Enrollment Management Revolution.* (253–280). Washington, DC: American Association of Collegiate Registrars and Admissions Officers.

——. (2002). Creating a student service culture. In D. Burnett & D. Oblinger (Eds.), Best Practices in Student Services. Washington, DC: Society for College and University Planning.

Brubacher, J. & Rudy, W. (1976). *Higher Education in Transition.* (3rd ed.) New York: Harper & Row.

Bryson, J. (1995). *Strategic Planning for Public and Nonprofit Organizations.* San Francisco: Jossey–Bass.

Burnett, D. & Oblinger, D. (2002). *Innovations in Student Services: Planning for Models Blending High Touch/High Tech.* Ann Arbor, Michigan: Society for College and University Planning.

Council for Adult and Experimental Learning (1999). Serving adult learners in higher education: Findings from CAEL's benchmarking study. Chicago, IL: Council for Adult and Experimental Learning.

Dolence, M. & Norris, D. (1995). *Transforming Higher Education: A Vision for Learning in the Twenty-first Century.* Ann Arbor, MI: Society for College and University Planning.

Dolence, M. (1997). Strategic enrollment management. In R. M. Swanson & F. A. Weese (Eds.), *Becoming a Leader in Enrollment Services* (107–133). Washington, DC: American Association of Collegiate Registrars and Admissions Officers.

Federal Reserve (2002, September 16). Flow of funds accounts of the United States. Washington, DC: Federal Reserve.

Frand, J. (2000, September/October). The information age mindset: Changes in students and implications for higher education. *EDUCAUSE Review.* 35(5): 15–24.

Goral, T. (2002, March). There's a hole in the bucket. *University Business.* 5(2): 32–35.

Graves, W. (2001, March/April). Virtual operations: Challenging for traditional higher education. *EDUCAUSE Review.* 36(2): 46–56.

Howe, N. & Strauss, W. (2000). *Millennials rising: The next great generation.* New York: Vintage Books.

Jafari, A. (2002). Conceptualizing intelligent agents for teaching and learning. *EDUCAUSE Quarterly.* 25(3): 28–34.

Johnson, A. (2000, Winter). The evolution of strategic enrollment management: A historical perspective. *Journal of College Admissions.* (166): 4–11.

Lovett, C. (2002, March/April). Cracks in the bedrock: Can U. S. higher education remain number one? *Change.* 34(2): 10–15.

Massa, R. (2001). Developing a SEM plan. In J. Black (Ed.), *The Strategic Enrollment Management Revolution* (149–171). Washington, DC: American Association of Collegiate Registrars and Admissions Officers.

Mortenson, T. (2002, July). State appropriations, public institution tuition rates and state student financial aid appropriations, FY 1975 to FY 2002. *Postsecondary Education OPPORTUNITY.* (121): 1–16.

——. (2002, August). College participation rates by state for students from low-income families, FY 1993 to FY 2001. *Postsecondary Education OPPORTUNITY.* (122): 1–7. Nelson, J., Flood, M., & Goodman,

R. (2002, December). *Tuition affordability challenges financial health of many private colleges* (Report No. 76841). New York: Moody's Investors Service.

Oblinger, D. (2002, November 12). *Redesign, relocate, and reconfigure: Creating integrated services in higher education.* Plenary presentation at the twelfth annual Strategic Enrollment Management Conference, San Diego, CA.

Page, D. (2000, October). Arthur Levine: Creating an education system for an information age. *Converge.* 3(10): 48–49.

Peppers, D., Rogers, M., & Dorf, B. (1999). *The One to One Fieldbook.* New York: Currency and Doubleday.

Rudolph, F. (1962). *The American College and University: A History.* (6). New York: Vintage Books.

Schwartz, J. (2003, January 2). Professors vie with web for class's attention. *New York Times.* [On-line]. Available: www.nytimes.com/2003/...2/technology/02WIRE.html?todaysheadlines.

U.S. Department of Education (2001, November). Enrollment, staff, and degrees conferred in postsecondary institutions participating in Title IV programs, by level and control of institution: Fall 1997, fall 1999, and 1999–2000. In *Digest of educational statistics, 2001.* [On-line]. Available: http://nces.ed.gov//pubs2002/digest2001/tables/dt170.asp.

U.S. Department of Education (2002, May). High school graduates, by control of institution, with projections: 1986–87 to 2011–12. In *Projections of education statistics to 2012.* [On-line]. Available: http://nces.ed.gov/pubs2002/proj2012/table_23.asp.

U.S. Department of Education (2002, September). Projections of the population, birth to age 24, by race/ethnicity and age: 1993 to 2020. In *Population projections of young people.* [On-line]. Available: http://nces.ed.gov/pubs/yi/y9602a.html.

Wallhaus, R. (2000). E-learning: From institutions to providers, from students to learners. In R. Katz & D. Oblinger (Eds.), *The "E" is for Everything: E-commerce, E-business, and E-learning in the Future of Higher Education.* San Francisco: Jossey–Bass.

Weigel, V. (2000, September/October). E-learning and the tradeoff between richness and reach in higher education. *Change.* 33(5): 10–15.